OUTLINE
OF
INDIAN PHILOSOPHY

OUTLINE
OF
INDIAN PHILOSOPHY

By

P.T. SRINIVASA IYENGAR

BHARATIYA KALA PRAKASHAN
DELHI (INDIA)

First Edition : 1909
Revised Edition : 2008

Published by **C.P. Gautam**
BHARATIYA KALA PRAKASHAN
3421-A, IInd Floor, Narang Colony, Tri Nagar,
Delhi-110035. Ph. : 32967505, Telefax : 011-27393083
E-Mail : bkp3421@yahoo.co.in

ISBN : 978-81-8090-187-4

Laser Type Setting by :
A-ONE GRAPHICS
Delhi-110088

Printed at
BDH Printer at Salasar Imaging System, Delhi

CONTENTS

PREFACE

I have, in the following pages, attempted to separate the varied threads of the tangled skin of modern Hindu philosophical thought and religious beliefs. Each school of ancient thought was based on a special point of view of its own and was promulgated for the purpose of emphasizing the particular standpoint which appealed to the persons that founded and elaborated that school. But "as the water that rains from the sky goes all to the ocean" and once mixed with the ocean, the countributory streams become indistinguishable from one another, so modern Hinduism has received the tribute of the Upaniṣads, the Sāṅkhya-yoga, the Vaiśeṣika-nyāya and the triple Āgamas, and its wonderful tolerance has intricately mixed up all these elements. I have endeavoured to separate all those elements and exhibit separately the teachings of these ancient systems.

In doing so, I have attempted to discuss the ideas of the earliest available exposition of each school. In India, thinkers, however independent they may be, whatever new vistas of thought they may open up, are compelled by inexorable orthodoxy to father their opinions on the ancients. The boldest thinker this country has produced, Śaṅkara, felt it necessary to seek the sanction of orthodoxy by deriving his new ideas from the old Brahma Sūtras and the older Upaniṣads. Being a philosopher, he had to pretend to be a scholiast. Obversely, each commentator on an older philosophical work, while professing to expound his author, imports some of his own ideas in the comment and thus unconciously helps on the movement of thought. Thus, to take an illustration from modern schools, when the canon may be expected to be definitely fixed, Sureśvara, the premier disciple of Śaṅkara, slightly alters the Advaita of his master. The author of Bhāmati, Vācaspati Miśra, gives it another twist; after him, Vidyāraṇya gives another; and so thought goes on ever changing, though not always for the better. So, too, the Viśiṣṭādvaita; of Yāmuna, Rāmānuja, Pillai (Lokācārya), Vedānta Deśika and Maṇavāla, each has introduced some alteration in the scheme of thought. Similarly, the early Vaiśeṣika Sūtras ignore a creator or a distributor of rewards and punishments: but the modern Tarka school it wedded to a thorough going theism. Hence in discussing the opinions of each school I have relied on the earliest available book and not on the commentaries thereon.[1] In the case of the Brahma Sūtras, I have made an attempt (the first, I believe, by any one) to indicate what I imagine to be the author's position distinguishable from that of the 'three' schools of interpretation, called the "three creeds" (trimata) which have engulfed it.

Though the Hindu venerates the Veda as self-revealed and takes great pride in calling himself aVedāntī and has recently proposed to himself to carry the light of Vedānta to the West, yet the living religion of India, what one may call the 'working faith' of the Hindus of today, is based on the Āgamas, Śaiva, Śākta, or Vaiṣṇava; less than a thousand years ago, the Āgamas were looked on as unauthoritative and Yāmuna, in founding the modern Vaiṣṇava Viśiṣṭādvaita school felt it necessary to write the *Āgamaprāmāṇya,* the authoritativeness of the Āgamas. Today, however freely scraps of the

1. How much even European scholars have succumbed to the influence of the commentator is proved by the fact that Max Muller, in translating certain passages of the upaniṣads has put into the text matter found only in Śaṅkara Bhāṣya ; Deussen's recent exposition of the philosophy of the Upaniṣads is vitiated by his identification of the position of the Ṛṣis with that of Śaṅkara. Is it any wonder that the average Hindu, to whom the seer and the scholiast are both prophets sees revolation in both text and commentaries.

Upaniṣads are quoted in discussions, the actual opinions and religious practices of the Hindus are taken entirely from the Āgamas. For this and other reasons, the Āgamas have been kept secret. I have attempted to give an account of them and their fundamental ideas, quoting from unpublished or untranslated works. I hope that this will direct the attention of scholars to a vast virgin soil of investigation likely to yield valuable results.[1]

In discussing the various schools my aim has been to combine the sympathetic insight which is possible only to one born and bred within the Hindu religious fold and the critical and impartial judgment of one who has shaken himself free from the shackles cf sectarian animosity and partisan enthusiasm. Whether and how far I have succeeded it is for the reader to judge. The only other works that can be compared with this one in scope are the *Sarva Darśana Saṅgraha* of Mādhavācārya and the *Sarva Vedānta Siddhāntasāra,* attributed to Śaṅkarācārya, but a late work. The former though written with a degree of impartiality very creditable in a Hindu of five centuries ago, has for its aim not the exposition of the fundamental tenets of the many Indian systems of thought, so much as the glorification of the Advaita as superior to the rest. Moreover Mādhava uses each school only to demolish the previous one and his exposition of every darśana (system) is limited by this circumstance, those only of the fundamental ideas being referred to which help him in his object. His account of the Āgama schools is very meagre; in fact he does not mention the Śākta Āgmas at all; possibly because he himself, being the reputed founder of the Sṛṅgeri mutt, was a Śākta as so many Advaitīs are and regarded its mysteries too sacred to be desecrated by being revealed to the public. Of the second work, I could get only a part. It is now being edited by Professor Raṅgācārya of the Madras Presidency College. Its treatment of Mīmāṁsā is good. The rest does not seem to be valuable.

1. Prof. Garbe alone of European scholars has realized the value of the Āgamas, but he does not seem to have done much for their elucidation.

In dealing with Sanskrit technical terms, I have preferred not to employ English substitutes especially in the 2nd and 3rd chapters. If Indian philosophy is at all to be understood by English-speaking peoples, they must learn to associate with Sanskrit terms their special connotations. No Sanskrit philosophical term can be equated to any English word. The word 'manas', for instance is usually translated 'mind', but the connotations of the two words are by no means identical. 'Manas' to a Hindu is a material, objective thing : it is not the brain, for the brain is 'gross', whereas 'manas' is subtle matter. But even a crass Western materialist who regards mind as a secretion of the brain will not admit mind to be matter in any sense of the word; he may deny its separate existence as an entity, but to him it is subjective and not objective. Hence the translation of manas as mind cannot but raise obstructive associations in the mind of the reader. The word 'Buddhi', again, is absolutely untranslateable. Ahaṁkāra is self consciousness, the basis of the cognitions, 'I am the doer of this', but Ahaṁkāra to the Hindu, is a function of matter, the object, and not that of Self, the subject. Another fruitful source of confusion caused by translating technical words is due to the fact that different schools of thought use the same word in different senses : thus, 'viveka' to the Advaitī is the distinction between the subject and the object; to the Viśiṣṭādvaitī, it is the choice of the proper food that leads to spiritual enlightenment. The word 'mūrta' in the Upaniṣads means that which has form and in the Vaiśeṣika it means that which moves. Obversely different words have been used for the same idea in different schools and this has contributed to the accentuation of their differences. It has therefore been thought that the synopsis given at the end of the book of such terms would be more useful than an index mechanically constructed. Yet no new Sanskrit technical term has been introduced in the text without some sort of explanatory word (suiting the context, but not pretending to be a translation) being added, for the use of readers who may not care for the subtle shades of difference but may like to acquaint themselves with the general trend of thought of the various systems discussed. One English philosophical word alone, I have taken the liberty to use freely, *viz.* 'consciousness'. This word I have used not in its usual connotation, in psychological works, of 'mental states', but in the sense of one's awareness of those states apart from the states themselves. Without realizing this sharp separation of the operations of the mind from the concurrent awareness of them, it is hopeless to understand Hindu philosophy. Huxley and the French School of psychologists headed by Ribot and Binet approximate to this use of the word and theirs is my authority for appropriating this word in this sense.

My system of transliteration is practically the same as that of most European scholars (barring, of course, Max Mūller's quaint system adopted in the "Sacred Text-books of the East"); but I must apologize to my readers for sundry inconsistencies in the transliteration due to the fact that the Tara Press has been trained to use a peculiar system of transliteration whereby, in violation of phonetics, the values of ṭ and t etc. are reversed; I must also beg the indulgence of the reader for errors due to defective proof-reading.

I cannot close this preface without referring to the invaluable help rendered me by my friend, Mr. Govinda Dāsa of Benares both by his criticism and suggestions and by giving and procuring loans of Mss., by the encyclopaedic scholar, Professor Gangānāth Jhā of Allahabad in the sections on Mīmāṁsā and Vaiśeṣika, and by Mr. P. Bhaṭṭanātha Swami of Vizagapatam, without whose help I could not have deciphered or interpreted parts of my Mss. material.

P.T. Srinivas Iyengar

CHAPTER - I

CYCLE OF IDEAS COMMON TO ALL PHILOSOPHICAL SCHOOLS OF INDIA

As it was in ancient Greece and Rome so it is in modern Europe and America; various schools of Philosophy are being propounded, each challenging every fundamental principle of the rest. Not so in India, where though the different Darśanas disagree about important questions, the ideas common to all these systems are so many and so vital that these deserve to be formulated by themselves under the name of Hindu Philosophy.

These ideas are as a rule assumed and not definitely expounded in the literature of the different schools; each school being naturally anxious to explain and justify by argument, the special points of doctrine and discipline which constitute its individuality, and differentiate it from its sister philosophies. These philosophical schools are commonly enumerated as six, called the Ṣaḍ Darśanas. Two of them are wholly based on the Vedic texts and are called the two Mīmāṁsās;[1] they are Pūrva and Uttara (Earlier and Latter), otherwise, Karma Mīmāṁsā and Brahma Mīmāṁsā, investigation of Dharma and of Brahma. The other four are based on reasoning and while paying homage to the supreme authority of the Veda do not derive their substance from Vedic texts, *viz* : Sāṅkhya, Yoga, Nyāya, and Vaiśeṣika, the disciplines of Enumeration, Effort, Reasoning and Definition respectively. Mādhava, in his *Sarva-darśana-saṅgraha* however, classifies the schools of his time as sixteen, *viz*, Cārvāka, Bauddha, Ārhata, Rāmānuja, Pūrṇaprajña,

Nakulīśapāśupata, Śaiva, Pratyabhijñā Raseśvara, Vaiśeṣika, Akṣapāda, Jaiminīya, Pāṇinīya Sāṅkhya, Pātañjala and Śāṅkara.[2] He professes to explain the specific teachings of each school, but one gets lost in this forest of philosophical systems and forgets that in them there is very much more community of opinion than diversity, which alone Mādhava emphasises. We shall discuss in this chapter these fundamental assumptions of Hindu thought, so as to prepare the way for the consideration of the different teachings of the various schools with regard to individual problems and to methods of philosophical training.

Philosophy to all modern western thinkers, is chiefly a matter of speculation; to them its interest is mainly intellectual, in that it solves problems that have troubled the mind; but to the Hindu as to the ancient Greek and Roman, philosophy has besides this theoretical, a practical interest, the regulation of life. "In ancient times," says Dr. Bussel, "The pursuit of wisdom was practical and implied adherence to a definite rule of life" (*Personal Idealism,* p. 342); and so it is in India even today. Philosophy has never been in India dissociated from life; hence each school sets about its investigations with the specific aim of discovering the means of man's attainment of a state of perfection called Mokṣa. This is the *raison d' etre* of each school. Unless it embodies a definite method of intellectual, ethical and spiritual training, leading a man up to perfection, it has according to Hindu ideas no justification for existence.

The only modern European philosopher that recognises this to be the function of philosophy is the semi-oriental Spinoza. The opening sentence of his *De Intellectus Emendatione* (Transl. Elwes), says, "After experience had taught me that all the usual surroundings of social life are vain and futile; seeing that none of the objects of my fears contained in themselves anything either good or bad, except in so far as the mind is affected by them, I finally resolved to enquire whether there might be some real good having power to communicate itself, which would affect the mind singly to the exclusion of all else; whether, in fact, there might be anything of which the discovery and attainment would enable me to enjoy continuous, supreme, and unending happiness."

As to Spinoza, so to all Hindus, philosophy begins with Vairāgya, estimation of pleasures and pains at their proper value, and ends with Mokṣa. The first impulse to philosophy is not intellectual but emotional and moral. "'What hast thou to do with riches? What hast thou to do with kin? how shall wives bestand thee, son! that shalt surely die? seek the Ātman, that which lieth hidden in the cave. Where are gone thy father, and the fathers of thy father?' Such was the teaching, still more ancient, addressed by an ancient Indian father to an ancient Indian son—addressed by Vyāsa to his son Śuka—Śuka who grew to be greater even than his great father. And such used to be the origin of philosophy in olden Indian." (Bhagavān Dās, *Science of he Emotions,* p. 9)

And such ought to continue to be always the power that inspires philosophy if it is to be something more than arid logomachy, laboured pounding of husk, fruitless and only too often leading to hypocrisy, to pharisaic self-righteousness, to pompous protestations and poor performance. The world has a moral value and philosophy ought to serve a nobler purpose than merely securing to its devotee the feeling of intellectual satisfaction in the acquisition of an idea by the path of speculation.

Philosophy, therefore, to a Hindu means not merely a body of opinions to be believed, but a life to be lived, a training to be undergone for attaining a state of release from bondage.[2] It is therefore unfair to these schools to judge of them as western writers invariably do, as theories to be argued about, apart from the practical training that they prescribe.

All these disciplines, except the school of crude philosophical Nihilism as expounded in the *Sarvadarśanasaṅgraha* under the name Cārvāka and attributed to Bṛhaspati, are agreed about the truth of the following propositions regarding the constitution of the cosmos, the nature of man, and the goal of human evolution.

(1) Man is a complex of consciousness, mind and body.

(2) The Ātmā is of the nature of consciousness and is immutable.

(3) Mind (antaḥkaraṇa), though an inner organ is material and is other than the Ātmā.

(4) Psychic life obeys fixed laws and hence all mental events are determinable.

(5) The five sense-organs (jñānendriyas) and the five action-organs (karmendriyas) are, like the mind, made of subtle matter.

(6) The eleven organs inhere in a liṅgadeha or subtle body, which is relatively permanent.

(7) The liṅgadeha is periodically connected with a body of flesh and blood, which provides man with sense-organs and action-organs of gross matter.

(8) Matter (prakṛti) is mutable but increate and obeys fixed laws.

(9) The world history is made up of alternating periods of activity (kalpa) and rest (pralaya).

(10) The subtle elements that make up all objects are five, corresponding to the five senses.

(11) All energy in the universe is personal, *i. e.* bound up with consciousness of varying degrees of intensity.

(12) This energy is prāṇa, which is intermediate between spirit and matter.

(13) The law of causation—karma—is supreme in the physical and mental worlds.

(14) Saṁsāra, the course of karma, is anādi, had no beginning.

(15) Mokṣa is the goal of human life and results from the training of the mind, and hence reaching the state of mokṣa is a definite mental event.

It is curious that these fundamental doctrines upon which all schools of Hindu philosophy are absolutely agreed, deal with questions about which western philosophers have been hopelessly divided from the time of Aristotle to modern days. It is also worthy of note that in this long list of propositions about which all these schools are agreed, there is no reference to God or to His relations with the cosmos. For while the Vedānta is a school of Pantheism, all the rest are, as expounded by their founders, what the European thinker would regard as atheistic; while all of them recognize the existence of the many powers of Nature, they exclude the conception of one Universal Being. The earlier Sāṅkhya, Vaiśeṣika and Mīmāṁsā works are frankly atheistic. The Yoga and the Nyāya Sūtras refer to a Deity, but the former makes him but an ancient teacher, and the latter but an adjuster of rewards and punishments and no more. The later expounders of all these systems have given a theistic twist to them, because in later days, the Vedānta became popular and hence he name Nirīśvara, atheistic, became a term of reproach.

We shall now discuss the fifteen propositions which are common to all these schools.

(1) Man is a complex of consciousness, mind and body

In western philosophy the concepts 'consciousness' and 'mind' are not mutually exclusive. They are sometimes used synonymously; as when 'states of consciousness' and 'states of the mind' are used as the names of the successive phases of the flux of the inner life; at other times 'consciousness' is treated as a quality or adjunct of mental life; but in Eastern philosophy these two concepts indicate two things absolutely distinct from each other; consciousness is Samvit the enlightener of the mind and the senses and their operations; whereas mind, antaḥ-karaṇa, is jaḍa, unconscious. In other words, mind is matter and consciousness is spirit. Samvit, pure consciousness, is what manifests to the man himself the operations of his mind and of his senses. To borrow an analogy from the senses, the eyes see the world when opened and directed towards objects. Similarly when Samvit, consciousness, is turned on mental processes, the spirit *sees* or *knows* the functioning of his mind. It is as if a ray of light proceeded from the spirit and enlightened the processes of perception, reasoning, etc. These mental functions exist whether consciousness accompanies them or not, just as the world exists whether beings see it or not. Sight manifests them to the individual; so the light of consciousness manifests the functions of perception, reasoning and conation to the man. Consciousness is not thought, for the latter is a procession of images, and the former the manifestation of them to the man himself. Even Hindu writers sometimes confound the two, for the word jñāna is used for thought as well as for consciousness; nor is the word caitanya devoid of ambiguity, because the idea of motion (which is a function of material objects) is associated with it.

'Pure consciousness' has to be distinguished from 'personal consciousness.' This latter is investigated by Prof. James in chap, xii of his *Text-book of Psychology.* He subdivides it into two parts (1) the self as known, the 'Empirical Ego', or the *me* and (2) the self as the knower, the 'Pure Ego', or the I. The former he subdivides into (1) the 'material me,' the body, etc, (2) the 'social me,' the recognition one gets from his mates, and (3) the 'spiritual me', the entire collection of one's states of consciousness; the 'pure Ego' he defines as the Thinker, the Agent behind the passing 'states of consciousness,' whose existence psychology has nothing to do with. This is the best commentary on the proposition that man is a complex. But elaborate as this classification is, it does not distinguish between 'pure consciousness' that is unchanging light and 'personal consciousness' which is mind as illuminated by the spirit, between citśakti, and citta-vṛtti as the Yogī terms them. 'Personal consciousness' is Aham, an ideal construction from experience, just as the world is an ideal construction and belongs to the conceptual plane. 'Pure consciousness' is Ātmā, a fact underlying all that is given by experience. The pure consciousness of the Puruṣa is that of which the personal consciousness bound up with mental or bodily activities, with which alone we are normaly acquainted, is a reflection in matter. When we move the muscles of the body we are conscious of pleasure and pain, of perception, conation, or judgment and we are conscious of ourselves as separate from the objects outside us. These are states of personal consciousness, each state being a complex. From it let us eliminate whatever is contributed by the body and by the mind. What remains is the consciousness that accompanies all mental processes, first differentiated by Plotinus among western philosophers and called the accompaniment—parakolon thesis—of the mental activities by the soul. This is the light of consciousness which manifests both the mental and the physical worlds. It is the power of pure intelligence—citśakti—which being unchangeable, cannot become the seat of perception, for this latter belongs to the mind. We have thus reached a vague idea of pure consciousness as separate from mental activity, by abstraction from the personal consciousness. Pure consciousness however, is not an abstraction but a reality, the greatest reality attainable by man. The realization of this life of the Ātmā is the aim of all schools of Indian philosophy.

What is called the inner life of man is termed 'the stream of consciousness' in western philosophy. Prof. James notes the following four characteristics in the flowing 'states of mind':—

(1) Every 'state' or thought is part of a personal consciousness.

(2) Within each personal consciousness states are always changing.

(3) Each personal consciousness is sensibly continuous.

(4) It is interested in some part of its object to the exclusion of others, and welcomes or rejects —chooses from among them. *(Text-book of Psychology,* chap. xi.) In this description, the conceptions of 'state', and of 'change' belong to matter; those of 'continuity' and 'choice' belong

to the Puruṣa and personal consciousness is due to the union of the two. Matter presents itself as a series of changing states, and spirit, whose light is continuous, chooses a few of them and illuminates or manifests them to himself by *seeing* them. Only we must regard all states of the mind—all cognitions, desires and actions as states of matter that is always in a flux, and not as belonging to the spirit, whose life is continuous and unbroken. Prof. James explains that the third of the above four propositions "means two things: (a) That even where there is a time-gap the consciousness after it feels as if it belonged together with the consciousness before it, as another part of the same self; (b) That the changes from one moment to another in the quality of the consciousness are never absolutely abrupt." (*Ib.*) This continuity is explicable only if consciousness is regarded as separate from mental states, and the relation between the two to be similar to that between a light and a procession of objects illuminated by the light. There is no change in the 'quality' of consciousness, but to strain the analogy a little, the *object,* in this case a state of mind, goes to the outermost fringe of the field of illumination and hence looks dim and no more.

G. F. Stout (*Manual of Psychology,* p. 8) notes two uses of the word consciousness:— (1) To indicate all mental states whether we have cognizance of them or not (2) the awareness we have of ourselves and of our own experiences, as states of the Self—an inner sense—the function by which we perceive the mind and its processes, as sight perceives material facts. Father Maher distinguishes three meanings generally attached to this word, (1) To indicate the sum total of our psychical existence, all cognitive, emotional and appetitive states which are capable of being apprehended. (2) The minds direct, intuitive, or immediate knowledge either of its own operations or of something other than itself acting upon it; in other words, the energy of the cognitive act, and not the emotional or volitional acts as cognized. (3) The reflex operation by which the mind attends to its states and recognizes them as its own. (*Psychology*, pp. 26-27.) The second meaning of consciousness, according to Stout and Maher approximates to some extent to the Hindu idea of it. Perception, Emotion and Conation are functions of the mind that take place according to mental laws, whether they are, or are not, illuminated by the light of the spirit and manifested to it. In ordinary psychic experience this consciousness of the spirit is inextricably and compulsorily bound up with the life of the mind; and can be understood only when it can be separated from the mind and contemplated apart from its mental colouring. This pure consciousness being the immaterial part of man is called Puruṣa —Man, *par excellence*. It is also called Jña, the knower, for he knows or becomes conscious of the functions of the mind, the senses, and the muscles and of himself as the Ātmā. Puruṣa is Svayam-prakāśa, manifesting his own being. He knows himself to be, unlike the mind and the body whose existence is manifested only when cognized by some conscious being. Hence consciousness is frequently compared in Hindu books to light. The light of the sun reveals itself to us directly and when it beats against any object it manifests the existence of that object also. So the Puruṣa reveals his existence to himself and also illuminates a mind or a body he is in contact with, which otherwise would be unconscious, unknown, unmanifested to him. European Idealism makes the existence of matter depend on its being made manifest by the mind. It holds that whether there be a noumenon behind what we cognize as matter or not, it is certain that sensations exist and that as sensations are mental modifications, no objective existence can be manifested in the absence of mind. Constructive Idealism represented by John Stuart Mill admits a permanent possibility of sensation behind the phenomena of the objective world; but the thorough-going Idealism of Berkeley does not. Indian thought is a much more profound Idealism than these; mind and matter are both objective to the Puruṣa; they are revealed by him, without whose illumination they are Asat, non-being, for Sadbhāva, manifestation of being, can never exist without the illumination of the Puruṣa. But to himself Puruṣa is always illuminated; consciousness is an ultimate factor of human experience and cannot be proved or need not be manifested by anything else. Descartes argued, "I think, therefore I am;" Hindu Philosophers argue, "I am, therefore I am."

2. The Ātmā is of the nature of consciousness and is immutable

The part of Man that we have called consciousness is variously named Puruṣa, Ātmā, Bhoktā, etc, and its characteristics variously described. Thus the Puruṣa of the Sāṅkhya School is pure consciousness, devoid of any quality. The Ātmā of the Vaiśeṣikas is characterised by desire, effort and so on. But in all Schools the essential nature of the Ātmā is Svayamprakāśatva, the power of illuminating or manifesting the mental and bodily functions which, but for the Ātmā, would go on unconscious and unknown. Itself is immutable, a steady light that knows not change. The immutability and hence the immortality of this immaterial part of man is involved in its very conception. Ātmā is vibhu, not limited by space; matter is aṇu, atomic. It is, in the words of Plotinus, "All in all and all in every part." Hence the Ātmā is neither divisible nor indivisible, neither a compound nor an atom, not susceptible of diminution nor of excess. It is futile to attempt to conceive the origination or destruction of consciousness, for consciousness is involved in that very conception. Creation and destruction are understandable if conceived as the beginning or the ending of one of a series of forms in which any noumenon manifests itself in relation to an observer; consciousness being from its very nature immutable can hence neither begin nor end. "The Ātmā is Jña, eternal consciousness, because it is increate. Eternal consciousness is the nature of the Ātmā, just as heat and light are of fire." (*Śaṅkara Bhāṣya* on *Ved. Sūt. II. iii, 18*). Moreover, Ātmā is by definition the opposite of Anātmā, matter. The essential nature of matter is its mutability, its capability to evolve into a procession of phenomenal forms; whereas Ātmā is unchanging. Therefore the beginning or the ending of consciousness is excluded from the very definition of Ātmā. He may shift his place of illumination from body to body; or rather, a series of bodies may be periodically brought near him and shine by his reflected light, but he is nitya, eternal. Some Bauddha schools alone, of Indian systems, reject the notion of the continuity of the life of the man's Ātmā, but Buddhism and Jainism are excluded from this brief survey of Indian thought, only the so-called orthodox schools being included, those that at least nominally admit the prāmāṇya, authority, of the Veda and do not openly denounce it as the followers of the Buddha and the Jina do.

3. Mind, though an inner organ is material and is other than the Ātmā

The mind of man is an organ made of subtle matter and is not immaterial or spiritual but prākṛta, made of matter. Sensation, perception, volition, etc., are in western philosophy called subjective states and treated as non-material. Hindu philosophy analyses them into two factors, *viz:* (1) a mental process internal but *not* subjective, and (2) consciousness accompanying the process and reflected from the Ātmā. The first is material and the second immaterial. Mental processes are variously classified in the various schools, the Sāṅkhya attributing to the mind all psychic life, and the Vaiśeṣika regarding it merely as the organ of attention, but all schools are agreed in regarding mind as matter. This apparent paradox of schools of philosophy, essentially idealistic, but holding to the view called materialism in the west, namely the view that mind is matter, has proved a stumbling-block to every western scholar. In western philosophy, the clear-cut concept 'consciousness' as we have formulated it above has not been attained; nor are definite marks attached to the concept 'matter.' Descartes made extension the only characteristic of matter. This "confusion of matter with space", as Clark-Maxwell called it, even Spinoza, the expounder of Descartes, rebelled against. In ordinary thought the so-called properties of matter are made to hang loosely from that concept, and the phrase 'states of consciousness' is held to imply elementary facts incapable of further analysis. When consciousness is eliminated from the facts of psychic life and when it is realized that mental functions are by themselves, jaḍa, unconscious, it ought not to be difficult to understand what the Hindu philosopher means when he says that antaḥkaraṇa is a form of matter. Antaḥkaraṇa literally means, the inner organ as opposed to the outer organs of sensation and action. The jña, the spirit, uses it as an organ, and therefore it must be other than he, "since there is a knower and an organ of knowledge." (*Nyàya Sūtra III. I. 17.)* This mind is objective to the spirit. He sees it quite as much outside him as he sees his body and the world outside him, whereas the knower cannot place himself outside like a perceived object. Objectivity to the conscious Puruṣa is the chief mark of matter; matter and mind possess this characteristic. Another idea involved in the concept 'matter' is its mutability, its ever-present flux, its capability of evolving in a series of ever-changing phenomena. Antaḥkaraṇa evolves in ever-changing phenomenal forms (called cittavṛtti by the Yoga school) like the waves and ripples and eddies on the surface of a lake, unlike the steady light of the Puruṣa which waxes not nor wanes.

These phenomenal manifestations of matter in a never ending kaleidoscopic flux of forms are subject to time and space; and mental events are both temporal and spatial. They succeed one another in time and are restricted in space to the brain which subserves them. Puruṣa is neither big nor small; he has no before and after. These spatio-temporal relations of the manifestations of mind are subject to the law of causation. They are prakṛti-vikṛti, related as cause and effect. But consciousness is a steady light and where there is no change, there can be nothing subject to the relation of cause and effect. Hence if, as modern Psychology admits, mental states are governed by the law of causation, mind is matter, not spirit.

Atomicity—indivisibility and invisibility— is a mark of certain forms of matter according to the Vaiśeṣika philosophers and mind is aṇu, atomic. Ātmā is vibhu, pervasive, everywhere and nowhere. Consciousness cannot be conceived as being restricted to any part of the body through which it manifests itself; but the mental processes of cognition, desire, etc., are certainly not "all in all and all in every part," but clearly localized.

Traiguṇya—being possessed of the three Guṇas or fundamental properties, resistance, motion and equilibrium—is the chief characteristic of matter according to the Sāṅkhyas. Whatever resists force, can be moved by it and reaches equilibrium under the action of many forces—that is matter according to this school. Antaḥkaraṇa displays all these characteristics, inertia, excitability and finally equilibrium. But consciousness by itself is not amenable to the influence of external objects. It cannot be quenched; nor can it be increased by their influence. Hence it is a category quite distinct from mind.

It is difficult to realize mind to be matter, because of the fact that it derives a pseudo-subjectivity on account of its being an inner organ. When our muscles act, our consciousness accompanies the action; but we can in thought separate the consciousness from the muscular action and realize the latter as a phenomenon of matter that is the non-ego, and all the more easily because in the case of other human beings than ourselves we observe these muscular actions without observing the consciousness that accompanies them. But mental action each man can study only in the operations of his own mind, and as these are accompanied by the light of his own consciousness, the separation of these two and the appreciation of the difference of the nature of consciousness and of mental action becomes a matter of difficulty.

Plato and Aristotle use such phrases as the "seeing of sight", "the perceiving of perception," the "thinking of thought" to indicate consciousness apart from mental functioning. *Kena Upaniṣat* uses strikingly similar phrases "what speech does not enlighten, but what enlightens speech," "what one does not think with the mind, but by whom they say the mind is thought", "what one sees not by the eye, but by whom seeing is seen", "what one does not hear by the ear, but by whom hearing is heard," "what none breathes with breath, but by whom breath is breathed, this is Brahma, not what people here worship." (I. *4-8.)* Plotinus, among ancient philosophers first clearly formulated this distinction. "Intelligence is one thing and the apprehension of intelligence is another. And we always perceive intellectually, but we do not always apprehend that we do so." (*Enn. IV. 3. 30,* Trans. Taylor.) This is the first clear indication in European philosophy of the existence of unconscious mental action, and of the idea that our so-called inner life is a complex of two different factors—consciousness and unconscious mental modifications. The idea that consciousness is not a necessary concomitant of mental operations was first clearly enunciated in modern European philosophy by Leibniz. "As a matter of fact our soul has the power of representing to itself any form of nature whenever the occasion comes for thinking about it, and I think that this activity of our soul is, so far as it expresses some nature, form or essence, properly the idea of the thing. This is in us and is always in us, *whether we are thinking of it or no." (Metaphysics,* Tr. by Montgomery, p. 64). "Perception should be carefully distinguished from apperception or consciousness. In this matter the Cartesians have fallen into a serious error, in that they treat as non-existent those perceptions of which we are not conscious." *(Ib :* p. 253*)*. Sir William Hamilton brought into prominence the conception of unconscious mental modifications. Dr. Schofield, in the opening chapter of his *Unconscious Therapeutics,* attributes the phenomena of hysteria to the power of unconscious mind, and justly complains that the powers of unconscious mind have been unduly neglected by investigators. But it has not struck western thinkers that mind is in itself always unconscious as muscle is always unconscious. Ribot, in *The Diseases of Personality,* uses the fact that the life of the mind is sometimes unconscious, to prove that consciousness is "a simple phenomenon, superadded to the activity of the brain, as an event having its own conditions of existence appearing and disappearing according to circumstances" (*Ib* : p. 4). Binet says, consciousness is "capable of disappearing without the corresponding nerve process being altered. Two similar images succeed each other in the mind. It matters little whether we did or did not notice the resemblance, for being similar, they will put a common cell element in vibration. This identity of seat will be sufficient to produce all the results which are produced by a resemblance which is recognised and judged by a conscious comparison" (*Psychology of Reasoning,* p. 126). "The formation of general ideas must take place without the intervention of the cell, in the same manner as suggestion by similarity and for the same reasons, by the sole virtue of the images raised; or in more accurate terms by the effect of the identity of the seat of the particular impression. Images have the property of organizing themselves into general images as they have the property of suggesting similar images" *(Ibid* : p. 27). This is true so far as it goes, but it does not go far enough. All psychic life is in itself unconscious, except in so far as the light of consciousness illuminates it and manifests it to the knower. Consciousness is unique; it exists for itself and of itself. Psychic life runs its own course, following its own laws, which are the same as the general laws of matter; this course is not affected by the light of Puruṣa that is sometimes shed on it thus bringing it within his field of vision. Psychic and physiological conditions are invariably bound together, both being material functions; consciousness is not a phenomenon or epi-phenomenon of material processes as it exists in its own right, neither beginning nor ending, never increasing, never diminishing. Not so the complex fact, which we have called personal consciousness, made up of the reflection of pure consciousness and of mental functions. All mental functions are in themselves unconscious; when the Puruṣa turns to them he illuminates them and makes them manifest; otherwise they would remain as unmanifest as the physical world would be in the absence of sentient beings. Mind is a material fact just as a muscle is a material fact. The action of the mind or the muscle may be or may not be accompanied by consciousness. In investigating the action of the mind or the muscle, consciousness has to be eliminated as an alien factor, and mind should be realized to be always unconscious in its own own nature, as muscle is. Western philosophy not thus distinguishing the nature of consciousness to be characteristically different from that of mind has raised an insoluble problem—"what is the relation of conscious mind and unconscious matter? Is it one of interaction, or of parallelism?" Either hypothesis is unthinkable. It is neither possible nor philosophically helpful to imagine that consciousness and modifications of matter, categories so characteristically apart from each other, can interact or run parallel to each other. Immutability and mutability cannot meet. Mind is matter and mental processes are material modifications. Consciousness may illuminate them, manifest them, or know them, but except this there can be no other relations between them and consciousness. Whether the mind be taken as identical with the nervous system, as western materialists do, or it be constituted of subtle matter as eastern philosophers hold, it is absolutely different from the Puruṣa that illuminates it; though he may out of ignorance identify himself with it, he is not really identical with it. The disciplines prescribed by the founders of the Darśanas are but means of training a man to realize the nature of the Ātmā to be different from that of mind. The bondage from which all the Darśanas except the Pūrva Mīmāṁsā propose to relieve the Ātmā is that due to adhyāsa, false identification of himself with mind, the consequent pain due to ignorance, and mokṣa is the actual realization of the difference of these two. Till this difference between the Ātmā and mind is grasped it is impossible to understand the philosophy of the East.

4. Psychic Life obeys fixed laws and hence all mental events are determinable

As the antaḥkaraṇa is a material organ, its modifications must take place under fixed laws. All matter obeys the law of causation. Hence every mental event is the resultant of previous events, so that if the causes were known, the effects could be calculated and predicted exactly as in any other sphere of matter. As all schools of Hindu philosophy thus regard mind as a form of matter, the problem of the freedom of the will was never raised in India. The 'will' is a metaphysical entity, that is one of which we cannot form a picture, which, in European philosophy, is supposed to be a factor of the mind and to introduce into phenomena, mental or bodily, a new force which can upset all known causes of those phenomena. Hindu philosophy analyses mental events into cognitions, desires and actions interconnected by causal relations, but does not postulate a will among them. The threefold life of the mind goes on under the triple law of Sattva, Rajas and Tamas, but neither the mind itself nor anything extraneous to it can constrain the mind. There is no other *vera causa* of its movements than Sattva, Rajas and Tamas, which are but the conditions of its modifications. Hence the so-called freedom of the will is a myth. That cannot be called free which obeys fixed laws and the course of whose modifications can be calculated beforehand. The mind is no more free than the apple which falls when it is released from the tree which gave it birth. Hence all Indian philosophy is deterministic. It regards all mental action as reflex; a current of energy (called Prāṇa, the analogue of nervous energy in subtle matter) from without, entering the mind and returning as an action. In the mind, deliberation may intervene between the in-going and out-going currents. During the deliberation, motives floating in the mind or buried deep within it may rise and influence the direction of the return current, but all is calculable, all is determinable. No mental function is "free" in the sense that the well known laws of matter are transcended by them.

The mind is not free, but the Ātmā may attain freedom from his bondage to mind. Consciousness is involved in most mental and bodily processes. We are generally conscious of our thoughts and motions. In the case of some of them, we can deliberately withdraw our consciousness from them. We can turn our consciousness away from a passing thought or a casual bodily activity; but an intricate train of thought or a complicated co-ordination of muscular contractions perforce drags the consciousness into it. This compulsory involution of the consciousness in mental or bodily life is bondage; the ability to withdraw the consciousness from mental or bodily events, however exciting, or again, the ability to stick to a thought which is being hustled out of the field of consciousness by other thoughts is the freedom which man is to gradually acquire by self-training. Thus freedom is the goal of human evolution; but this is not freedom of the will, but the liberation of consciousness from being compulsorily mixed up with bodily and mental events. The Mukta, he who has reached perfection, is said to be "free." It is not freedom of the will that he develops, but the freedom from the compulsory interlocking of his conscious self with his mind and his body. He may turn away from matter and thus escape its tyranny, but if he uses a mind, he can do so only by recognizing its laws and by utilizing them by judicious obedience to them just as man uses the forces of the physical world by understanding them and obeying them. In this sense, the greatest God, nay Īśvara Himself, is said to be not above the Law of Karma.

The two profoundest thinkers of modern Europe Spinoza and Leibniz had no illusions on the question of free will. "In the mind there is no absolute or free will; but the mind is determined to wish this or that by a cause, which has also been determined by another cause, and this last by another cause and so on to infinity" (Spinoza, *Ethics,* 18, 48, Transl: Elwes). "All our thoughts and perceptions are but the consequence, contingent it is true, of our precedent thoughts and perceptions, in such a way that were I able to consider directly all that happens or appears to me at the present time, I should be able to see all that will happen to me or that will ever appear to me" (Leibniz, *Metaphysics,* Transl: Montgomery, p. 25).

The theory of free-will has been re-started in recent western Philosophy by the argument that it is a datum of consciousness. In the interest of this theory Munsterberg has propounded an illogical antithesis between "truth of life" (Free Will) and truth of science (Determinism). The function of Science is to group the facts of life under ideal schemes, and hence there cannot be any antithesis between the two. The new Oxford School of Hmanism, led by Dr. F. C. S. Schiller, holds the view that determinism is a postulate, a methodological assumption in the sphere of science, the truth of which is strictly relative to its explanatory function. Similarly freedom is a postulate in the moral sphere with as good a right to exist if it can be used with like profit. But common sense rebels against the adoption of two opposing postulates to explain the same phenomena. The real cause of the difficulty is this:—determinism is a fact of the mental world and freedom, possible or actual, belongs to the sphere of Ātmā. Western philosophy treats the mind enlightened by the consciousness of the Ātmā as one single category, whereas a so-called state of consciousness, *i.e.* a psychical event, is a complex of two factors—one unique, at present in bondage but with the possibility of acquiring freedom, and the other, working under fixed laws. With regard to this mixed category, called personal consciousness, disputes have raged. Some looking at one side of the question have maintained it is free and others have protested against the idea. Hindu philosophy escaped being caught in the vortex of this dispute, because it started with a clear analysis of a psychic state into its constituent elements (1) consciousness and (2) a flux of psychic phenomena and saw, from its inception that freedom as a datum of consciousness, and determinism of the psychic series as a scientific conception are not incompatible, because thy refer to different categories. In popular religious thought, the question is still further confused by the importation into it of alien problems. The problem of evil supposed to be introduced into the world by a personal devil and the idea of the moral responsibility of man for the proper use of powers he was supposed to be gifted with by a personal God have confounded the real philosophical question at issue. The irrepressible anthropomorphism which ruled early human cultures and inspired the ideals of so many world-scriptures erected God into an autocratic Ruler who gave life and human faculties to man and ordered him to use them according to certain ordinances on pain of punishment for violation. But science has abolished this God made in man's image and this divine law which was but a glorified copy of human laws.

Others maintain that effort depends on free will. Effort is roughly proportional to stimulus, and belongs as much to matter, as force does; for what depends on stimulus from without cannot in any sense be spiritual or free.

A few again fight shy of a frank acceptance of determinism from a fear that it will render impossible man's guiding his self-improvement. This fear is groundless. The supersession of the capricious Gods of nature of the early days by the recognition of natural law in the material Universe has in no wise tended to strangle human efforts to utilize nature for human purposes. So, too, will the recognition of natural law in the mental and moral world not prevent human efforts in mental growth; but on the contrary, it would make self-training intelligent and effective and prove it necessary. Ignorance of the laws of the mental world and a blind faith in its being outside the law of causation can never help effort. On the contrary a knowledge of the conditions of mental life, of what is possible and what is impossible in mental training, and of the means whereby we might co-operate with nature in the evolution of our minds is the best possible help to individual effort for self-improvement.

5. The five sense-organs and the action-organs are, like the mind, made of subtle matter

Subject to the mind are the five Jñānendryas (organs of knowledge) and the five Karmendriyas (organs of action). These also are made of subtle matter. The nervous system is the physiological counterpart of these eleven subtle organs, one "internal" and ten "external." They are all made of Sūkṣma bhūta, the five kinds of subtle elementary matter to be discussed later on. The organs of knowledge are those of audition, touch, vision, taste and smell. The organs of action are those of speaking, handling, walking, excretion and procreation. These ten organs are conceived as being primarily modifications of invisible subtle matter, which evolve into those of the visible physical body. Their ten functions are controlled by ten different subtle lines of force and they are subordinate elements of psychical life, while the functions of the mind are its principal elements. Like the mental functions they enter the field of consciousness only when the light of Ātmā falls upon them. At first sight it looks like a violation of the law of Parsimony that the senses are conceived as existing both in the physical and super-physical matter. But if it is true, as all Hindu Yogis assert, that the sense functions are exercised by a man separated from the physical body during life or after death, the subtle organs ought to exist separate from the gross ones. The division of muscular functions (Karmendriyas) into five classes is against the modern physiological idea that motor impulses of all kinds are one and the same; but so long as physiology has not yet been able to make up its mind as to what a nervous impulse is, it cannot object to the Hindu idea of there being five different kinds of motor impulses in the subtle body.

6. The Eleven organs inhere in a Liṅga-deha which is relatively permanent

The mind of man and the other ten organs inhere in a body of subtle matter called Liṅga-deha (characteristic body) also called ayonija (nonuterine body) and[5] subdivided variously into several subtle bodies by the different schools. It is the companion of the Ātmā during his long wanderings (Saṁsāra) in akalpa (world period). It is bhūtāśraya, composed of elementary subtle substances. It is also Karmāśraya the store-house of saṁskāras, potential deposits of man's thoughts, desires and actions. It is the vechicle of his prāṇas, nervous energies of various kinds. The union of Puruṣa with the Liṅgadeha, during the long period of his manifested life (Kalpa) is for the purpose of enabling him to experience pleasure and pain (bhoga) and finally reach apavarga (emancipation). Pleasure and pain are not primary attributes of physical or psychic life. The action of the outside world on man through the sense organs produces a reaction in the shape of a motor impulse. This motor impulse is a flow of prāṇa towards muscles. This flow if uninterrupted is called pleasure and if interrupted is called pain. Both in normal and morbid conditions pleasure and pain are frequently confounded and people find pleasure in pain and vice versa; thus proving that the flow or interruption of prāṇa is the primary fact and pleasure and pain but an interpretation thereof. This is all in harmony with the Hindu ideas; but this flow or interruption of energy takes place in the Liṅgadeha, whose special function is Bhoktṛtva, capability of subserving sensibility.

The Neo-platonists believed in the existence of a Liṅga-deha. Plotinus speaks of "a separable portion of the soul," a "common, dual, or composite nature which is the subject in perception," and which is an intermediary between soul and body. (Whittaker's *Neo-platonists, pp.* 46-49). This doctrine dropped out of European philosophy in the darkness of the middle ages. On account of the severance of the Greek philosophic tradition during this period of the obscuration of European intellectual life it is impossible to find out what the ancients really meant by the terms psyche and mens, nor can we trace the exact correspondence between Greek and Hindu philosophy; only it is certain that the modern English translations of Greek terms are as inadequate as those of Saṁskṛt terms and there was more unity of thought between the ancient Greek and the ancient Indian than the English translations of Greek and Saṁskṛt works indicate.

7. The Liṅgadeha is periodically connected with a body of flesh

This is the Sthūla-deha, the "gross body" by means of which man acts on nature outside him. The addition of this Sthūladeha completes the man. The personal consciousness as already pointed out is the result of the conjunction of the Saṁvit of Puruṣa, the Bhoktṛtva (sensibility) of the Liṅgadeha and the Kartṛtva (capacity for action) of the body of flesh and blood. While in this body the world offers man pleasures to be enjoyed and pains to be avoided. These call forth his activities in manipulating nature. When he acts on the world he gets a knowledge of the world as object and of himself as actor. The resulting pleasure and pain intensify this knowledge of self as apart from the not-self. Desires and experience of pleasure and pain interact on each other, and he thus establishes relations between himself and other men. He therefore periodically returns to incarnation for the fruition of his hankerings and the satisfaction of the bonds established between himself and others. When Rāgadveṣam (desire and aversion) is transcended, compulsory incarnations cease.

Super-human beings also who normally have but subtle bodies sometimes take birth in human bodies. This is called Avatāra, a crossing over of the boundaries that usually separate the currents of human and super-human lives. This may be a voluntary or a compulsory incarnation. Kṛṣṇa in the *Bhagavat Gītā* IV. *6-8* says, "Though I am not a being subject to birth and death and the Lord of born beings, I by my wonder-working power enter into prakṛti that is mine and am born in a body. Whenever there is a decay of right action and increase of lawlessness, then I make for myself a body, O Bhārata; for the protection of the well-doers and destruction of ill-doers and the establishment of laws I come to birth age after age." The *Purāṇas* abound in tales of superphysical beings being made to take physical births as a punishment, but an incarnation voluntary or involuntary is a limitation to the being that undergoes it, for while in a physical body, the laws of physical matter cannot be transcended even by the highest. But the body also affords the super-physical being opportunities to hold intercourse with human beings and affect their destinies in a much surer fashion than otherwise, as is indicated in the Ślokas quoted above. If superphysical beings should from their own spheres act directly on the brains of man, it would be at the cost of upsetting the nervous, and hence the mental and moral, equilibrium of the man acted on. Inspired prophets have always been abnormal men in whom pathological conditions have been prominent and to them perfect sanity as we understand it has been impossible because their evolution has been so different from ours. For even an Īśvara is not omnipotent in the sense that laws of being (material or immaterial) can be suspended by him. The only way He can directly affect human beings is by birth among them as a man. As Antaryāmī (inner controller) he turns the wheel of life; he is onlooker, approver, supporter, enjoyer, greatest sovereign and highest self in the body (*Bhag: Gītā* XIII. 22), but laws of nature (Prakṛti) are immutable and she is the root of all mutations and qualities (*Ib* : 13-19).

Avatāra is popularly understood as a "descent" of Īśvara into mundane regions. This is absurd. Īśvara is everywhere and hence a "descent" would be to Him an impossible feat. Hindu writers take care to explain that what actually takes place in Avatāras is but the manifestation, generally temporary, of a ray of Him, through the body of an advanced human being, more than He is manifested in the heart of the ordinary man. Even Kṛṣṇa said to be a "full" Avatāra a became an ordinary man sometime before his death.

8. Matter is mutable, but increate and obeys fixed Laws

Matter like the Ātmā is increate and indestructible. Creation exnihilo and dissolution again into nothingness have been notions always obnoxious to Hindu thinkers. The Saṁskṛt root Sṛj means to pour out, emit, beget and Sṛṣṭī means emission or emanation. In the Vedas the self-existent is always spoken of as emitting or emanating matter as well as living beings by means of tapas, meditation. Leibniz among European philosophers agrees with the Hindus in regarding creation "as a kind of emanation just as we produce our thoughts" (*Metaphysics,* tr. Montgomery p.23). The chief characteristic of matter is that it is dṛśya, perceptible, that which becomes an object to the knower. It is jaḍa *i.e.,* its existence could be manifested only by the spirit that is the seer; it is not svayam-prakāśa, *i e.* it cannot of itself manifest its being. It is prakṛti-vikṛti, mutable. It transforms itself into a series of phenomena during a cycle of manifestation (kalpa), each phenomenon being a modification of a previous something and itself soon modified into something else. This susceptibility to change of name and form, nāmarūpa, as well as its objectivity are the primary characteristics of matter. Matter is also atomic, Bhinnā, whereas the Ātmā, cannot be broken up into minute parts. It has three primary characteristics or Guṇas which are the fundamental laws of its being—Tamas, Rajas, and Sattva . In the physical world, Tamas is the property of inertia and sums up the facts that particles of matter or material objects tend to retain their states of motion or rest and offer resistance to any force acting on them. It is the fundamental Law of all beings and is the primary definition of objective existence. Rajas indicates the second property of matter, by which we conceive of it as "not only that which offers resistence to change of motion, but also that which causes change of motion in other portions as of matter : it is not only the object on which force spends itself, it is the seat of this force." (Merz, *Hist. Eur. Thought,* i. 336). Rajas, therefore, is the Law of Force, embodying the Second fundamental property of matter as it shows itself to our senses. Sattva is the Law of equilibrium by which atoms and molecules, paramāṇus and dvayaṇukas, when they are parts of objects act and react on each other so as to reach equilibrium and to hold together and remain as objects. These three properties of matter, or guṇas as the Hindus call them, follow from the fact of the existence of material objects. If they have to exist at all they must have those guṇas, hence they constitute the materiality of matter. They constitute, as it were, three cases of the so-called Law of self-preservation. If we try to imagine a physical world without one of these three guṇas of inertia, force and equilibrium we shall find that our world will dissolve into thin air before our mental vision. Hence they are guṇas more properly than Laws. This explanation of the action of the three guṇas in the physical world makes them exactly the same as Newton's famous three Laws of motion. It is being gradually recognised that Newton's Laws are not so much Laws of motion as factors that make up the concept 'matter'. The first and third Laws can scarcely be called Laws of motion. The second is as much a Law of motion as of matter. They are more properly the fundamental properties, guṇas, of matter, that which differentiates matter from what is not matter. They define matter and indicate the conditions of its manifestation. Matter manifests itself while in motion; that is why they are also called Laws of motion. In the earlier days, motion was regarded sometimes as an ensrationis, sometimes as a thing in itself, because the Cartesian conception of material substance as consisting merely in extension was prevalent. But we can see "that matter without motion is as inconceivable as matter without extension, so that Descartes' assumption that matter was there first as an inert lump and motion was put into it afterwards is illlegetimate and irrational" (Pollock, *Spinoza His Life and Philosophy,* p. 115).

These three Guṇas condition mental modifications also. Mental events are of three levels, according as cognitions, desires and actions predominate in them. In the lowest level, Tamas, Rajas and Sattva appear automatic action, excited action, and deliberative action. In the level of desire, the three manifest themselves as all-compelling desire, the struggle of motives and Vairāgya, or regulated desire. In the level of cognition, the three Guṇas operate as ignorance, clouded intellect and perfect knowledge. The general tone of the mind, under the influence of these guṇas, is indifference, pain and pleasure. Thus the mind is as traiguṇya, conditioned by the three guṇas, as the body.

Thus we see that the conception of the three Guṇas is the widest and most helpful generalization that has been reached by philosophy. It embraces within its wide sweep all states of perceptible objects and all states of mind that we know of, everything that is mutable, everything that is objective to the

Puruṣa, and binds them in one general concept, Guṇas differentiated into the three conditions of the manifestation of the objective Cosmos. The inertia of physical objects, the automatism of the mind, its subjection to desire, the failure of its powers of apprehension and insensibility to pleasure and pain are all comprehended under the one word, Tamas. Tamas is literally, 'being choked', hence darkness, and sums up in one word these characteristics and forms one of the conditions of the manifestation of matter. Rajas similarly sums up motion under the constraint of force, excitement, struggle of desires, wrong apprehension and pain. Rajas, literally, the cloudy coloured illumination of the intermediate sphere between the dark earth and the bright heaven, aptly denominates this condition. The common factor of equilibrium, balance, self-control, right apprehension and pleasure is conceived as Sattva, real being.

These three guṇas are not qualities of any substance, but the laws of matter, the modes in which matter can manifest itself. Karl Pearson defines scientific method to consist in "the careful and often laborious classification of facts, in the comparison of their relationships and sequences, and finally in the discovery, by the aid of the disciplined imagination, of a brief statement, or formula, which in a few words resumes a wide range of facts." Such a formula is a scientific law. In this sense, the Guṇas are the fundamental laws of matter. The word, law, associated as it is with the idea of a Law-giver is a rather unsatisfactory word unless we, as Lotze says, "give up the customary view according to which the Laws of reality are regarded as a self-subsistent power controlling the real and actual. They are nothing more than general forms of thought in which, a spirit contemplating the course of the world and comparing its different movements might sum up the whole system of it in one brief expression. What is thus briefly expressed is the thing realized by and through the own nature of things themselves, which are what they are and act as they act of themselves, so making it possible for us to comprehend their behaviour as a case of this or that law. Everything which we regard as a law or ordering of the world is just the world's own nature, and it is only our incorrect, though hardly avoidable way of looking at things which represents it as a rule separable therefrom and having already an authority from some other source to which this nature must submit" (*Philosophy of Religion,* p. 76). In other words, the activity of matter found the laws and not the laws the activity. The three laws, or Guṇas, condition the manifestation of matter everywhere. What is not matter—Puruṣa, consciousness—can alone never be affected by the Guṇas, which do not belong to the sphere of the immutable Ātmā.

That matter is also subject to Space and Time and causality follows from its being atomic in constitution and Traiguṇya in nature. But though the evolution of matter is subject to time, matter itself is indestructible. The individual Puruṣa may turn from it and ignore it but it ceases not to exist. And when The Lord of the Universe withdraws His energies from it its - evolution is but interrupted, for during Pralaya, matter continues to exist as Asat, Avyakta, unmanifested "as the shoot within the seed (*Śaṅkara)*.

9. The world-history is made up of alternating periods of activity and rest

Matter is in a constant state of flux. The largest periodical flux is that of pralaya and kalpa. Pralaya is the period when matter is avyakta, undifferentiated. It cannot then be cognized. The Guṇas are in a state of quiescence. Puruṣas are then also avyakta, unmanifest. Kalpa is the period of the manifestation of a world, or a system of worlds. Western scholars are of opinion that the doctrine of periodical manifestations and obscurations of the universe did not exist in the earliest period of the *Veda* notwithstanding the assertion of *Ṛgveda,* V. 190-3, that "Brahmā created as before. "But western scholars are apt to forget that the three *Vedas* are, after all compilations for purposes of Yajña (sacrifice), and were never intended to be religious treatises; for the matter of that, even the *Upaniṣads* are but manuals of Upāsanā (meditation) and religious doctrines can, if they appear at all in them, do so only by way of allusion. Hence the paucity or even the absence of references to any doctrine in these books cannot by itself be treated as evidence to prove that the doctrine had not been worked out by the ancient thinkers. It was just because the whole of the *Veda*—the former and the latter parts, the portion of ceremonial work and that of meditation, was merely a manual of ritualism that mīmāṁsās were required to elucidate the theory and practice of the rituals. Therefore there is nothing to disprove the traditional view accepted in India that the doctrine of periodical dissolution and creation belongs to the earliest ages of Indian thought.

Nor is the doctrine so difficult or complicated as to presuppose a long previous course of philosophical development. Man naturally works from his own constitution to that of the cosmos. In the earliest savage times he attributed his own thoughts and sentiments to rocks and trees and animals around him. So today he extends the conceptions of force and of energy which he is conscious of in his own body to the objects about him and thence seeks to explain the cosmos. Just so, in olden times he extended the daily alternations of activity and sleep of his own body, jāgrata and suṣupti to the universe and formulated the ideas of Brahmā's activity (Kalpa) and sleep (pralaya). There is nothing specially modern in this conception that should compel the historian of Hindu thought to assign to it a later age.

Here it must be noted that the word Nitya, usually translated eternal, means not an illimitable future, as is understood in the West. Eternity is but time with its boundaries thrown to a great distance, just as infinite space, is but limited space, but with its bounds thrown far apart. Both phrases are freely used and few realize they are but words without any definite meaning behind them. On the contrary, Hindu philosophy invariably understands by Nitya, up to the end of this Kalpa; a śloka of the *Matsya Purāṇa,* says "By immortality (amṛtatva) is meant (life) until the destruction of all beings (i.e. until Pralaya sets in). Immunity from reincarnation is life as long as the three lokas last." Indeed it is meaningless to extend Time, as we know it, into the state, called Pralaya. Time is related to the change of states of a perceiving mind and hence cannot exist, when the minds themselves are no more. The Hindu philosophy divides Kāla (Time) into two classes, Khaṇḍa, and Akhaṇḍa, discrete and continuous. The former alone, is time as we know it. The latter, duration, independent of change of states of mind, we can scarcely understand, since it transcends human experience. *Mait. Up*. vi. 15. says:—"There are two forms of Brahma, Kāla and Akāla, Time and No-Time. That which is before the Sun is Akāla, devoid of parts; and that which is subsequent to the Sun is Time, with parts." It is in this sense of Akhaṇḍa, that kāla is hymned as the source and ruler of all things in *Atharva Veda* xix. 53, 54. and that Kṛṣṇa speaking as the Īśvara, says in the *Bhag. Gītā* xi. 32, "Time am I, the destroyer of the worlds."

10. The subtle elements that make up all objects are five corresponding to the five senses

The subtle elements, sūkṣma bhūta, are conceived as elementary sensations. Thus smell, taste, light, touch and sound exist in a rudimentary, ethereal form outside man and also in his sensorium. They are called in many schools, tanmātra, lit., that alone, the pure root of sensation. Corresponding to the five senses, there are five tanmātras which by their combinations produce the sthūla bhūta, the objects of the world.

Western Science explains "the ultimate element of material constitution to be an electric charge or nucleus of permanent aethereal strain". "Each sub-atom with its permanent electric charge must be surrounded by a field of permanent or intrinsic aethereal strain, which implies elastic quality in the aethereal instead of complete fluidity; the portion must therefore be in whole or in part a nucleus of intrinsic strain in the aether, a place at which the continuity of the medium has been broken and cemented together again (to use a crude but effective image) without accurately fitting the parts, so that there is a residual strain all round the place" (Larmor, *Aether and Matter,* pp. 26. 27).

Thus have Western Scientists, with extraordinary experimental and mathematical skill, framed a picture of Ākāśa, Aether, modified to serve as the basis of light vibrations. Clerk Maxwell proved light and electricity to be identical, and hence the Aethereal strain charged with electricity is explained as the particular structure that helps us to imagine what corresponds to Rūpatanmātra or rudimentary light. But no Western Scientist has as yet started the question of what are smell, taste and touch. Are they also strains in the Aether and if they are, what kinds of strains? Most Hindu schools say that they also are modifications of Ākāśa, tanmātras, roots of sensation, the Vaiśeṣikas only regarding them, as well as light, to be qualities and not modification, of atoms. Thus four different kinds of strains in Aether would be required to explain the roots of these four sensations. Then there is sound, which Hindu Philosophy conceives as a quality or modification of the unstrained, unmodified, non-atomic Ākāśa. Modern Science explains sound to be vibrations of air. The Hindu idea is that behind the air vibrations there is a modification of Akāśa, not of the kind that constitutes an atom, and this is the basis of sound. There is nothing inherently improbable in this idea that the five sensations are five different modifications of Aether. Outside the human body they exist in a Tamasa or resisting form and constitute the elements of the Universe. Inside the sense-organs the same Aethereal modifications exist in their Sātvika, equilibrated form and hence the man perceives them as sensations. Western Science pictures the external causes of the various sensations as modes of vibration. This has led to the insoluble problem, how can a vibration outside the body become a sensation after it impinges on a nerve. To conceive of light or sound as vibrations as the physicist does, helps him to investigate their properties, but from thence to assert that the vibration is a fact, a noumenon, a reality independent of our thought, and that the sensation is a phenomenal representation of this fact by consciousness to itself is absolutely unphilosophical. For vibration is but a concept of the mind manufactured from experience of the motion of our bodies and itself but a phenomenal representation. It is equally unphilosophical to talk of consciousness responding to vibrations in the forms of sensations. This is (in the words of the *Yoga Sūtras)* a vikalpa, a form of words without any fact corresponding to them (1.9). The only idea we can attach to consciousness is, as Hindu Philosophy points out, that of enlightener, what manifests or illumines that whose existence would otherwise be unmanifest. To speak of consciousness as responding to vibration is to attribute activity to that which cannot be conceived as acting. It is not an active agent, a manipulator of vibration into a sensation, a déus ex machine that mysteriously changes a vibration, a harmonious displacement of molecules of matter into a taste, a smell, etc. Such an explanation is metaphysics in the worst sense of the word —the use of language to conceal ignorance and not to clarify thought. Consciousness can enlighten, render conscious, make the man know what would otherwise be unconscious sensation, unknown to him, but it is impossible to imagine how it can respond to, *i.e.*, change itself, in the form of a sensation, when a vibration falls on it. The physical explanation of sensation that "sound light, heat, electricity and even the nervous influx " is due to "vibratory movements, varying only by their direction and their periods" is, as Binet lucidly points out, "but an artifice, a symbol or a process convenient for classification in order to combine the very different qualities of things in one unifying synthesis—a process having the same theoretical value as a memoria technica, which, by substituting letters for figures, helps us to retain the latter in our minds. This does not mean that figures are, in fact, letters, but it is a convenient substitution which has a practical advantage " (*The Mind and the Brain,* p. 33). Motion is not less of a phenomenon, more of a reality than the five sensations, but is more easily capable of measurement. Otherwise the physicist can conceivably explain all sensations and motions, *i.e.* all phenomena in terms of form, or, as the Hindu mystic does, in terms of sound. From a philosophical standpoint it is a mere accident that our visual and muscular sensations seem to have acquired such a supreme importance that we invent theories explaining other sensations by imaginary visual and muscular events. But it is as valid to explain a sound as a vibration, as to explain a motion as a sound. "To measure the length of a body instead of applying to it a yard wand, one might listen to its sound; for the pitch of the sound given by two cords allows us to deduce their difference of length, and even the absolute length of each," (*Ib.* p. 4). Thus all scientific theories may be reconstructed in terms of auditory events, and sound held to be the parent of all material form; and we may understand why the Hindu calls sound (nāda), the first manifestation of the unmanifested. Hence the idea that vibration is an ultimate fact and sensations are its phenomenal forms, though it underlies all modern European thought, is philosophically absurd.

Moreover to say that a vibration affects consciousness is to attribute mutability to that which is immutable. The Hindu explanation is at least intelligible. Sensation is the same outside the body as it is inside the body. But inside the body it is illuminated by the conscious subject, who is then said to "know", and till it is known it is what we may call "unconscious sensation." Sensation exists outside the body as sensation and the five sensations by their combination constitute the objects of the world. It is in this sense that they are the five elements of the world. Hence also is the world perceptible by a mind. Thus sound inside the auditorium or in the universe, is but a special modification of Akāśa. The perceiving organ of audition and the perceived object, sound, are of the same nature, both being Ākāśa or Śabdatanmātra, pure sensation of sound; only Ākāśa outside the body is not pure, unmixed, like the one in the organ of hearing, but compounded with air, etc., and hence the Śabda (the essence of sound) in the external Ākaśa before it can reach the hearer must first be manifested as nāda or dhvani, or vibrations of air. As a commentator on Jaimini's *Mīmāṁsā Sūtras,* 1. 13, says, "the still atmosphere which interferes with the perception of sound, is removed by the conjunctions and disjunctions of air (undulations, vīcī-taraṅga) issuing from the speaker's mouth and thus sound becomes perceptible." Similarly in the case of the other senses cognition is rendered possible by the fact that the same substance exists inside the sense-organ as in the outside world. These are the five elements, so much misunderstood and hence ridiculed. This Hindu view of the existence of five tanmātras or five elements or five modifications of Aether to account for the five sensations and five sensibila is not as all opposed to reason or to modern ways of thought.

11. All energy in the Universe is personal, *i.e.* bound up with consciousness, though of varying degrees of intensity

Besides consciousness and unconscious matter, the great generalization made from the phenomena of the universe is Energy. Energy is the link between these two. The only manifestation of energy of which we have first hand knowledge is the energy we expend in re-acting on the objects around us by changing their position or conditions. Hence when we observe bodies altering shape or position, we infer that some energy has been acting on them. That the manifestation of energy in the world other than by animals is not accompanied by any degree of consciousness is what is called the mechanical view of the world, and this view dominates modern thought. The opposite view, that all manifestation of energy in the universe proceeds from conscious beings, visible or invisible, is the animistic theory of the cosmos, the adhidaivata explanation of it accepted by all Indian-schools of philosophy. Of these theories the adhidaivata theory is certainly the more plausible, for the conscious exertion of energy by us is a concrete reality of our lives, whereas the idea of energy unaccompanied by consciousness is only an abstraction from our experience. The mechanical theory, like Euclid's theory of space, has been a concept of much assistance in understanding the cosmos, but neither theory is a percept of the world of experience. The extraordinary growth of modern science inspired by the mechanical explanation of the universe has made people forget that it is an abstraction and not a reality of conscious experience.

Of this trio, Consciousness, Energy and Matter, one view isolates Consciousness as Real Being and regards Matter and Energy as being prakṛti or object. This is the view of the *Bhagavadgītā,* vii. 4— 6:-"My atomic Prakṛti eightfold, is Earth, Water, Fire, Ākāśa, Manas, Buddhi and Ahaṁkāra. This is the lower; learn now, O mighty armed, my Prakṛti, higher than this, that which becomes living (Jīva) and by which the Universe is upheld. Know that these two are the wombs of all beings." Another view isolates Prakṛti, and regards consciousness and Śakti, or Energy, often personified as Ambikā, the world-mother, as the chief factor of the cosmos. As the opening stanza of *Ānandalahari* says "Śiva can create only when united with Śakti." This is the Śākta view that has affected later Hindu thought so much. The view that modern science has evolved, which makes Nature, that is, Matter moved by Energy, the reality behind the Universe to the entire exclusion or neglect of Consciousness is nowhere represented in Hindu thought; for all Hindu Philosophy is animistic. Even the Sāṅkhya, Yoga, Pūrvamīmāṁsā and Vaiśeṣika Sūtras, which ignore a Supreme Real Being:—Parabrahma or even a moral Governor of the Universe, accept this scheme of the Adhidaivata hierarchies, troops of gods (devas and asuras) that inhere in nature and cause its operations. These gods are, some of them at least, not spiritually or morally higher than man; for man is the microcosm in whom all the elements of the cosmos exist. Himself is the Puruṣa; his mind, sense organs and action organs represent the various devas, and his bodies represent the subtle and the differentiated elements. Hence the Universe is represented in him in miniature. But the gods, though the field of their operations is much larger, are parts of the macrocosm. They have each one element to deal with and one kind of organ to control it by; nor are many of them capable of the high moral and intellectual advancement that man can attain to. The animistic theory prevails in crude forms among the savage races of the world. Hence the West regards it as a theory fit only for savages, but the true philosopher does not estimate the value of philosophical theories from feelings of racial superiority. The modern impatience with animism is but a phase of the materialism that has obsessed the Western mind; and surely an idealistic savage may have better intuitions than one who is the flower of modern civilisation but blighted by the canker of materialism. The prejudice against animism is, like the prejudice against determinism, due to a feeling that the conduct of conscious beings must be capricious irreducible to fixed laws.

But conduct of man or of nature, depending as it does on mind and body, takes place always according to fixed laws. The informing consciousness that accompanies it either in the human body or in Nature has no power to make it fitful or unamenable to the eternal Laws of matter. Hence the unerring mechanism of Nature's operations is quite compatible with its being enlightened by the conciousness of the gods.

The name animism is an unfortunate one suggesting as it does, totemism and similar associations. But the theory that personality of various kinds or degrees underlies all operations of Nature is not at all crude. Many of the greatest thinkers of the world have accepted and expounded it, some admitting one Personal God, and others assuming many personal beings, calling them Gods, Angels, Powers, Devas, Asuras, etc. Materialism alone opposes it.

Leibniz, who shared with Newton the honour of presiding at the birth of modern scientific thought, perceived the danger of that thought lapsing into a forgetfulness of the intelligence behind nature and vigorously protested against it. In section 19 of his *Metaphysics* he acknowledges the validity of the mechanical explanation of nature so far as it goes, but adds that to neglect totally the intelligence behind nature would be "as if, in order to account for the capture of an important place by a prince, the historian should say it was caused by the particles of powder in the cannon having been touched by a spark of fire expanded with a rapidity capable of pushing a hard, solid body against the walls of the place, while the little particles, which compose the brass of the cannon, were so well interlaced that they did not separate under this impact—as if he should account for it in this way instead of making us see how the foresight of the conqueror brought him to choose the time and proper means, and how his ability surmounted all obstacles" *(Ib.* p. 35). Leibniz uses this argument to establish the intelligence of the one God behind nature, but it does not affect the argument if to that one supreme intelligence be added many subordinate intelligences. Animism, then, is not so terribly primitive a conception as it is said to be.

12. This energy is Prāṇa, which is intermediate between spirit and matter

Western science conceives all forms of energy as motion, molar or molecular. We must remember that this picture of energy of all forms as motion is not a reality independent of our mind. It is a concept formed by us to help our halting thought to deal with the various physical phenomena which we desire to bind into one notion, and is not necessarily true outside the world of ideas. Hindu philosophy regards Prāṇa and not motion as the fundamental energy of the cosmos. Prāṇa is conceived as a power coming from or started by the Puruṣa and acting on matter. This conception of Prāṇa as power charged with consciousness which manifests itself as energy when it acts on matter and thus becomes visible outside the Puruṣa is a necessary corollary of the Adhi-daivata explanation of the world.

The Sāṅkhya cannot admit that Prāṇa can start from the Puruṣa. The utmost that this school and the allied school of Yoga would allow is that Prāṇa starts into activity in matter when there is a union of Puruṣa and Prakṛti.

If nature-powers (Devas) exist behind nature all her energy must ultimately be immaterial in origin. The energy exerted by an animal or a man is primarily nervous energy. All the energy of animals is nervous energy till it leaves the muscles and acts on outside objects. This nervous energy is called Prāṇa.

Western Science has for a hundred years unsuccessfully tried to explain nervous energy as a form of mechanical motion; Eastern Philosophy reverses the process and derives mechanical motion from Prāṇa, or energy accompanied by consciousness.

Prāṇa, corresponds to the Psychikon pneuma, animal spirits, of Greek philosophy, a category which is intermediate between spirit and matter, and brings them into relation with each other. Matter is ever changing, always in a state of flux. Puruṣa is immutable. He reflected, "What is it by whose departure I shall depart (from the body), by establishing whom (in it) I shall remain established (in it)? He emitted Prāṇa" (Praś. *Up*. VI. 3-4) as his empirical representative. Matter is atomic and unconscious; Prāṇa is continuous, that is, not discrete, and charged, as it were, with the consciousness of the Puruṣa. Puruṣa being above space, cannot himself move or be the direct cause of motion in matter. Prāṇa is spoken of as Vāyu or air, for air is the best symbol of an immaterial something which is the cause of motion, but is not at the same time pure spirit. The energy of the Universe is but the Prāṇa of cosmic beings. Prāṇa is Śakti regarded as a material fact and not as conscious somebody. Being an intermediate category between Ātmā and matter it partakes of the nature of both. It is capable of more or less, like matter, and is at the same time accompanied by consciousness, it connects as a bridge Ātmā and matter whose characteristics are so opposed to each other that to speak of their union or their interaction will be as absurd as to say that linear magnitude is mixed with whiteness. Students of European philosophy are familiar with the difficulties of the connection of body and mind. This intermediate category solves all such difficulties.

This doctrine of Universal Prāṇa is developed in the Upaniṣad and Āgama literature and not fully worked out in the other Darśanas. It is not incompatible with their special points of view, but is not discussed by them because the Darśanas concern themselves with the discipline that they advocate, and do not refer to theories not immediately connected with the special mental training they prescribe.

13. The Law of causation—Karma—is supreme in the physical and mental worlds

The Law of Karma is the supreme law under which the manifested Universe works. The binding nature of the relation of cause and effect is part of the conception of the Prakṛti. Both the physical and mental worlds being evolved from matter come under this Law. All beings that possess bodies, even if it be the highest being incarnated cannot be independent of this Law. The free spirit that has reached the self-realization, is alone above it, for spirit being immutable is "free". The fundamental idea of the Law of Karma is this. Every mental or physical process, every thought, desire, or force exerted on bodies is followed by a consequence which when not immediately visible, is called Apūrva, *Adṛṣṭa*, whose nearest English equivalent is "potential energy," which manifests itself when suitable conditions arise.

"The experiences of the seen (physical world) and the unseen (subtle worlds) have their resting place in Karma and their root in Kleśa (the afflictions of ignorance, egoism, etc.); as long as the root exists it fructifies as birth (in human or non-human bodies), life (therein), and experiences (pleasurable or painful). They lead to joy or grief according as they originate in good or evil" (Yoga *Sūt.* ii. 12-14). Every experience is a Saṁskāra, a modification of the subtle body, which has a tendency to reproduce itself; and every man is "bound" by the Saṁskāras. They form the atmosphere which must influence the course of his thoughts, desires, and deeds in the present. It is not every one of the Saṁskār as that can operate every minute of his life. For potential energy can become kinetic only when the proper conditions present themselves. That portion of a man's past that is operative in influencing a man's mind and the course of his experiences during an incarnation is called prārabdha (lit: begun to act). Those that yet lie deep within the inner recesses of his liṅgadeha and have not yet begun to manifest themselves during an incarnation are called saṁcita (accumulated), while every present act, every present thought, every present desire becomes stored in his subtle body as agāmi (augmentative), which goes to enrich his atmopshere of Karma and will react on him in the future.

The present course of a man's life, the circumstances in which he finds himself, the pleasures and pains that will reach him, the thoughts and desires that will rise in his mind and the actions that he will be constrained to do, all depend upon prārabdha. The Law of Karma[3] reigns supreme in the mental and physical worlds.

Hence all schools of Hindu philosophy are rigidly deterministic. Man is not free but bound by his past conduct, is absolutely determined by the desires that operate on the mind and the prārabdha determines what desires should rise under any given combination of circumstances. Desires, actions, even the mind, being all material processes, the supreme Law of matter—the Law of causation —inviolably constrains man. Even the mukta, the liberated man must experience his prārabdha Karma.

14. Saṁsāra, the course of Karma, is anādi, had no beginning

Karma, the sum total of causes, that remains potential during a period of pralaya and manifests at the beginning of a world-period (Kalpa) is described as Anādi, beginningless. Anādi is defined in the Hindu books to be "like a flowing stream whose origin beyond the circle of vision is unknown." In tracing events to their causes we can push back our inquiries up to the point when the present world manifestation began. Beyond that point, it will neither be possible nor profitable to trace the current of causes. It is unphilosophical to assume that these currents must have started at some past point of time, for there are no grounds for such assumption. We know that matter is in constant flux under the Law of causation; but cannot think that there was a period when there was no such flux. If it did not exist at some past point of time it could not at all have been originated. Hence the course of Karma is Anādi, has always existed.

So too, Mūlaprakṛti, causal matter, whether it be the non-existent Nescience of the Advaita, or the germ of objectivity of the other schools. The individual spirits (jīvātmā) too are Anādi, for if they did not exist at any time no cause could have arisen to bring them into being. The Brāhmaṇas and the Upaniṣads very frequently speak of a beginning—Agra. This Agra always means, before the present Kalpa—world-period—and no more. Anādi does not mean eternal. Hindu books speak of two kinds of beginninglessness, (1) Ajanyatva rūpa anāditva, beginninglessness of the kind of never having been born. This belongs only to Absolute Being. (2) Pravāha anāditva, the beginninglessness of a flood, above explained. All Hindu speculations about Nityatva, enternity, ought to be understood only in the second sense; thus the Nitya muktas, eternally free beings, of the Rāmānujīyas are those who were 'free' at the beginning of this Kalpa and the Nityanārakikas the eternally damned, of the Mādhvas are those who will remain "bound" at the end of this Kalpa.

15. Mokṣa is the goal of human life and results from the training of the mind and hence reaching Mokṣa is a mental event

All human beings are baddha, bound, by the course of karma, the causes they have set going, also by the laws of the matter that constitutes their minds and bodies. The object of philosophy is to teach them to escape this bondage and to lead a life uninterrupted by compulsory incarnations. When this is transcended, man is mukta, emancipated. So long as the conscious spirit does not realise its nature and identifies itself with its body or its mind, it is not free. So long as the man's life is but the life of the material body and the material mind, which act according to fixed laws, all life is bondage.

What, then, is mokṣa, the state of freedom to attain which is the true goal of human life? The constant unbroken recognition of the difference between the nature of spirit and of matter, the knowledge that the operations of mind are foreign to, outside of, the real man, the consequent freedom of the spirit from involution into psychic life, and the perfection to which man may bring his mind by knowing the laws of its working. In the physical universe the modern scientific man conquers nature by obeying and utilizing its laws; the same the mukta does in the psychical world. The training for mokṣa therefore is a process of knowledge, a process of "discrimination of Puruṣa from Prakṛti Ātmā from Anātmā." As the Sanskṛt aphorism has it, "Jñānādevatu kaivalyam," liberation is through knowledge alone. One necessary concomitant of the realization of man's true nature as a spiritual being is "deathlessness." For when he knows himself to be not his body but the immutable Ātmā, "the Lord of death runs away" from him, for the Lord of death has control over bodies alone and not over the eternal Ātmā. Another concomitant of the discrimination of man's real being from the unreal phenomenal forms of matter is the cessation of pain (duḥkha, kleśa, tāpa). Pleasure and pain and are but interpretations by Buddhi of incidents of the flow of Prāṇa in the subtle bodies. Hence when the spirit, after his long weary pilgrimage, knows himself to be other than the subtle body or the mind, he feels pleasure and pain to be outside him. Life is no more a ceaseless storm of desires tossing the helpless mind about; the long pilgrimage of man is over; no more under the sway of something external to him, but self-ruled, self-determined, he reaches supreme peace.

This discussion of the common points of all the Hindu Darśanas, however brief, shows that they are practically agreed in regard to all vital questions regarding the constitution of man, the constitution of the cosmos, and the lines of the past and the future evolution of humanity. It is impossible to point out such a surprising unanimity other, or the schools of philosophy of any other nation in the world. Hence it is that neither the extraordinary complexity of the subdivisions of sects that so distract the inquirer, nor the great changes of ritual and external manifestations of religion that the Hindu Dharma has undergone during the many thousands of years it has swayed the lives of the Indian peoples, nor again the impacts of the diverse foreign cults that have at various times assailed it, have at all impaired its vitality, but have only helped to show that it rests on the bed rock of truth, and will continue to prevail in the distant future when many modern philosophies will have been forgotten.

REFERENCES

1 Rāmānuja defines *mīmāṁsā* to be "a discussion of sentences of the Veda for the purpose of specially determining the *nature* and modes of (the things referred to in the Veda)."

2. Mādhava's chapter on Śāṅkara darśana, so long believed by all scholars to be identical with the book called *Pañcadaśī,* has been discovered in the Tanjore Library by Govinda Dāsa of Benares and incorporated in the recently published Anandārama edition of the *Sarvadarśanasaṅgraha.*

3. Even the Pūrva Mīmāṁsā, though this is not commonly recognized, proposes to lend to a state that can be properly called Mokṣa for, as Naciketas says,—"Those who live in the Heaven world teach immortality." *Kaṭhopaniṣat,* i. 13. vide Yam's reply, *Ib.* i 17-18.

4. Different Schools mention different subtle bodies, intermediate between the permanent liṅgadeha and the perishable sthūladeha *i.e.* chāyā. Yātanādeha, etc, perishable bodies that the man is provided with during his post-mortem peregrinations; but here we are concerned only with the general principles underlying all Hindu Schools and not the special teachings of any particular School.

5. An oft quoted śloka shows the use of Karma as one of the names of the universal cause against which use some scholars have protested. "He, whom Śaivas worship as Śiva, Vedāntīs as Brahma, Buddhists as Buddha, the Naiyāikas skilled in proof, as the Creator, those that delight in the Jaina scriptures as Arhan, the Mīmāṁsakas as Karma, may he, Hari, the Lord of the three worlds, give us the fruits of our desires.

CHAPTER - II

METAPHYSICS

Ever since man began to think about the relations between himself and the world about him and to distinguish the hosts of passing phenomenal forms from the possible permanent noumenon of which these forms may be temporary modifications, he has followed two different and opposed tendencies of thought, which may be called individualistic and monistic.

The first tendency is inspired by the ineffaceable sense of continuous personal existence which men feel and which refuses to be abolished under any circumstances. The other is the equally potent intuition which men have of the unity of all things, of the oneness of the life that pulsates in all beings. Hence philosophy has grown in two directions— two opposing theories have been advocated by thinkers—one in which the individual man is declared a real permanent factor of the cosmos, the other in which the manifold world is conceived as aspects of one Reality—whether that reality be a conscious Brahma, or unintelligent Nature. These latter theories are rightly called monistic; but the name dualism usually applied to the former is scarcely accurate, for they recognise, not two, but at least as many real Beings as there are human individuals, besides the real substances behind nature. Hence the name individualistic or pluralistic seems to be a more correct designation of these theories.

Kṛṣṇa in the *Bhagavad Gītā,* ii. 3, divides men into two

classes—Sāṅkhyas and Yogis, those fit for Jñāna yoga and those fit for Karma yoga.[1] To the former, meditation on the Self appeals; the latter prefer a life of action, one of loving service of the Lord of the Universe, or of some monistic abstraction, like the humanity of the Positivists. This difference between these two classes of men seems to be due to the preponderance of the representative or the affective elements of psychic life, of 'intellect' or of 'will' as Schopenhauer calls them. "If the normal man is made up of two-thirds will and one-third intellect, the man of genius consists of two-thirds intellect and one third 'will' (Schop, *"On the Primacy of the Will.* Quot. by Ribot. *Psych. of Emot.,* page, 390). The names Sāṅkhyas and Yogīs given above to these two classes of men have nothing to do with the Schools of Philosophy, so called, but only imply that the former are inclined to the discipline of Contemplation and the latter to that of Effort; abstract thought attracts the former, concrete images the latter. In India, as in other countries, both kinds of philosophical theories have been expounded and vigorously upheld by their followers; those called Vaiśeṣika, Nyāya, Sāṅkhya and Yoga are individualistic : whereas those schools of thought which are derived from the *Upaniṣads* and *Āgamas* are directly or indirectly monistic. In this and the succeeding chapters the different metaphysical, cosmological and psychological theories of these schools as propounded in their earliest available expositions will be discussed. In later Indian philosophy, the doctrines of the sharply distinguished lines of thought of the six Darśanas have been mixed up. Hence, the original Sūtras or Kārikās will be quoted as far as possible, and the commentaries will be, as a rule, avoided, for they were made by later thinkers who mixed up the ideas of the different schools, partly because in their days, the Vedānta came to be regarded as the final truth, and partly because the absence of a historical spirit made it impossible for them to expound accurately the ideas of schools which were widely divergent from their point of view.

Metaphysics attempts to answer the question :—what is

the ultimate reality behind the changing phenomena of the Cosmos? Phenomenon means showing, nāmarūpa, name and form, and pre-supposes a noumenon, or "thing as such," which shows itself as phenomena. How many noumena are necessary to explain the Cosmos, and what is the essential nature of each noumenon are the fundamental problems of metaphysics; and these have been solved variously in India as in the West.

The Vedānta[2] believes the ultimate independent Reality to be One—Param-Brahma. The Sāṅkhya and the Yoga schools posit two noumena, Puruṣa and Prakṛti, to produce the Cosmos. The schools of the Vaiṣṇavas and the Śaivas postulate the tattvatraya three ultimate realities, the Lord, the individual and the unconscious (matter). The Śāktas also admit three, which they conceive as the absolute consciousness, the active consciousness and matter. The Nyāya and Vaiśeṣika schools predicate no less than nine ultimate dravyas (substances) which unite to produce the manifested worlds. We shall briefly discuss the metaphyical theories of each of these schools.

SECTION I. VEDĀNTA

The *Vedānta* teaches that there is but one Reality behind the world of matter and of individual beings and that is Param Brahma. The earliest attempt to describe the Supreme Being, the one Reality that underlies what we call spirit and what we call matter is the well-known *Nāsadīya Sūkta, Ṛg-Veda* X. 129. "Then Asat (proto-matter) did not exist. Sat (manifested being) did not exist. There was no air nor sky above. What enveloped (all)? Where, in whose protection? Was it water, the profound darkness? Death was not, nor immortality. There was no differentiation of night or day. That one breathed without breath, self-supported. There was nothing different from or above it. In the beginning darkness existed, enveloped by darkness. Undifferentiated was all this. That one which lay void wrapped in Nothingness was developed by the power of meditation." This is a description of the one Reality during the period of world-repose—Pralaya. Now follows a description of the same during the world-activity, Kalpa. "I will propound to you the Jñeyam (that which is to be known) knowing which one tastes deathlessness, the Supreme Brahma. It is called not Sat and not Asat. It has hands and feet in every direction, eyes, heads, and mouths on all sides, ears everywhere. It stands enveloping all things in the world. Devoid of all organs, it shines with the functions of all organs. It is unattached, yet the supporter of all. Without Guṇas, yet enjoyer of Guṇas. It is without and within all beings. It is movable and withal immovable. It is unknowable on account of its subtleness. It is far and near. Indivisible, yet dwelling amidst beings as if divided. It is to be known as the supporter of all beings, their devourer and generator. It is the Light of Lights,, is said to be beyond Darkness. This jñeyam is consciousness seated in the hearts of all, and is to be reached by consciousness" *(Bhag. Gītā,* xiii. 12—17). "Root above, branch below, Aśvattha they call it, indestructible, whose leaves are hymns; who knows it is the knower of Veda. Downwards and upwards spread forth its branches, nurtured by the Guṇas, the sense-objects its twigs. Downward its roots stretch, the bonds of action in the world of men. Its form is not here beheld, nor its end, nor the beginning, nor its foundation. This Aśvattha of well grown roots with the strong weapon of dispassion having cut down, then the path has to be trodden, which having reached, no one returns. I follow indeed that primal Puruṣa whence has streamed forth the ancient energy" (*Ib.XV.* 1-4).

He is not Asat (the root of matter) for "There is no other seer than He, there is no other hearer than He, there is no other perceiver than He, there is no other knower than He. In that Akṣara (imperishable), then, O Gārgī, the Akāśa is woven, like warp and woof" (*Bṛh. Up. II.* viii.-11). He is not Sat (manifested being), for "That, verily, O Gārgī, the Brāhmaṇas call Akṣara, not gross, not minute, not short, not long, not red, not fluid, without shadow, not dark, without air, without Akāśa, not attached, without taste, or smell, without ears or eyes, without speech, without manas, without seed, without Prāṇa, without mouth, without measure, having no inside or outside, it does not consume anything, nothing does consume it," *(Ib. III. viii. 8.)* He is above the three limitations of space, time and causality (Desakālanimitta). "This Brahma has no earlier or later, no inside or outside" *(Ibid. II. v. 19)*. "Beyond good, beyond evil, beyond what is made, beyond what is not made, beyond what has been, beyond what shall be" (*Kaṭh. Up.* ii-*14)*. This Supreme Being is creator in the sense that he emitted matter and then entered it as its soul. "He wished, may I be many, may I propagate. He meditated. After he meditated, he emitted all this, whatever there is. Having emitted it, He entered it. Having entered it he became Sat (Being) and Tyat (? Non-Being), defined and undefined, supported and unsupported, consciousness and unconsciousness, reality and unreality. The Reality became all this whatsoever. That is Truth, they say" (*Tait. Up. II. 6)*.

Param Brahma, the one Reality is thus the one behind unconscious matter, the one behind all puruṣas (conscious beings). He is the immutable Being underlying the various manifestations of conscious lives due to the union of innumerable puruṣas with forms of matter. Unlike them, he is the Enjoyer without means of enjoyment, the Seer without an organ of vision, the Actor without organs of action. He is the source of the Energy that plays in the Universe. He is the matter of which the worlds are made, as well as the maker of these worlds. He is the Inspirer of all actions of all beings and yet the Dispenser of the fruits of those actions.

The Vedānta Sūtras of Bādarāyaṇa were intended as a *Mīmāṁsā,* an exegesis, embodying the principles of interpretation to be applied to the *Upaniṣads*. These latter being manuals of meditation, Bādarāyaṇa proposes to teach by his Sūtras how the various symbols and words used by the Ṛṣis have to be interpreted, and how meditation is to be practised. The Vedānta Sūtras do not primarily constitute a manual of philosophy so much as a manual of exegesis. Incidentally, Bādarāyaṇa attacks the other disciplines prevalent in his days, like the *Sāṅkhya,* the *Vaiśeṣika,* the *Bauddha,* the *Bhāgavata,* the *Pāśupata,* etc. and proves their philosophical implications to be opposed to the revealed Śruti and to reason. In philosophical discussion which is so common in India, solitary sentences of the *Upaniṣads* or the Sūtras of the *Uttara Mīmāṁsā* embodying philosophical doctrines are frequently quoted; hence people imagine that these are philosophical works. It is time that they are recognised not to be such, but that the former are manuals of Upāsana, heterogeneous collections of various methods of meditation, advocated and practised in ancient India, and of utterances embodying mystic experiences while in an exegesis or state of ecstasy, and the latter, but a manual of the same. Nor are the Sūtras complete in the sense that they contain unmistakeably Bādarayāṇa's ideas. For the word Sūtra means a thread. The Sūtras are series of single words, or phrases, or sentences, on which were hung the explanations and lectures of the Ṛṣis to their disciples and were a sort of *memoria technica* intended to remind the disciples of the teachings of the Master. In many aphorisms, neither the subject treated of, nor what is predicated, is at all referred to; *e. g.* "From connection" *(Ved. Sut. I. iv. 15);* "On account of the connected meaning of the sentences" *(Ib. I. iv. 19)*. In course of time the lectures were lost, the 'threads', alone remained, without the pearls, lending themselves to the ingenuity of the commentators to hang whatever they liked on the Sūtras; this and the wonderful dialectic skill of the Ācāryas have in the case of the Vedānta Sūtras made it all but impossible for an unsectarian investigator to find out exactly the opinions of Bādarāyaṇa on many points.

Yet there is no ambiguity about the fundamental position of the Vedānta Sūtras. "Then therefore the enquiry into Brahma. From which the origin, etc. of this (Cosmos). From being the source of the Scripture. That, again, from its close connection. From seeing (*i. e.* consciousness) being attributed to the cause of the world, unconscious matter is not (the cause; for it is) unscriptural" (*Ved. Sūt.* I. i. 1. 5). The reality behind the Cosmos is thus a conscious Being. The Sūtras then explain that this Being is referred to in the *Upaniṣads* for purposes of Upāsana (meditation) by various personal names—Ānandamaya, the Blissful person (*Ib.* I. i. 12-19), Hiraṇmaya Puruṣa, Golden person (in the Sun), Akṣipuruṣa, person within the eye *(Ib.* i. i. 20), Manomaya he who consists of mind (*Ib.* I. ii. 1-8), etc.; this Being is also referred to in the *Upaniṣads* by names of material substances—Ākāśa *(Ib.* I. i. 22) Prāṇa *(Ib.* I. i.-23), Jyotis, light (*Ib.* I. i. 24-27), etc.

This Brahma is the operative (Nimitta) cause of the world. "He is declared as described to be the cause with regard to Ākāśa etc' *(Ib.* I. iv. 14). Because the world is called (His work)" *(Ib.* I. iv. 16). He is also the material cause of the world. "The material cause also, on account of its not being in conflict with the promissory statements and the illustrative instances" *(Ib.* I. iv. 23). But he is formless. "He is without form verily, that being the most important. (He is) as consisting of Light (which manifests forms), (this discription) being not devoid (of meaning)" *(Ib.* III. ii. 14-15). "For this very reason (are used) comparisons such as (images) of the sun, etc." (*Ib.* III. ii. 18). "He is a vyakta, undifferentiated, so (the scripture) says. But (He is apprehended) by propitiation, according to pratyakṣa and anumāna" (*Ib.* 111. ii. 23).

He is the Supreme, though he is described in the *Vedas* by means of phrases indicative of limitations of place, as a bank (setu), a boundary etc. "On account of the designation of bank, measure, connection, and separation, (in the Śruti), one might think there is some thing higher than He; but (it is not so, for He is only called a setu) on account of some resemblance (between a bank and Him). (Such phrases only) subserve the purposes of the mind; as when we speak of his four feet. (The statements of connection and difference) are due to difference of place, as in the case of light, etc. (being spoken of as shining in particular places, though all pervasive) and on account of the possibility (of only this sort of connection between Him and other existences). Thus from a denial of everything else (He alone is the) Highest. His omnipresence (is proved) from declarations of (His) extent" *(Ib.* III.ii. 30-36). He is also the moral governor of the world, the distributor of the rewards of actions. From Him, the fruit; for (that alone) is possible. And because that is declared by Scripture" (*Ib.* III. ii. *37-38)*.

Thus there is no ambiguity about the main Vedānta position. The noumenon of the world is one. In Pralaya that one can neither be regarded as conscious Being as we know it (Sat) nor as the unconscious (Asat). He is above Sat and above Asat. These two are aspects of Him, but yet are apprehended apart from Him. He is the one source of life, the one goal of aspiration to be reached by conciousness (Jñānagamya).

Plotinus, in the third century A. D., learnt these Vedānta teachings, and taught them in Rome in words that recall the phraseology of the *Upaniṣads* and the *Bhagavad Gītā*. "In order to perceive the one it is necessary to receive from intellect a declaration of what intellect is able to accomplish. Intellect, however, is able to see either things prior to itself, or things pertaining to itself, or things affected by itself. And the things indeed contained in itself are pure; but those prior to itself are still purer and more simple; or rather this must be asserted of that which is prior to it. Hence, that which is prior to it, is not intellect, but something more excellent. For intellect is a *certain* one among the number of beings, but that is not a *certain* one, but prior to everything. Nor it is being (Sat); for being has, as it were, the form of *the one*. But That is formless and is not even without intelligible form. For the nature of *the one* being generative of all things, is not any one of them. Neither, therefore, is it a certain thing, nor a quality, nor a quantity, nor intellect, nor soul, nor that which is moved, nor again that which stands still, nor is it in place nor in time; but is by itself uniform, or rather without form, being prior to all form, to motion and permanency. When we say that the one is the cause of all things, we do not predicate anything as an accident to it, but rather as something which happens to us, because we possess something from it, the one in the meantime subsisting in itself (Enn. III. ix. Tranl. Taylor). Spinoza, among modern European philosophers approaches nearest to the Vedānta metaphysical position. " God, or substance, consisting of infinite attributes, of which each expresses eternal and infinite essentiality, necessarily exists. Whatsoever is, is God; and without God nothing can be, or be conceived. God is the in-dwelling and not the transient cause of all things. God is the efficient cause not only of the existence of things, but also of their essence. Intellect, in function finite, or in-function infinite, must comprehend the attributes of God and the modifications of God, and nothing else." (*Ethics,* I Props. 11, 15.18,25,30.) "Thought is an attribute of God, or God is a thinking being. Extension is an attribute of God, or God is an extended thing" *(1b.* II. Props. 1,9). Pollock thus translates Spinoza's metaphysical position in language suited to modern habits of thought. " We know the world under the attributes or aspects of extension and thought (Asat and Sat), and in each kind the sum of reality appears to be inexhaustible. Our world consists of modes of extension associated with modes of thought. But we have no right to assume that this is the only world; for this would be to set bounds to infinite being" *(Spinoza, His Life and Philosophy,* p. 167).

It is curious that one of the half-a-dozen sentences (logia) which modern research has traced to Jesus, but which is not found in the Gospels, is pure Vedānta. Such Vedānta logia were carefully eliminated from the Christian Gospels, possibly during the time when the early church parted company with myticism in the 3rd and 4th centuries of the Christian era, and Christianity entered a phase of materialism from which it has not yet emerged.

The *Vedānta Sūtras* also discuss the relation between the individual souls and Supreme Brahma as well as the relation between Him and matter. But the different Ācāryas have made these Sūtras yield different meanings absolutely opposed to each other. Thus, III. ii. 11, literally translated would run, "Not on account of place, though of the Supreme, two-fold characteristics; everywhere, verily" Śaṅkara reads this as "Not on account of (difference of) place also can twofold characteristics belong to the Supreme; for everywhere (Scripture teaches Brahma to be without difference)."

Rāmānuja makes this out as, "Not on account of place even is there any imperfection in the Supreme; for everywhere (He is described) as having twofold characteristics." According to Mādhva, it is, "Even from difference of place, no essential difference between the manifestations of the Lord should be supposed; for (Śruti declares of Him the identical character) everywhere." Again, III. ii. 17 runs thus :—"It is seen (in Śruti); and also is remembered (in Smṛti)." Śaṅkara comments on this—That Brahma is without difference is proved by passages from the Śruti. The same teaching is conveyed by Smṛti." Rāmānuja comments on the Sūtra as follows—"Hosts of *Vedānta* passages (prove) His being devoid of faults and being the treasure-house of auspicious qualities; so, too, the Smṛtis". Mādhva makes out this sūtra to mean that Śruti shows that perfect bliss is the form of the Lord and Śmṛti shows that the Lord's form consists of intelligence. Again that famous sentence of the *Upaniṣads,* "Tat Satyam Sa Ātmā Tattvamasi," has been the battle-ground of the Ācāryas. Śaṅkara in comments on it says, "In the sentence 'Tattva-masi' That thou art) it is taught that 'thou' refers to S a t, real Being......By 'Tattvamasi' (he) directly teaches the identity of the Self and Sat, Pure Being" (*Com. on Ch. Up*. vi. 16.) Rāmānuja explains it as follows:—"The word 'that' refers to Him who is the cause of the world, a mine of hosts of all auspicious qualities, without imperfections, without change, and 'thou' refers to the same Brahma specialised in the mode of a Jīva who is his own body, by his forms of the inner controller of Jīvas ." (*Vedārthasaṁgraha,* p. 35).

Madhva remarks on this passage, "the statement of non-difference (between the individual soul and Brahma) is due to his essential nature being knowledge, bliss, etc.; which are qualities of Brahma (also)" (*Bhāṣya on Ved. Sūt.,* II. ii. 29).

In one of his *Prakaraṇas,* called *Viṣṇu Tattva Nirṇaya,* section *Navakṛtobhyāsa,* Mādhva cuts the Gordian knot by proposing to read "Sa Ātmā, Atattvamasi," "He is the Ātmā , Thou are not that." This is the *reductis ad absurdum* of the favourite Hindu method of deriving new ideas from old texts.

The Ṛṣis of the *Upaniṣads* spoke as Upāsakas. Sentences like "tattvamasi" were intended to give pointed expression to experiences reached during the practice of Vidyās, methods of meditation, which abound in the *Upaniṣads.* They are psychological facts, at least to the one engaged in the mystic contemplation; facts to be verified by following the methods of meditation prescribed, and not to be treated, as the Ācāryas, and more especially their later expounders have done, as texts to be wrenched out of their context and made the foundation of a philosophical structure built with a heavy load of argumentation. The Ṛṣis spoke of Brahma from the intuitions reached during the rare moments of ecstatic communion with Him, arrived at after steady attempts at keeping down all mental activity and reaching a plane above the storms of human passions. By the more or less contradictory statements of the Real being scattered in the *Vedas,* and especially in the final sections of the *Vedas* called the *Upaniṣads,* the human mind tries to represent to itself what must ever be realized by transcending the mind; mind being but an organ made of matter, human language, which is the expression of the human mind, can contain only expressions descriptive of objective material categories. To attempt to describe in such language what is not mind, and further what is not conscious being as men know it, must necessarily lead to the use of contradictory ideas and phrases. The Ṛṣis, who spoke from intuition, did not realise the difficulties that cold logic could raise against the contradictory statements that alone are possible when we attempt to describe the indescribable, to limit in forms of speech what is unlimited, to imprison in symbols of the mind (pratīka, that which is formed by out-going activity of the mind) what for ever soars in an atmosphere which the mind cannot reach. The

Ācāryas of a later age were anxious above all to construct a self-consistent theory. Logical consistency can apply only to the systems built by the mind. An extension of the laws of mind to the region of the Absolute, which is above mind as It is above all regions of relativity, must lead to profitless logic-chopping, as it has done in the sectarian squabbles of the minor subdivisions of the Vedānta.

The principal commentators of the *Vedānta Sūtras* among those that have founded sects, namely Śaṅkara, Rāmānuja and Mādhva, have imposed on them three widely different, but self-consistent philosophical and disciplinary systems called Advaita, Viśiṣṭādvaita and Dvaita. Their followers have accentuated the differences among these three, and minimised their points of agreement, and thus carried on the sectarian movement till the modern Vedāntic sects are hopelessly divided. Later, but original, commentators have formed other theories out of the same Sūtras. We shall briefly indicate the main line of divergence of these three original sects of the Vedānta.

Śaṅkara starts from the position of one who attempts to realize the nature of the Ātmā, the Self manifested in the heart of the individual, of one "who apprehends in the moment of the rise of knowledge (*i. e.* in the moment of realization of the Supreme) his Self and no second" *(Dakṣiṇāmūrti Stotrai)*. When the consciousness is released from the bounding adjuncts of matter and mind, there is no more duality, no more relativity, all is One and that One is the Self. In such a state of exaltation the world appears unmanifested, "like the shoot within the seed." Hence Śaṅkara allows only phenomenal existence to the individual Self, Jīvātmā (the self living in the world) and to matter. The following quotations from his Bhāṣya on the *Brahma Sūtras* indicate his view on these questions.

"We meet with two forms of Brahma (described in the Śruti, one) conditioned by the different kinds of name and form, and (the other) the opposite of this, devoid of all conditions whatsoever. Thus where there is duality (or relativity) then one sees the other. When all becomes his Self, whom does he see and by what (organ)?" *(Br. Up.* IV. x. 15). " When he sees naught else, that is the high (state); when he sees something else, hears something else, perceives something, that is the low (state). That which is the high, that is the immortal (state); that which is the low, that is the mortal (state)" (*Ch. Up.* VII. xxiv. 1). "The wise one, who, having perceived all forms and made all names, sits calling (them by their names)" (*Tait. Ār.* III. xii. 7). "Without parts, without actions, peaceful, without faults, taintless, the supreme setu (bank) of immortality,. like a fire that has consumed its fuel" (*Śvet. Up.* VI. 19). "Not so, Not so" *(Bṛh. Up.* II.iii.6). "Not great, not small" *(Ib.* III-viii. 8). "One place is defective, the other perfect". These texts and a thousand others point out the double form of Brahma, according as it is the object of Vidyāor Avidyā, knowledge or Nescience" (*Ved. Sut.* I. i. 11). "(It is argued that) He who maintains the nature of Brahma to be immutable (Kūṭastha brahmātmavādī) contradicts the tenet of Īśvara being the cause (of the world); because the absolute unity (of Brahma) precludes the relation of the Ruler and the ruled. (To this we reply), No, for omniscience (and other qualities) of Īśvara depend on the evolution of the germs of name and form, which are of the nature of Nescience.........Forming (as it were) the very soul of the omniscient Īśvara, are name and form, produced by nescience, incapable of being described as Its nature or as the nature any other than That, which constiute the germs of the phenomenal universe. This is the wonderworking power (Māyāśakti) of the omniscient Īśvara, Prakṛti, as we learn from Śruti and Smṛti. The omniscient Īśvara is other than those two (name and form)......Thus Īśvara is dependent upon the conditions of name and form, produced by nescience, just as space is dependent upon the conditioning objects, jars, pots, etc. (before it becomes differentiated as the space inside a jar, the space inside a pot, etc.). From the standpoint of the phenomenal universe he is the Sovereign of those who are called Jīvas, (individual souls), Vijñānātmās (lit. knowing selves, those capable of perception and knowledge), who are his very self, but who depend on (bodies that are) the aggregates of organs of action, produced by name and form, based on nescience, resembling in this the space in a jar; hence Īśvara's Lordship, omniscience, and omnipotence depend on the limitation of condition of the nature of nescience. From the standpoint of the noumenon the activities (involved) in being the Ruler, the ruled, the omniscient, etc., cannot subsist in the Self, cleared of all limiting adjuncts by right knowledge (Vidyā)." *(Com. on Ved. Sut.* II. i. 14). "In the supreme Brahma, there is no duality; this concept excludes no second being, real or unreal. The concept Īśvara necessitates the concept of a causal 'fore-state '(prāgavasthā) of the world, dependent on the Īśvara, but without which Īśvara cannot become a creator. This causal state of the world is called Avidyā, nescience, for it is destroyed by Vidyā, knowledge of the Ātmā which secures for the Mukta, the released, once for all, the realization of the absolute unity of all life. It is also called Avyakta, unmanifested, for before creation it cannot be perceived; sometimes it is spoken of as Māyā, illusion" (*Bhāṣya on Ved. Sūt.* I. iv. 3). The theory that Prakṛti is Māyā, unreal, the non-existent simulating reality, was started by Śaṅkara and done to death by his later followers. He himself is guarded in his statements, as might be noticed in the above quotations, and seems to insist more on Avidyā (ignorance) being the cause of the imaginary duality where there is but unity; but later Advaitīs have, with the fatal, but dangerous, facility with which phrases devoid of content are handled by metaphysicians, created Māyā into a non-entity that masquerades as an entity, and read this doctrine into the *Upaniṣads*. All other schools of Hindu thought that have any touch with Vedānta—Vaiṣṇava, Śākta and Māheśvara Schools have always protested against the notion of the world being an unreal non-entity, as it is based on the real Brahma. Among European scholars, Colebrooke first noticed that Māyā was always used in the early (and genuine) *Upaniṣads* and *Bhagavad Gītā* for the wonder-working power of the Lord, and the use of Māyā for non-entity or for Prakṛti was invented by the Advaita School. It is curious that Gough and, in our day, Deussen, should have so far allowed their critical faculty to be obscured by their familiarity with the Advaita Vedānta as to attempt to read the modern Māyā doctrine into the ancient *Upaniṣads*. To these scholars as to most Indian Advaitīs, the word Vedānta means advaita; the Śāṅkara teaching and that, too, in its later developments, identical with that, of the *Upaniṣads*. They forget that Śaṅkara, though a great philosopher, claims to be but a Bhāṣyakāra, a commentator, and that he did not even profess, as Rāmānuja professes, to expound the Sūtras in accordance with tradition. If Śaṅkara quotes any previous commentator it is but to criticise him; he boldly starts a new line of thought following the logical necessities of his stand point and brushes aside any textual difficulties that might obstruct him. All system-builders that base their philosophical system on ancient inspired texts have to twist them to suit their purposes; but Śaṅkara does this more self-reliantly than the other Ācāryas who support their interpretations by quotations from other books of doubtful authority. Śaṅkara relies chiefly on argument for this purpose.

The Advaita was first propounded by Gauḍapāda,a generation before Śaṅkara,in his Kārikās on the *Māṇḍūkya Upaniṣad*. It is noteworthy that Gauḍapāda and his disciple's disciple, as Śaṅkara is said to be, were both of them Śāktas, and base the whole Advaita doctrine on the fundamental fact of their realization of the unity of all life in the ecstacy of contemplation. It is to them a fact of experience, a "datum of consciousness" reached after undergoing a special discipline. Śaṅkara defines those whose "vision is superior" as those who are able to realize that the Ātmā alone exists (*Com. on Māṇḍūkya Kārikā,* iii. 16). He again speaks of the "Advaitadṛṣṭi (vision of oneness) of us, the disillusioned" (*Ib.* iii. 18). Whereas all their critics later than Rāmānuja, and, what is more curious, all their followers and exponents, too, treat it, not as a question of fact, but as a question of argument, not as a question of discipline, but of exegesis. This has led to the fearful degeneration of Advaita in India, where we find people who talk monism all day long, but lead the most selfish life imaginable.

Rāmānuja controverts the fundamental metaphysical positions of the Advaita. (I) He does not allow that a non-differentiated substance could be established by any one's consciousness, because consciousness always implies difference. (2) He holds that the Śruti does not also teach a Brahma free from all difference (nirviśeṣa Brahma). To accentuate his opposition to this theory he delights in piling adjective on adjective describing the divine attributes. "The one cause of the evolution, maintenance, dissolution and release from Saṁsāra of the universe of sentient and non-sentient objects, of a nature different from all things other than Himself, on account of being hostile to all evil, and being one with infinite auspiciousness, of hosts of lovely qualities, boundless and unsurpassable, Universal Ātmā, Supreme Brahma, Supreme Light, Supreme Essence, Supreme Ātmā, known in all Vedānta by various words like Sat, etc. the Lord, Nārāyaṇa, Exellent Puruṣa" (Rāmānuja's *Vedārtha Saṁgraha,* p. 11.) (3). He also holds that the theory of a beginningless Māyā (Nescience) cannot be proved by the accepted methods of proof. (4). Nor can such Nescience act on supreme reality so as to become the cause of creation, etc. For he argues that a perfect Being cannot become a prey to ignorance; hence, according to him, creation and relativity are due not to Māyā, but to the Love of the Supreme Deity for man and other individual souls. He allows the validity of the realization of Unity (Advaitānubhava) of Gauḍapāda and Śaṅkara, but explains that this ecstatic consciousness of unity is not the consciousness of the Supreme Brahma, but that of the Self as apart from the limitations of matter (Prakṛti Vīyuktātmādarśana). A higher experience than this is the intuition of Param Brahma by constant loving meditation on his divine attributes (bhakti, upāsana).

He regards metaphysical questions from this standpoint and hence he teaches that Brahma is Saviśeṣa, characterized by attributes. He is the Self of both the individual souls (cit) and matter (acit) and yet different from them. His views of the relation of the Supreme to individual Ātmā and matter can be gathered from the following:—"It is proved from the *Antaryāmi*

Brāhmaṇa (Brih. Up. III. viii. 3-23), etc., that Cit and Acit (conscious and unconscious beings) in their gross effected state (during a Kalpa) and in their subtle causal state (during Pralaya) form the body of Param Brahma, and Param Brahma is their Soul........From words like Ārambhaṇa, etc. *(Chand. Up. VI.* i. 4. etc.), it is known that the world is not other than the Supreme cause, the Param Brahma. Now this is the truth—it is Brahma that is denoted at all times by all words because of His having for his body Cit and Acit.

Sometimes (during pralaya) notwithstanding His possession (of these) as His own body the body of Cit and Acit attains a Subtle State, in which it is incapable of being designated apart from Him. This is Brahma in the causal condition (Kāraṇā-vaṣṭhā). At other times (during Kalpa) the body of Cit and Acit attains a gross state in which it is capable of being treated as something apart from him. This is the effected condition (Kāryāvaṣṭhā) (*Śrī Bhāṣya* on *Ved. Sūt. II.* i. 15).

Thus according to Rāmānuja, the Reality is one, the Supreme Brahma and Cit, the conscious individual souls, and Acit, the unconscious forms of matter, are his bodies, Avyakta, indistinguishable from Him during Pralaya, but during Kalpa in a period of manifestation; not only Vyakta, distinguishable from Him, but related to Him in the Śeṣiśeṣabhāva, the relation of the Disposer and the disposable.

The Viśiṣṭādvaita has undergone a degeneration quite as bad as that noticed in the case of the Advaita. Rāmānuja preached an Īśvara of unimaginably excellent qualities, the goal of loving thoughts uninterupted like a stream of oil, of whom all humanity and all nature was the body. His followers today have become an exclusive sect, marked off from the rest of the Hindus by glaring white and red marks covering their person and substituting an elaborate mummery for the simple life of loving meditation on the perfections of Īśvara and service of men that the founder preached. It is also curious that Rāmānuja speaks more often of Īśvara, though he maintains Nārāyaṇa to be the chief form of Īśvara; but his followers call themselves Vaiṣṇavas, the devotees of Viṣṇu, one of the Hindu Trinity. Rāmānuja, while controverting the psychological possibility of cognizing a Nirviśeṣa Brahma, an absolute Being devoid of attributes, fully recognised the validity of the Advaita experience of the unity of Ātmā as one of the goals of humanity, as legitimate as a means of immortality as the Bhakti he advocated. (*Vide, Bhag. Gītā, Rāmānuja Bhāṣya* on viii. 20). So, too, Yāmuna, his predecessor and the early Āgamas. Similarly Śaṅkara, while specially advocating jñāna yoga in all his writings, admits that Kṛṣṇa taught the easier Karma Yoga to his friend Arjuna in preference to the *more difficult* path of contemplation. (Vide *Bhag. Gītā Śaṅkara Bhāṣya* on xii. 13). But the disciples of these teachers have developed an intolerance which the founders of the Advaita and the Viśiṣṭādvaita did not feel, and always tried to be-little each other's system and to abuse each other.

Before going into Mādhva's views on these questions, it must be pointed out that Śaṅkara's and Rāmānuja's interpretations of the *Vedānta Sūtras* agree in most points, except when in sundry places their special doctrines come into conflict. Madhva's interpretations differ widely from these. Thus according to the former two, *Ved. Sut.* II. 42-45 deal with the Bhāgavata doctrine, but according to Mādhva they deal with the Śākta doctrine. By comparing Śaṅkara's and Rāmānuja's Bhāṣyas, Sūtra by Sūtra, a comparative study of their common points and divergences can be made. But Mādhva's Bhāṣya strikes such original lines, that therein is visible most plainly how the traditional interpretations of the Sūtras having become lost, the Bhāṣyakāras, commentators, were untramelled and could make out whatever they wanted from the Sūtras.

Mādhva's views can be gathered from his Bhāṣya on *Ved. Sūtras,* II. iii. 28,29." The Jīva, individual soul, is certainly separate (from the Lord), for *Kauśika Śruti* argues, The supreme is different from the multitudes of individual Souls. The Supreme is inconceivable. He is full, the group of individual souls is not full. He is eternally free, from Him release from bondage (is to be obtained). Hence he is to be sought: Since the essential nature (of the individual soul) is knowledge and bliss (which are also) the qualities of Brahma, the individual soul is spoken of as not different from Him. Brahma is spoken of as the Ātmā of all (the universe) in the text. All this is indeed Brahma' (*Ch.* III. 14. I) because all qualities belong to him". Under *Ved. Sūt.* 11. iii. 7, he quotes the following from *Bṛhat-Saṁhitā:*—"The One, Supreme Puruṣa, Indivisible is called Viṣṇu. Prakṛti, Puruṣa, Time, these three are divided (*i.e.* limited) ....That Supreme, Hari, is immutable. Being undivided, He is of Supreme bliss, eternal, of eternal attributes; what is divided is of little power". The following quotation from Chapter V of *Sarvadarśana Saṅgraha* shows how very vigorously the Mādhvas protest against the Advaita doctrine which they consider an insult to the most High :—"As stated in the *Tattvaviveka,* Tattva (ultimate substance) is acknowledged to be two fold, independent and dependent; The Independent is Viṣṇu, the Lord exempt from imperfections and of endless excellence. From inference, too, difference (between the Supreme and the individual) is ascertained. The Supreme Lord is different from Jīva, as (the former) is the object of his service. He who is to be served by another is different from him, as a king from his attendant.........On account of their thirst to be one with the Supreme Lord (they make) a statement that the excellent attributes of Viṣṇu are like mirage and this resembles the cutting of the tongue in the desire to gain a fine plantain; since it will result in their entering Andhaṁtamas (Hell of utter darkness) on account of their offending Viṣṇu.........The grand revelation, 'A difference between Jīva and Īśvara, and a difference between matter and Īśvara, a difference of Jīvas each from others, a difference between matter and Jīva and a difference of material beings each from others, this is the fivefold difference in the universe.' This is real and beginningless; if it had a beginning it would have an end; but it has no end; nor is it illusorily imagined, for if it were imagined merely, it would cease; but it never ceases.........As the *Mahopaniṣad* says, 'Like a bird and the string (tied to it), like the juices of different trees, like the rivers and the seas, like fresh water and salt water, like the robber and the robbed, like man and the objects (that he sees), so are the Jīva and the Īśvara different, eternally differentiated from each other'"

Starting from these three different standpoints numerous theories, all calling themselves Vedānta have been evolved by later expounders. Each system attempts to be a self-consistent whole, displaying the keenest logical and exegetical skill. The *Bhāṣyas* and *Vṛttis* on the *Vedānta* Sūtras so far discovered amount to over 30 and the commentaries on them run into hundreds each giving a slight twist to the original doctrines. It would not be possible to summarize the teachings of these schools; nor would it be of much interest as the points of difference that endow each school with individuality are so minute and so much apart from modern interests. These three have been noticed partly because they are so popular in modern India and partly because they seem to have been originally conceived as compromises between the Vedānta and other metaphysical theories. The Advaita is a compromise between the Vedānta and Sāṅkhya. It accepts the specific Sāṅkhya ideas of the immutability of spirit and of action and experience belonging only to matter, but adds that neither the Puruṣas nor Prakṛti are really existent but are imagined to exist on account of nescience. Buddhism and Jainism also influenced the evolution of the Advaita philosophy though Saṅkara like every other Ācārya, did not always clearly and correctly understand their position as is evidenced by his criticisms of them. The Dvaita is a compromise between Nyāya and Vedānta. It accepts the specific Nyāya teaching of the absolute differences among Īśvara, Jīvas and matter and grafts them on Vedānta as far as possible. The Viśiṣṭādvaita attempts to find a meeting point for the monism of Vedānta, the evolution and individualism of the Sāṅkhya and the theism and realism of Nyāya.

We can not in this book pursue the later developments of Vedānta in this country. They form a vast mass of profitless literature in which the old philosophical schools have been jumbled up in inextricable confusion. In them argument takes the place of psychological experience, bigotry takes the place of meditation, and abuse of other sects takes the place of inspiration. Among them they have raised the innumerable sects that divide modern India and deprive philosophy of its power of consoling man in his troubles and elavating him to a place of peace.

SECTION II. A. SĀṄKHYA

The Sāṅkhya analyses the universe into two independent and sharply contrasted factors— Puruṣa and Prakṛti, spirit and matter, subject and object. Puruṣa is not the Ego, for Egoity is a function of matter and the ordinary human consciousness involved in the notion of 'I' is but the reflection of the Seer on the instrument of cognition. The pure consciousness of the Puruṣa is reached only when the man has attained Kaivalya, aloneness, absolute separation from Prakṛti and is devoid of the distinction of I and not-I. This Puruṣa is not the noumenon underlying all the puruṣas of the universe, for each puruṣa, whether he be in the body of a Deva or of a man, is independent of and different from other puruṣas of the Universe. His attributes are the reverse (viparīta) of those of Prakṛti; he is immutable, not affected by the Guṇas, the conscious Seer of objective, phenomenal forms, separate from other puruṣas, the enjoyer (bhoktā) of pleasure and pain *(Sāṅ. Kār.* xi). He is neither prakṛti nor vikṛti, neither the antecedent nor the consequent state of a changing object (*Ib.* iii). The existence of the knower is established by the following proofs, (1) The objects of the universe apparently exist not for their own but for another's use. (2) The existence of matter with three guṇas pre-supposes the existence of puruṣa without guṇas. (3) Man has the power to control his body. (4) Man has the power of 'enjoyment'. (5) Man is impelled to seek kaivalya—the state when he is the pure seer, separated from contact with objects

(*Ib.* xvii). Hence the puruṣa is the solitary, inactive witness of the operations of Nature, bystander, spectator, passive (*Ib.* xix). Being immutable he does not change into phenomenal forms like prakṛti, but by his union with forms of insentient matter, buddhi, etc., they assume the appearance of sentiency and the inactive puruṣa appears active though it is the guṇas that are the source of all activity (*Ib.* xx). These puruṣas are many in number, because birth, death and the organs (buddhi, etc.) are severally allotted to individuals, their activities are simultaneous, and the three guṇas are differently distributed in different men (*Ib.* xviii). As the Sāṅkhya teaches the existence of many puruṣas. each living eternally separate from the rest, it may best be described as a school of individualism.

Prakṛti, the other constituent of the universe is of two forms, one causal, and homogeneous the other, effected and discrete (vyakta.) The latter (vyakta), is an effect (hetumat), inconstant, unpervading, *i. e.* bounded, mutable, multitudinous, phenomenal, mergent (in its noumenon), divisible and dependent. The former is the reverse (*Ib.* x). Pradhāna, or Mūlaprakṛti as the noumenon of material forms is called, is that from which the organs of knowledge and action and the objects thereof are evolved. It is not a modification of anything antecedent (vikṛti); hence it is a noumenon (*Ib.* iii). It can not be apprehended by the organs of knowledge on account of its subtility and has to be inferred from its effects buddhi, etc., some of which are similar to it, others dissimilar (*Ib.* viii). It differs from its phenomenal manifestations (vyakta) in having no antecedent, being indestructible, pervasive, inactive, unique, unsupported, indissoluble, indivisible, uncontrollable (*Ib.* x). It is curious that mūlaprakṛti, the root of matter is, in the Saṅkhya school given all the negative attributes that the Vedānta attributes to Param Brahma. It is also noteworthy that similar negative attributes are attributed to ether by modern science. Agnes Clerke, in her *Modern Cosmogonies* describes ether in words strikingly similar to the Sāṅkhya description of Mūlaprakṛti allowing for the difference of standpoint between the metaphysical and the scientific. "To the very brink of that mysterious ocean, the science of the 20th century has brought us; and it is with a thrill of wondering awe that we stand at its verge and survey its illimitable expanse. The glory of the heavens is transitory, but the impalpable, invisible ether inconceivably remains. Such as it is to-day, it already was when the Fiat Lux was spoken; its beginning must have been coeval with that of time. Nothing or everything according to the manner it is accounted of, it is evasive of common notice, while obtrusive to delicate scrutiny. Its negative qualities are numerous and baffling. It has no effect in impeding motion; it does not perceptibly arrest, absorb, or scatter light; it pervades, yet has (apparently) no share in the displacements of gross matter. Looking, however, below the surface of things we find this semi-fabulous quintessence to be unobtrusively doing all the world's work. It embodies the energies of motion; is, perhaps, in a very real sense, the true primum mobile; the potencies of matter are rooted in it; the substance of matter is latent in it; universal intercourse is maintained by means of the ether; cosmic influences can be exerted only through its aid; unfelt, it is the source of solidity; unseen, it is the vehicle of light; itself non-phenomenal, it is the indispensable originator of phenomena. A contradiction in terms, it points the perennial moral that what eludes the senses is likely to be more permanently and intensely actual than what strikes them."

Besides these negative attributes Pradhāna or Mūlaprakṛti has some positive attributes which are common to it and the phenomenal forms evolved from it. It is affected by the three Guṇas, it is unconscious, objective, common to all Puruṣas, insensible to pleasure and pain and immutable *(Ib.* xi). The existence of this Pradhāna , (lit., chief principle) or Mūla-prakṛti (or root of matter), this noumenon behind phenomenal material objects, is proved by the following considerations; (1) these objects being discrete, can only be conceived as being carved out of an indiscrete something; (2) certain common properties are found in all objects thus indicating a common substratum; (3) objects remain discrete only so long as the energy of their cause acts in them; (4) an effect is different from its cause; (5) the whole universe of multitudinous forms is one object (*Ib.* xv). This noumenon of matter operates by means of the three Guṇas . The three Guṇas are not three qualities of some substance other than themselves; but they "are substances, yet called Guṇas, qualities, as they are the accessories of the Puruṣa" (Bhāskararāya. *Com. Lal. Sahas.* 604).

They are three strands into which primal matter differentiates itself when its homogeneity is first disturbed. Their manifestations as the so-called Laws of motion in the physical world, as mental characteristics in the world of mind and as feeling-tones in the moral sphere have been described in Chap I. They are "things (dravyāṇi) and not specific qualities." "In speaking of qualities, however, the term Guṇa is not to be regarded as an insubstantial accidental attribute, but as a substance discernible by soul through the medium of the faculties" (Wilson's *Com. on Sah. Kār.* xii). The origin of the theory of the three Guṇas is shrouded in obscurity. It appears all on a sudden in the Sāṅkhya philosophy. The only references to it previous to the are of Sāṅkhya philosophy is found in *Atharva Saṁhitā X. viii.* 43. "The knowers of Brahma know that spirit (Yakṣa) which resides in the lotus with nine gates, invested with the three Guṇas." This verse is repeated in *Ath. Sam,* X. ii. 32, but the latter half is changed into "in the sheath (Kośa) made of gold of three spokes, of three supports". The Vedic age divided regions into three, Pṛthvī, Antarikṣa, and Dyu, the earth, the intermediate sphere and the sky. Possibly this triplet was developed into the triplet of Guṇas. This idea is rendered probable by the fact that Rājas, the second of the Guṇas is also the name of the middle region, Antarikṣa. In Pṛthvī, the earth, there is a preponderance of Tamas, in Antarikṣa, the middle region there is a preponderance of Rajas and in the Dyu, the sky, there is a preponderance of Sattva. In later times a fourth region and a fourth Guṇa was worked out and described in the *Āgamas* and the *Purāṇas*. This region was beyond the sky; in this region the three Guṇas are absent; instead of them, there is Śuddhasattva, illumination accompanied by knowledge, whereas the lower three regions are characterized by Miśra-sattva—a mixture of the three Guṇas in different proportions. Tamas literally means the condition of being choked or exhausted, hence darkness. Rajas is colour, the coloured radiance of the cloudy regions, obscuration, Sattva is illumination, brightness. These are the three fundamental blue, red and white threads out of which the universe is woven.

These two categories of the Sāṅkhya, Puruṣa and Prakṛti are thus absolutely opposed to each other. There is nothing common between the two. Each Puruṣa is independent of the rest. There can be no common substratum underlying all Puruṣas, for the Puruṣa is the pure immutable consciousness and not a phenomenon. He can understand his nature as Puruṣa only by an intellectual analysis of man's life and putting away all that is contributed to it by matter and thus realizing his Kaivalya, aloneness. The Sāṅkhya reached this conclusion because it began by rejecting the ritual of the *Vedas*. "The revealed mode (of salvation) is impure, because it requires animal sacrifices, while its rewards also are susceptible of diminution and excess." *(Ib. ii)*. The Sāṅkhya proves its conclusions by the intellectual analysis of human experience and not like the *Vedānta* by exegesis. In this path each man can start only with his own experience; and starting therefrom, he denudes it of all that is' not himself. He strips from his experience sensation, perception, egotism, and volition, all that matter has contributed, and finally knows himself to be the pure Jña, knower, when there is an end to ignorance and pain. Hence when he is Mukta he remains a separate entity, in other words he reaches Kaivalya, aloneness.

The history of the rise of the Sāṅkhya school of thought is wrapped in impenetrable obscurity. Most scholars now admit that it was developed before the age of Buddha. The *Kapila Sūtras* as we have them, has been proved to be a work composed not earlier than the XIV century, A. D., though it probably contains words and phrases belonging to a very much earlier *Kapila Sūtras,* now lost. *The Tattva Samāsa Sūtras* which Max Müller regarded as an ancient work strikes us as being a rather late index of some pre-existing Sūtra work. Īśvara Kṛṣṇa's *Sāṅkhya Kārikā* composed probably in the age immediately preceding the beginning of the Christian Era, is the earliest exposition of the Sāṅkhya that we have. Kārikā, means the versified form of a pre-existing Sūtra. Pañcaśikha, an early Sāṅkhya teacher is quoted by Vyāsa in his commentaries on *Yoga Sūtras* II. 13. He is also quoted in the *Sāṅkhyasāra*[3] by Bhāva Ganeśa Dīkṣit, a disciple of Vijñāna Bhikṣu. All this early Sāṅkhya literature is now lost; but yet there is no room for doubting that the system was worked out in the form it now exists in the age that preceded the birth of Gautama Buddha and Mahāvīra. This system, so ancient in birth and so modern in spirit, must have taken some centuries to be developed. Philosophical systems do not start straight from the head of a thinker, as the finished Minerva from the head of Jupiter. The Sāṅkhya, as we know it, is a final product with no mark of the hesitancy which characterizes an evolving system. It holds definite views on many questions, the nature of Saṁśara and of Karma, the functions of the three Guṇas, the nature of the Puruṣa, the materiality of Antaḥkaraṇa, and the unreality of bondage, most of which were scarcely known to the thinkers of the early *Upaniṣads.* The Sāṅkhya is a finished metaphysics and a finished psychology. How many centuries intervened between the fluid state of thought we meet with in the later Vedic age and the co-ordination and crystalline polish of the Sāṅkhya, what has become of the intervening literature which alone can show how the one evolved out of the other, who can say? Between the schoolmen with their doctrine of "occult qualities" and "sympathetic virtues" and the modern pellucid scientific conceptions of energy, etc., so many centuries of quick-moving thought have elapsed. Whether ancient thought moved as quick, what helped on the ancient Sāṅkhya movement to gain independence of the trammels of revealed scriptures and boldly take its stand on reason, is a problem which at present defies solution. Of one thing we may be sure. The Sāṅkhya could not have been evolved by one man, of however commanding genius, as Prof. Garbe thinks (vide Introduction to his translation of Aniruddha's *Commentary*).

Another equally curious fact is the fate of the Sāṅkhya system after its promulgation. The *Vedānta Sūtras* make a definite attempt to oppose it (*Sūt*. II. i. 1-2 and II. ii. 1-10). The Buddhists controverted some of its teachings. The Vaiśeṣikas from the beginning opposed its fundamental principle of Satkāyavāda, the axiom that effects pre-exist in a potential form in their causes. But very soon and especially outside these schools, the Sāṁkhya came to be regarded as a revelation and absorbed bodily and welded firmly into later Indian thought.

The *Āgamas,* on which has been based the Hindu religion of the past two thousand years took in the Sāṅkhya wholly. The Ācāry as except that they oppose one Sāṅkhya tenet— that a Supreme conscious being is not the cause of the world—treat the rest of the Sāṅkhya teaching as revealed truth and base their exposition of the Vedānta on the Sāṅkhya. This has cut short the further evolution of the system and it remains exactly where it was two thousand five hundred years ago. Whether a future Indian Renaissance, inspired by the science of the West will take up the work thus interrupted is a problem whose answer is concealed in the womb of the future.

(B) Yoga

The metaphysics of the Yoga school is practically the same as that of the Sāṅkhya. Puruṣa and Prakṛti are called by the more expresive names of Draṣṭa and Dṛṣya the Seer and the Seen. Sight (Dṛṣṭ) is the word used in this school to express the function of conciousness, as other schools prefer light (Prakāśa) or Jñāna (knowing). The Seer sees the operations of the 'inner organ', which in this school is called Chitta, not to be confounded with the Chitta of the later Advaita schools whose function is merely memory. All mental activity, the unceasing succession of 'states of conciousness' (as they are called is Western philosophy) is termed Cittavṛtti in the *Yoga Sūtras* and the Puruṣa sees these 'states of conciousner'; hence he is the Seer. Yoga is the inhibition of the ceaseless flow of Cittavṛtti and while it ceases flowing, the Seer abides in his true nature (Svarūpa) of pure conciousness *(Yoga Sūtras* I. 2-3). "Dṛśya (The Seen) has the three qualities (Śīla , Guṇa) of illumination, activity and rest and is the noumenon of objects and organs (and exists) for the enjoyment and emancipation (of the Seer)". *(Ib.* II. 18) Prakāśa , Kriya, Sthiti of the *Sūtra* just quoted, stand for Sattva, Rajas and Tamas.

The noumenon of the Dṛṣya is called Alinga (lit, the indistinguishable), Avyakta, as it is called in other Schools. It is the Pradhāna of the Sāṅkhyas. "The Draṣṭā, mere vision, (conciousness), though pure *(i.e.,* devoid of any mutation), immediately perceives images of objects, common to others besides him (who has reached Kaivalya.) The conjunction (of the Seer and the Seen) is the cause that they attain the nature of the possessor and the possessed." *(Ib* II. 20-23.) On account of this conjunction the Seer evolves into the possessor and the Seen is then apprehended as possessed. But when ignorance is removed, the real immutability of the Seer is grasped. Thus we see that, except for a complete change of technical terms, the metaphysical theories of the Yoga are absolutely identical with those of the Sāṅkhya. The *Yoga Sūtra* designates itself Sāṅkhya Pravacana, exposition of Sāṅkhya. The *Sarvadarśana Saṅgraha* sums up the Yoga arguments regarding the immutability of the Seer in these words:—"Citiśakti (lit. the power of 'knowing', conciousness) is devoid of mutation because it always 'knows' (the mental modifications). If this Puruṣa were mutable, he could not always know mental modifications, as the mutable is inconstant (in its action). As the Puruṣa who is of the nature of consciousness remains always the Superintendent, his essentially pure nature is always maintained. Whenever it (his nature) is (apparently) affected (lit. clouded) by (the shadow of) any object whatsoever (that is perceived by him), it is the Dṛṣya , the object that always receives his light and is illuminated by it. Hence the Puruṣa is (really) unaffected (during a perception) and it follows he is always knowing and is always above the suspicion of mutability. The Citta it is that is (really) affected by objects and then that object is perceived. When it is not affected (by an object), it is not perceived. Objects resemble magnets and the Citta resembles iron and is susceptible of mutation because it is the seat of attraction and repulsion (by objects) which causes their being known or unknown. Now (it may be objected that) as the Citta and Indriyas (sense organs) which are of the nature of egoism are all-pervasive and hence always connected with all objects, therefore must be produced knowledge of (all things always and everywhere. (It is replied that) though all-pervasive, when the Citta is modified in any one body and by certain objects in contact with that body, in that body alone is knowledge (of those objects) produced; not in other bodies. As this limitation is absolute, it is held that objects are like magnets and affect the Citta which resembles iron by their coming into contact with it through the channels of the sense-organs. Hence modifications belong to the Citta and not the Ātmā" *(Ib.* chap. xv).

Dṛṣya (matter) evolves as Bhūta, objects, and Indriya , organs, by which the Draṣṭā comes in contract with objects. Objects and organs are Dharmī, the seat of Dharma or qualities. Citta, the inner organ, being a mode of Dṛṣya, matter, cannot illuminate or manifest itself but must be lighted by Puruṣa. The whole universe is but the Citta tinged by the Seen (on the one hand) and the Seer (on the other) (*Yog. Sūt.* iv. 22). The Seer illuminates it and the Seen colours it a mixture of white, red and blue, the three colours representing the three Guṇas. As Vyāsa in his comment on this Sūtra says, "It is but Citta that, tinged by the Seer and the Seen, manifests as non-ego and ego becomes conscious and unconscious, though material, appears immaterial, and is called the totality of objects."

Among the innumerable Puruṣas that are in this world

there is one called Īśvara. The mention of Īśvara in the *Yoga Sūtras* has made many people describe the Yoga as a School of theism; but this is extremely inaccurate; for the Īśvara mentioned in the Yoga is in no sense God. He is neither the ruler of Nature nor the moral governor of the Universe. Out of the multitude of Puruṣas in the Universe, he is a special Puruṣa who was never touched by Kleśa, the defects of ignorance, egoism, desire, aversion, and clinging to life, and by the mental deposits left by Karma and their fruition *(Ib.* i. 14). In Him is fully developed the seed of Omniscience which every Puruṣa has. He is the ancient teacher whose life is unbroken by Time as ours is *(Ib.* i-25-26). The Īśvara of Yoga Darśana, therefore, is neither the reality behind Nature, nor any Universal Being in which human selves find their unity. Except omniscience and mastery over time, He has no other divine attribute, His only function being that of an ancient teacher. Hence Yoga is in its tenets as atheistic as Sāṅkhya. Yoga is called in India Seśvara Sāṅkhya, the Sāṅkhya which acknowledges the existence of an Īśvara; but when this phrase is translated 'theistic Sāṅkhyas, as is frequently done by English Scholars, it becomes absurd. For the Īśvara here referred to is not the Lord of the world, but the Lord only of his devotee, and He is his Lord only in the sense that he figures Him in his heart as the mystic syllable 'Om' and this makes it easy for him to reach his own inner consciousness. Though the Īśvara of Yoga is an inactive Puruṣ a, it accepts, like the Sāṅkhya, the adhidaivata, animistic, explanation of the life of nature. But this doctrine of the adhidaivata cannot make any philosophy 'theistic' in any sense of the word. On account of the great spread of Vedānta in modern India, later writers like Madhusūdhana have regarded Sāṅkhya and Yoga as stages leading to Vedānta. German mysticism also, whether it appears as the realistic monism of Haeckel, who sees in matter the one noumenon of the universe, or the more popular Pantheism of many modern philosophers, discounting as it does the abiding value of the individual, arrogates to itself the title of final truth and calls all individualistic or dualistic theories empirical. This is absurd. Both monism and dualism are equally valid explanations of the cosmos. It is a question of individual temperament which explanation appeals to one. The human mind which forms general concepts to explain the cosmos to its own satisfaction is swayed by the temperaments. The man of the rich, emotional cast of mind whose mainspring is his love to the Lord of the universe, whose greatest pleasure is service of the Lord of his heart follows the path that leads to monism; for to him everything is his Lord, all beings, conscious or unconcious, but the Lord's body, and he thus reaches the concept of the one noumenon. If he shuts himself out of touch with the spiritual side of the universe and thus cannot reach the conception of Īśvara, he invents the idea of nature or clothes with flesh the abstract idea of humanity and erects them as the objective of his emotional outflow. On the other hand, the man of the stern intellectual cast of mind prefers the path of meditation, trains himself in Viveka, distinction of Self and Not-self and reaches the dualistic interpretation of the cosmos. He may, like the Advaitī try to explain away the Not-self as really illusory and only empirically true and thus reconcile his theory with monism, but he is a dualist all the same, for his path is one of discrimination. Nor must we forget that after all both theories are but concepts of the mind, and not experiences of the spirit. Before the spirit can realise itself or the devotee can realise his Lord, Manas has to be transcended and the stage of theorizing has to be passed; and when there is realization, concept-making is neither necessary nor possible.

SECTION III. ĀGAMA

The early Vedic religion was a cult of magic, a system of propitiation or constraint of Nature-powers (Devas) by means of sacrifices (Yajñas), offerings of animal fat (ghī, vapā, etc.) and fermented liquor (Soma), poured into fire regarded as the mouth of the Gods, and accompanied with the chanting of mantras. Some of these mantras were incantations of praise, and others combinations of sound having no meaning, being sometimes inarticulate cries ("like the bellowing of a bull, etc."). They were believed to please or constrain the Devas and thus to secure the fulfilment of the sacrificer's desires, whether these were the acquisition of material objects in this life or the enjoyment of pleasures in post-mortem states (Svarga). In the alignment of the Yajña Śālā, the sacrificial hall, were embodied the early notions of the structure of the Macrocosm, for even in the earliest days the idea of the world being a macrocosm and the individual man being a microcosm, a minified copy of the cosmos, was worked out. The well-known Puruṣa Sūkta which though later than the earliest hymns is certainly much anterior to the age of the *Upaniṣads,* proves this. The moon sprang from (the Cosmic Puruṣa's) manas; from (his) eyes the sun was born; from (his) mouth Indra and Agni, from (his) prāṇa, vāyu was born. From (his) navel was the middle region (antarikṣa) from (his) head was the sky; from (his) feet the earth, the quarters from (his) ears." *(R. V.* X. 90. 13, 14). This subject is referred to in numerous passages of the Vedas (*Vide Śat. Brāh.* X. iii. 3. 8., XIV. 2. 13. *R. V.* X. 16. 3. etc.). Since all the gods were represented in the human body, methods of getting into communion with them other than by means of sacrifices were invented. These attempts were, in the first instance, but the conversion of the bahiryāga, outer sacrifice, into antaryāga, inner sacrifice, bāhyapūjā (exterior worship) into mānasapūjā (mental worship). The intermediate stage between bahiryāga and antaryāga is represented by the following quotation from *Śatapatha Brāhmaṇa XI. ii* 6. 13. "One should say 'this is the Deva yājī'and 'this is the Ātma yājī. He is the Ātmayājī (lit: self-sacrificer) who knows, 'by this rite this member of my body is rectified,' 'by this rite this member of my body is restored'... He is the devayājī (god-sacrificer) who thinks 'I worship the gods with this, I offer (it) to the gods;... (The latter) does not conquer so great a world as the other." Gradually the form of sacrifice was kept up but transferred to the region of the mind. An early example of this is quoted from

Tait. Āraṇ. III. i., where is described the cidyāga by means of which Prajāpati created the world. "Thought (was) the sacrificial ladle (sruk); citta (mind),—the ghi; voice (vāk), the altar (vedi); purpose, the grass on the altar; desire, the fire; knowledge, the (second) fire; the Lord of voice, the hotā (priest); manas, the Upavaktā (assistant priest); prāṇa, the offering; equanimity, the adhvaryu." From these were developed the genuine vidyās, methods of meditation, which are collected in the various *Upaniṣads,*[4] each of which contains the vidyās traditionally taught in the Vedic School to which it belongs.

Meanwhile other influences worked on the Hindu mind and carried religious thought in other directions. The multifarious gods of the Vedas were grouped under three classes, thus laying the foundation of the later doctrine of the Trimūrti. The irrepressible instinct for unifying the multiform cosmic phenomena under one grand concept also worked from very early times and thus was evolved the idea of Brahma, the indefinable reality behind the Devas, the power that resides in the Mantras and hence can be utilized by the Mantravit, the knower of the Mantras, the Brāhmaṇa, for the purpose of constraining the Devas, the same power that in the Macrocosm drives the Universe. Through fear of Him the wind blows, through fear the sun goes; through fear of Him, Agni and Indra (do their work), and Death runs, the fifth." (*Tait. Up. II.* v. 3.) This same Brahma is the power within the innermost Self of the man. "Who dwells in the Earth, is other than the earth, whom the earth knows not, whose body the earth is, who rules the earth from within, he is thy Ātmā, the inner ruler, the immortal." *(Br. Up.* III. vii. 3.) "Who dwells in the (individual) Self, is other than the Self, whom the Self knows not, whose body the Self is, who rules the Self from within, he is thy Ātmā, the inner ruler, the immortal." *(Ib.* III. vii. 22.) This identification of Brahma with the Ātmā, of the God of the Universe with the God within the man, led to the development of the Supreme Science, the Parāvidyā, which is the specific Vedānta discipline and attempts to soar to the greatest heights of meditation man is capable of.

But it is very few that can seek the Supreme in the silent recesses of the heart. In most men 'the senses run out, not towards the Self; and they seek Brahma in the Cosmos without, in the world of object and not the subject. When the Paramātmā is thus thought of as the object He appears as the power of Nature, for That can never become the object, but is "the consciousness, to be reached by consciousness (in-turned), seated in the hearts of all." (*Bhag. Gītā* xiii. 17). Search for Him outside as Indra did. "He ran to That. That vanished from his view. He beheld in that very space, a woman, very brilliant, Umā of golden hue." *(Kena Up.* iii 12.) She is the Supreme power "by which this Universe is upheld," symbolized by Gāyatrī in *Ch. Up.* iii. 12 and *Bṛh. Up.* v. 14. This concept of Śakti, the Power of Nature, was developed from the much earlier one of Aditi, defined in the Nirukta as Adīnā devamātā, the mighty mother of the Gods. Even in the earliest hymns of the *Ṛg Veda* she is an embodiment of Power and the supporter of the Universe. She is described as "the luminous Aditi, the Supporter of the Earth, living in Heaven" (*R. V. I.* 136. 3). Not only is she the mother of the Gods, but she is "the great mother of the devotees (Suvratānām), the mistress of the rites, the strong in might, the ever-young, the widely-extended, the protecting, the skilful in guiding" (*Vāj. Sam.* 21. 5). When the power behind Nature and that of Mantras was erected into one objective entity—the world-mother, she absorbed all the functions of the ancient Aditi. Gradually this idea, that Brahma if sought as an object, and not the subject of introspective vision is Śakti, that the objective form of the One without form is Cosmic Power, grew and appealed to the religious imagination. Śakti, Cosmic Power, became the recipient of worship, both outer and inner; both Pratīka Upāsanā, worship of symbols in temples and at home, and Mānasapūjā of Ambā, the world-mother spread in the country[5] and largely supplanted Vedic Yajñas. This gave birth to the literature of the Āgamas (literally, revelations), also called Tantras (lit. skilful acts).

At the same time the ancient movement, already referred

to, of reducing the many Gods to three classes, each class under the headship of one chief God developed in different lines. The *Nirukta* of Yāska, and the *Bṛhaddevatā* were the earliest attempts at what we may call the higher criticism of the *Vedas,* while portions of the *Brāhmaṇas* represent the lower criticism. The critical movement of the *Nirukta* was snuffed out by a later ebullition of the mythoepic instinct, which seems so congenial to the Indian mind. The *Nirukta* taught, "There are three Gods, according to the expounders of the *Veda,* Agni whose place is the Earth, Vāyu or Indra, whose place is the middle region, and Sūrya, whose place is the sky." In the *Kenopaniṣad* Agni, Vāyu and Indra are spoken of as the chief Gods. This must have been the general belief in the age when the hymns of the *Ṛg Veda* were compiled into a Saṁhitā (collection), for we find that the first hymns of each Maṇḍala of the *Ṛg Veda* (except the ninth, devoted to Soma) are those in praise of Agni, the next generally of Vāyu and the last of Indra. In the *Taitirīya Upaniṣad,* Sūrya takes the place of Indra, but Indra (or Śakra) continued to be a chief God during the age of Buddhism. Indeed he was worshipped in temples in Southern India and Jāva, in the early years of the Christian era, when Buddhism was the state religion, as we find from Tamil Epics of eighteen hundred years ago. But long before this another Trimūrti had been worked out; Brahmā, Viṣṇu and Śiva who were minor dieties in the Vedic age, Brahmā being called Brahmaṇaspati or Bṛhaspati, and Śiva being called Rudra, supplanted the earlier Trinity. Śiva absorbed the functions of Agni besides those of some popular Dravidian phallic deity and Viṣṇu those of Indra and Sūrya.[6] Later on, Śiva with some and Viṣṇu with others became the chief person of the Trimūrti, on whom the heart might lean and round whose feet the emotions of the devotee might twine themselves.

Brahmā, though one of the Trimūrti, the Indian Trinity of the age that succeeded the final compilation of the *Mahābhārata* never became a supreme God like Viṣṇu or Śiva. This has puzzled European Scholars who cannot understand why the creator, the first and greatest person of the Trinity in their religion, should be considered a secondary person in the Hindu Trinity. The Hindu framed the concept of the one noumenon of the universe not as a person, but as a substance behind Sat and Asat, personal consciousness and the unconscious (*R. V.* x. 129). Considered as an *object* of thought, the *same* was the active power behind the phenomenal universe, identical with the power of the mantras, the golden hued Brahmā, Brahmaṇaspati, the Lord of Hymns (*R. V.* ii. 23, i. 40 etc.), later on conceived as a female deity, Śakti. Brahmā (male) never became a supreme personal God, for the Jñāna Yogīs, men of the intellectual temperament naturally preferred the higher concept of Brahma (neuter), the Impersonal Reality behind the Cosmos to be reached by āvrittacakṣuḥ, introspective meditation, as the eternal, immutable Subject, the ātmā; and the Karmayogīs, men of the emotional tempera-ment, when they did not worship Viṣṇu, the active God of the developing universe (the Vedic Sūrya, the nourisher of all that is) or Śiva who manifests himself when the individual turns his back on the world and becomes an ascetic (the vedic Agni who burns the universe), preferred the concept Śakti, universal power as a wider generalization than Brahma (male), the same power exercising the one function of creation. Another reason why Brahmā did not attain to the position of Viṣṇu or Śiva is that, being the creator, he is no more an active deity and could scarcely reward or punish his devotees. It is the hope of reward and fear of punishment that is the basis of most of what passes for Bhakti (religious devotion) and Brahmā could not satisfy these human emotions. In later times Brahmā was degraded to the position of an Individual Soul (jīvātmā). Hence so few traces are found of any worship of Brahmā in India. The cults of Viṣṇu were called Bhāgavata or Pāñcarātra and those of Śiva, Pāśupata or Māheśvara. These cults were in existence before the Christian Era. The Bhāgavatas are alluded to in an inscription of the second century before Christ. The *Mahābhārata,* which most critics now assign to the third century B. C, refers to the Pāśupata and of the

Pañcarātra systems; and the part of the *Mahābhārata* where they are referred to is certainly not a later interpolation, but is at least as ancient as the bulk of the poem.

These monotheistic movements, the Vaiṣṇava and Śaiva, inspired by the need of a single, supreme, personal God felt by those who could not rise to the high levels of meditation on the absolute spread to South India, where they received a great accession of strength, especially when oppposed to Buddhism, which they killed out after a severe struggle which lasted a few centuries. This great development of monotheism in southern India was perhaps influenced by the monotheism of the Semitic races with whom southern India had commercial intercourse from early times. The sterner and more repulsive features of Śiva as well as the extremely realistic phallic emblems which represent him remind us of the Jahve of the Hebrews, and the sexual aberrations associated with Viṣṇu worship remind us of similar excesses in the valleys of the Euphrates and the Tigris. The specific tenets of the Pāñcarātra and Śaiva schools were formulated in Northern India, for we find them referred to in the *Mahābhārata* and their technical terms are all Saṅskṛt; but the movements became all powerful in Southern India, from whence they spread back to Northern India and have taken a more prominent hold of the Hindu imagination than any other of the numerous schools of thought or worship developed in India. The final extinction of Buddhism and obscuration of Jainism in India was due to these two waves of Viṣṇu-worship and Śiva-worship that spread North from the South about 5 centuries after Christ. By that time Buddhism and Jainism were themselves choked with Tantra practices, though without provision for devotion to a personal God and therefore easily gave way to Tāntrika religions which provided for this Bhakti, so necessary to the emotional man. These cults utilized the architectural developments of Buddhism and Jāinism and hence arose the Temple architecture of southern India. This architecture was probably also influenced by the Egyptian temple architecture, for southern India had from early times a steady commercial intercourse with Egypt as with Babylonia. Temple ritual was elaborated on a grand scale. This ritual was primarily based on the ceremonies of fetish-worship of the Dravidian races, many of which are still observed in villages and under wayside-trees in all their primitive barbarism. Into the Temple-ritual was welded elements from the sacrificial ritual developed by the Aryan Ṛṣis. Thus was evolved the gorgeous ritual of the Temples which more effectively killed out the Vedic Yajñas (sacrifices) than the gentle banter of the *Sāṅkhya* and the *Bhagavad-gītā* or the more passionate denunciations of the founders of the Jaina and the Bauddha cults. Similarly the old fire-worship of the home (Ekāgni gṛhya ceremonies) gave way to domestic idolatry, a minified copy of the temple worship. And the vidyās of the *Upaniṣads* became supplanted by mental worship of the two gods and the one goddess that now supplanted the innumerable gods of the vedic Pantheon and the countless local and tribal deities worshipped from pre-Āryan times.

The worship of Śakti, Śiva and Viṣṇu by means of meditation, and of symbols and idols both in houses and temples gave birth to the three classes of Āgamas, called Śākta, Śaiva and Pāñcarātra. The Āgamas like the *Upaniṣads,* were the ultimate developments of the *Brāhmaṇas* (though they contained other elements besides); hence the followers of the Āgama schools sought to prove their orthodoxy by interpreting the *Upaniṣads* in accordance with their own tenets. They even gave the name of Saṁhitā to them, as also the name Smṛti, thus indicating their claim to be, what they really were, based on and regularly evolved from tradition. This movement gave birth to most of the later *Upaniṣads,* which unlike the earlier ones do not denominate the Supreme Being Param Brahma, but are expressly Vaiṣṇava, Śaiva or Śākta in their tone and are probably in many cases but Āgamas under the name of *Upaniṣads*. Many of the Āgamas themselves are called *Upaniṣads,* though not included in the recognized 108.

The *Bhagavad Gītā* which is called an *Upaniṣad,* also the

Smṛti, *par excellence,* and the *Śvetāśvatara Upaniṣad* are works of Vedānta, but show clear traces of the influence of the Āgamas. Garbe has pointed out the influence of the *Bhāgavata* (Vaiṣṇava) *Āgamas* on the former. The latter bears equally clear traces of the influence of the Śaiva cult. Both works seem to be due to an ancient synthesizing movement in which was attempted a higher standpoint than the monism of the *Upaniṣads,* the pluralism of the Sāṅkhya and the Vaiśeṣika and the three tattvas (triple reality) of the Āgama Schools, a standpoint from which all three can be reconciled and treated as different aspects of the higher point of view.

The influence of the Āgamas or Tantras, as they are more familiarly known, on Indian life has been profound. The living Hindu religion of today from Cape Comorin to the remotest corners of Tibet is essentially Tāntric. Even the few genuine Vedic rites that are preserved and are supposed to be derived straight from the *Vedas e.g.* the Sandhyā, have been modified by the addition of Tāntric practices. Equally profound has been the influence of the Āgamas on the development of Vedānta philosophy. Śaṅkara was a professed Śākta and his advaita exposition of the Vedānta, though overtly independent of the Śākta Āgamas, is influenced by Tāntric theories and his discipline by Tāntric practices. Rāmānuja who, according to Dr. Thibaut, expounds a less forced form of Vedānta and more near to the ideas of Bādarāyaṇa, the author of the *Vedānta Sūtras,* than Śaṅkara, was a Vaiṣṇava and regarded the Vaiṣṇava Āgamas as authoritative, though he too seldom quotes them to support his exposition. Mādhva is so much under the Āgama influence that his *Bhāṣya* is but a string of Āgama texts with a few words thrown in here and there to connect them.

The Āgamas have all been kept secret, very few having been printed or being easily available in Mss. The names of 108 Pāñcarātra Āgamas, 28 Śaiva Āgamas and 77 Śakta Āgamas are given as the authoritative books of these schools. Hundreds more are quoted in the commentaries of the new books that one can get at. The few Āgamas that are available now belong to different ages. The *Lakṣmī Tantra,* for instance, among the Vaiṣṇava Āgmas which is predominantly Śākta in tone, the *Pādma Saṁhitā,* which is nearer to advaita than the modern Vaiṣṇava relishes, being decidedly ancient, and the *Parāśara Saṁhitā* and the *Bhāradvāja Saṁhitā* which are highly sectarian and support specific recent tenets being decidedly of a very late age. In the case of the Śaiva and Śākta Schools, their common tenets are so many and specific differences so few that this test of age cannot be applied, but many of the existing Āgamas are anterior to the age of Śaṅkara.

And we must also remember that, in the of these writings, as in that of the *Rāmāyaṇa,* the *Mahābhārata,* the *Purāṇas* and the metrical-*Smṛtis,* portions of the substance are very ancient, but the form has grown with time. The contents of the Āgamas are of unequal value. Here and there we meet with snatches of high philosophy, subtle psychological analysis of ecstatic mental states, and valuable descriptions of centres of prāṇa and lines of force in the subtle body, but the bulk of the Āgamas is but grovelling superstition, mostly of a revolting form, and endless details of dull ritual. Besides the Āgamas, this school has given birth to a whole series of philosophical works—of Sūtras, Kārikās,[7] Bhāṣyas. Vṛttis and Vārttikas, besides independent works—an immense literature jealously guarded from the prying eyes of the modern investigator, but slowly sacrificed to the omnivorous poochies .

The Āgamas are generally divided into four parts (pādas,) Jñāna, Yoga, Kriyā, and Carya. "Jñana is knowledge of the Lord; that knowledge is called release" *(Pādma Saṁhita* I. ii. 6.) "Yoga is the restriction (bandha) of the unagitated citta to one subject" *(Ib.* II. i. 3.) 'Kriyā (embraces all acts) from ploughing the ground (for laying the foundations of the temple) to establishing (the idol) *(Ib.* III. i. 6). Caryā is "the method ot worship" *(Ib.* IV. i. I*)*. The Śaiva Āgamas regard that the last three parts together constitute Tapas to be learnt from a human teacher and that the first, *i. e*., Jñāna can be taught only by Śiva who comes as the Guru to the ripe disciple at the psychological moment and gives him an initiation (Dikṣā) into wisdom.

In the earlier Āgamas of all the three cults the Supreme Real Being of the Universe, corresponding to the Brahma Paramam of the *Upaniṣads* and called Nārāyaṇa in the Vaiṣṇava tantras and Maheśvara or Śiva in the other two tantras retreats to the background and all cosmic functions are attributed to Śakti treated as his wife but the really the predominant factor.

But in the Vaiṣṇava and Śaiva schools the male god soon acquired a prominent position and they also broke up into different sects. Yet these numerous schools have some common characteristics : They acknowledge three tattvas—ultimate realities, (1) A supreme Being with the male or female aspect predominant. (2) the class of individual souls (3) the objective Universe. These three Realities (tattvas) are given different names in the different schools, but their attributes and mutual relations do not vary much, though the terminology varies from school to school. These schools are also all agreed in opposing the Māyāvāda, the doctrine of the unreality of the world, developed from the teachings of Gauḍapāda and Śaṅkara and reduced to absurdity by their modern followers. Says the *Pauṣ kara Āgama*. "If, (as the Śāṅkaras say) the world is an illusive appearance of conscious being, the effected world will be a hollow unreality; how can the world which is established to be really existing by all methods of proofs be a false transmutation of consciousness" (*Ib*. ii. 5).

The Āgamas do not regard the world as a false show; as Bhāskararāya says in *Lalitā Sahasranāma Bhāṣya,* under the name *Mithyājagad adhiṣthānā* No. 735, "Really according to the belief of the Tāntrikas, who hold (the doctrine that) the world (is) a transmutation of Brahma, the Universe is real; because as there is absolutely no difference between Brahma and the world just (there is no difference) between a pot and the clay (of which it is made), the reality of the universe neccessarily follows from the reality of Brahma. As we accept that the difference (between Brahma and the Universe) is false, we accept all the texts declaring non-difference. From the unreality of difference (between Brahma and the Universe) it follows that the relation of supporter and supported is false. Hence the Vedānta theory of the illusoriness of the world cannot be accepted."

Intense Bhakti, personal Devotion, to the world-mother or to the world-father whether called Mahādeva (Śiva), or Nārāyaṇa, characterises these schools. The root of this attitude of Bhakti to a supreme Being can be traced to that spirit of the vedic Ṛṣis, which made them praise as the Highest, whatever God, high or low they happened to invoke at any time—the spirit which Max Muller has labelled Henotheism. The development of the Āgama schools gave a great impetus to Bhakti by concentrating the attention on one Deva and this resulted in an extreme development of Bhakti, a devotion that expressed itself in an absorbing love, a complete self surrender, which the want of a sense of humour to such ridiculous extremes that the devotee's became one orgie of singing and dancing and worse.

Another common characteristic of these Āgama Schools is their intimate association with abnormal manifestations of the sexual instinct The emotional nature of man is the common root of devotion to a superhuman being as well as to human beings and the habit of self-abandonment to a divine being which grows with devotion easily degenerates into self-abandoment of different kinds. Hence there exists in India to-day debased forms of Śakti-worship, Śiva-worship, and Viṣṇu-worship much too revolting to be described.

This devotional movement has, as in another countries, given a great stimulus to Art; Temple architecture, especially in Southern India, and Lyric (devotional) Poetry, especially Sanskṛt, Tamil and Hindī have reached a high order of perfection; only for want of cultivation of the powers of observation, this poetry is not noted for any wealth of poetic images, but is oppressed as other departments of life in India are, by a load of soul-suffocating convention. Music, Dancing (Nāṭya) and gesticulation (abhinaya) have also been evolved under the influence of religious devotion; but the last art has degenerated into gross sensuality as its modern expounders are the women euphemistically called 'slaves of the Gods' (devadāsīs) attached to the Southern Temples.

The following notes regarding the early references to Śiva and Viṣṇu temples in inscriptions so far discovered and deciphered have been drawn up by my friend, Mr. T. A. Gopinatha Row, of Srīraṅgam and are extremely useful.

References to Viṣṇu-cult.

1. Udayagiri cave inscription of...........ḍhala, son of Viṣṇudāsa, grandson of Chhagala and vassal of the Gupta King, Candra Gupta II, dated the Gupta era 82(401-2 A. D.) Sanskrit dedication of a rock-cut shrine to Viṣṇu.
2. Bhitarī stone pillar inscription of Skandagupta, undated, recording the intallation of the image of the God Śārṅgī and the allotment of a village to it.
3. Junāgaḍh inscription of Skandagupta, dated G. E. 138 (457-8 A. D.) Repairs to the lake Sudarśana by the governor Parṇadatta's agent, Cakrapālita. Cakrapālita caused to be built a temple to Carabhrit.
4. Gangdhār inscription of Viśvakarmā. dated 423-4 A. D. The inscription belongs partly to the Vaiṣṇava and partly to the Śākta (?) form of religion. It records that a person built a temple for Viṣṇu, the Sapta Mātṛkas and a well of drinking water.
5. Eraṇ stone pillar inscription of Budhagupta, G. E. 165 (481-5 A. D.) Erection of a dhvajastambha to Janārdhana by a Mahārājā Matṛviṣṇu and his younger brother Dhanya-viṣṇu.

6. Khōh copper plate of Mahārājā Saṁkṣobha. G. E. 209 (528-9 A. D [begins with the famous " twelve-lettered mantra" (Om namo bhagavate Vāsudevāya), of the Bhāgavatas].

7. Khōh copper plate of Mahārājā Jagannātha G.E. 177 (496-7 A.D). Grant of the village of Dhavaṣaṇḍika to a number of Brāhmaṇas for the purpose of a temple of Bhagavān.

8. Khōh copperplates of Mahārājā Śarvanātha G. E. 192 (512-3 A. D).

9. Gaḍhwa stone inscription of G. E 118 (467-8). found in the Daśāvatāra temple.

References to Śiva-cult.

1. Udayagiri cave inscription of Candragupta II. undated. Records the excavation of a shrine of Śambhu.

2. Bilsaḍ stone inscription of Kumāragupta of G. E. 96 (415-6 A. D) Records the building of a number of minor buildings in the temple of Swāmī Mahāsena.

3. Bihār pillar of Skandagupta.

4. Mandasōr pillar of Yaśōdharma.

5. Kōsam (Kauśāmbi) inscription on the stone image of the time of Bhīmavarmā G. E. 139 (458-9 A, D.)

These facts show how much these two cults were advanced in the Fifth century A. D, and that they must. have had behind them many centuries of development.

We shall now discuss the fundamental tenets of the Āgama schools.

(i) The Śākta or Devī Āgama

(The 77 Āgamas of this School are subdivided into three, (I) 5 Śubhāgamas, also called Samaya, which teach practices leading to knowledge and liberation (2) 64 Kaulāgamas, which teach disgustingly dirty practices supposed to develop magical powers (318) Miśrāgamas, aiming at both. The 64 Kaula Āgamas are said to deal with occult arts, causing illusions, killing people by means of magic, exorcising demons, alchemy and sundry dirty practices of worship. They are called Kaula, because they advocate the worship of Śakti residing in kula, the perineum. This is also called the left hand path. The eight Miśra Āgamas deal with Śrividyā also and are hence the mixed path. The names of these Āgamas are Candrakalā, Jyotisvatī, Kalānidhi,Kulārṇava,Kuleśvarī,Bhuvaśneśvarī, Bārhaspatya, and Dūrvāsamata. The five Śubha agamas describe the right hand path, also called also Samaya ācāra, the worship of Devī throughout the Suṣumnā. They are the Saṁhitās named Vasiṣṭha, Sanaka, Śuka, Sanandana, Sanatkumāra.[8] Philosophical ideas are referred to only incidentally in these Āgamas but are apparently regularly expounded in the Śakti Sūtras, a work which, it will be worth the while of Mss. hunters to bring to light. Nine Sūtras from this work are quoted by Bhāskararāya in different places of his Lalitā Sahasranāma bhāṣya. The opening Sūtra says, "Consciousness, which is independence is the cause of the production of the Universe." Another Sūtra says "when one does not realize this he gets confused by his own Śakti and enters Saṁsāra." The next Sūtra adds, "when he realizes it, and his mind is turned inwards and mounts up towards the knower, he reaches (pure) consciousness." The various stages leading to liberation are indicated in the following:—"When one attains the bliss of (pure) consciousness, (he reaches) Jīvanmukti, which is unshaken identity with cit (pure consciousness, though he retains the consciousness of body, prāṇa etc." "This attainment of the bliss of (pure) consciousness (Cidānanda) is due to Madhyavikāsa ", *i. e.,* "by the destruction of doubt." "When he attains bala (power of will), he makes the universe his own," The last Sūtra describes the goal of life to be "the attainment of the Goddess of True Consciousness and the mastery over the Cakras (the centres of energy)." Judged from these quotations the Śakti Sūtras, if discovered, will prove a very valuable find. Many other works of this School are known only by name or by stray quotations by commentators].

The three tattvas (ultimates) of this school are (I) An impersonal, inactive Being called Prakāśa or Śiva (to be distinguished from the active Śiva of the Śaivāgamas), of the nature of pure consciousness like the Puruṣa of the Sāṅkhya School, but differing therefrom in being omnipresent (akhilā-nugata). (2) an active, personal Being, called Vimārśa, Śakti or Tripurā of the nature of Pūrṇāhambhāva (full egoity), personal conciousness, who includes all individual souls; she is also called Ahaṁtā, I-ness (3) The insentient universe of matter, also called Idaṁtā, this-ness. Illumination, power and object thus form the triune manifested universe. In the Śaiva and Vaiśṇava āgamas, the first Being of this trinity is an active Being, and the Second, His Śakti, occupies a subordinate position and in the latest developments of these schools almost disappears from view. The extreme Śākta view is embodied in the opening śloka of *Saundaryalahari*. "Śiva, when he is united with Śakti, is able to create; otherwise, the God is unable even to move." Kṣemarāja in his Śiva sūtra Vimarśinī ,[9] quotes the following from the Mṛtyujidbhaṭṭāraka. "That Parāśakti, my Icchā potent, born of Nature (Svabhāvajā; is to be known as heat in fire, as of the form of the rays in the sun, that Śakti is the cause of all the worlds." Another famous tantra says, "Tripurā is the Supreme Śakti, antecedent to jñānā and other Śaktis, O dear one. She is differentiated as gross and subtle and becomes the mother of the origin of the Triloki (triple experience of man). Her form is that wherein the totality of the (36) tattvas is dissolved. All evolution being hers, the Supreme is not required (to be active in the world process;. The Supreme (Śiva) devoid of Śakti, is unable to do anything. He becomes omnipotent when he is united to Śakti. O, Supreme Lady, without Śakti, the subtle (unevolved, potential) Śiva has no name or support. Even though (he is) known, O Mahādevī, there is no use (lit. no gain of name or virtue).' When he is meditated on, (there results) no grace, no steadiness of mind. When she is in the supreme path, she is of subtle form and thence attains the states of the seed and the plant (the subtle and gross universes) which had been absorbed in her." (*Vāmakeśvara Tantra* iv. 4-9).[10]

Prakāśa and Vimarśa are explained by Bhāskararāya (the famous śākta scholar of the 18th century, who was a paṇḍit of the Tanjore Court and who has been already referred to) in his *Bhāṣya* on *Vimarśarūpiṇi,* 548th name in *Lalitāsahasranāma.* The spontaneous (svābhāvika) vibration of Parabrahma, who Prākāśa, is called Vimarśa. It is said in the *Saubhagyasudhodaya,* 'His *Śakti* is spontaneous vibration, vimarśa. It is she that creates the mobile and the immobile (creatures of) the universe, and also destroys this world." The third member of this trinity, matter, is defined and subdivided as in the *Sāṅkhya* School. In fact the *Āgama* schools have completely absorbed the *Sāṅkhya* philosophy so far as the analysis of the material universe is concerned. They have elaborated them in sundry directions and superadded other tattvas to those of the *Sāṅkhyas* and thus, to some extent, destroyed the clarity and philosophical purity of the *Sāṅkhya* concepts. Instead of the 25 tattvas of *Sāṅkhya* this school divides the universe into thirty-six tattvas (principles) which will be explained in the next chapter. These thirty-six tattvas are again classified as three tattvas (ultimates), called (I) Śivatattva, the supreme, (2) Vidyā tattvas, the subtle manifestations of *Śakti* and (3) Ātmātattvas, the material universe starting from Māyā and ending with the earth. These three ultimates are the same as Prakāśa, Vimarśa and Idaṁtā. These three concepts are very clearly explained by Bhāskararāya in his *Bhāṣya* on his own *Varivasyārahasya.*

"Brahma called Prakāśa is the pure knowledge resulting from the consciousness implied in the first person in 'I desire', 'I know, etc. It is associated with Omniscience, Lordship, Omnipotence, Plenitude, Immanence, and other powers. The vibration of a ray of Prakāśa of the nature of bliss is called Parāhaṁtā, the Supreme Egoism, Vimarśa, the Supreme Lalitā, Bhaṭṭārakā, Tripura-Sundarī [names of the world-mother]. It is said in the *Viśvaśarīra Skandha* of Virūpākṣa Pañcāśika "Lordship is Omnipotence (Power of Action), Self-dependence and consciousness. These are said by Śambhu to be the names of Parāhaṁtā. As objectivity (Idaṁtā, literally, this-ness) is not manifested without the subject (Ahaṁtā lit, I-ness) on account of the relativity of I and This (Self and not-self), the object, which is the content of the notion 'this', is caused by the power of Ahaṁtā (the subject; or by Brahma who is other than it. That object is evolved from it." (*Varivasyā-rahasya,* commentary on I. 3).

Prakāśa is illumination; it is the purest distillate of experience or rather the attentation of experience to purest consciousness of Being, the barest consciousness without being stained by the least touch of relativity; the nearest approach to Pure Being, to the Absolute that human thought or human language can hope to reach.

Ambā (the world-mother) is the first appearance of a vibration in the absolute Prakāśa , the first assertion of relation, of Vimarśa, distinction, which gives birth to all this universe. She is the power (Śakti) latent in Prakāśa beginning to manifest herself and give birth to Gods, men, and other beings. The motion that starts from Ahaṁtā goes over to the other pole of Idaṁtā, (This-ness) objectivity, matter. These three ultimates of the Tāntrikas, Illumination, Power, and Object may be compared to Hegel's three doctrines of Logic—Being, Essence and Notion, and Idea. "Being is the notion implicit only" its special forms have the predicate 'is' ... Pure being makes the beginning; because it is on the one hand pure thought, and on the other immediacy itself, simple and indeterminate; and the first beginning cannot be mediated by anything, or be further determined...Being-for-self, as reference to itself, is immediacy, and as reference of the negative to itself, is a self-subsistent, the One...The terms in essence are always mere pairs of correlatives, and not yet absolutely reflected in themselves: hence in essence the actual unity of the notion is not realized, but only postulated by reflection. Essence, which is Being coming into mediation with itself through the negativity of itself is self-relatedness only in so far as it is in relation to an other—this other however coming into view at first not as some thing which *is,* but as postulated and hypothetised—Being has not vanished : but firstly, Essence, as simple self-relation, is Being, and secondly as regards its one sided characteristic of immediacy, Being is deposed to a mere negative, to a seeming or reflected light—Essence accordingly is Being thus reflecting light into itself......The Essence lights up in itself or is mere reflection: and therefore is only self-relation, not as immediate but as reflected. And that reflex relation is Self-Identity .... Essence is mere Identity and reflection in itself only as it is self-relating negativity, and in that way self-repulsion. It contains therefore essentially the characteristic of Difference. The Notion is the power of the substance self-realised. It is a systematic whole, in which each of its constituents functions, is the very total which the notion is......The onward motion of the notion is no longer either a transition into, or a reflection on something else, but development. The realisation of the notion,—a realisation in which the universal is this one totality withdrawn back into itself and which has given itself a character of 'immediate unity by merging the mediation : this realisation of the notion is the Object." (*The Logic of Hegel, 2nd* Edition trans. by Wallace, Sect. 83, 84, 86, 96, 112, 115, 116, 160, I6I, 193).

(ii) The Śaiva or Māheśvara Āgama

The Śaiva schools are so intimately allied to the Śākta schools that the literature and doctrines of one are quoted as authoritative by the other. The chief characteristic of the Śaiva school is that Śiva is the predominant Being and, especially in the later developments of these schools, Śakti is almost a negligible factor of the cosmos. The characteristic Theism of the Āgama schools led to Śiva being regarded as the Final cause of the Universe. But the Śaiva system became divided into three different schools in regard to the question how far causal efficiency belongs to the will of Śiva and how far to the actions of beings.

These schools are called (1) the Lakulīśa-Pāśupata school of Gujarat, which prefers to call the Supreme Being Paśupati (lit. the Lord of cattle); (2) the Śaiva Siddhānta of Southern India, intimately allied to the Śākta; (3) the Pratyabhijñā school of Kashmir, so-called because the fundamental teaching of the sect is that pratyabhijñā (recognition) of the Lord in the knower as well as in the known leads to liberation.

With regard to the question of the respective causal efficiency of Śiva and of Karma, the Pāśupata School maintains that Śiva is a cause independent of the actions (karma) of individuals but that "the efficiency of actions depends upon (an individual's) power of action (kriyāśakti) being unobstructed on account of conformity with the infinitely potent will of the Lord" *(Sarvadarśana-saṁgraha chap.* vi). The Siddhānta school regards Śiva as the Universal agent, but not irrespective of individual Karma. "(The fruition of) the two *(i e.* good and bad) actions reaches (individual) souls by the order of the Highest; His dependence on the karma of the individual does not detract from His independance, just as a king's depending on his guards to protect his city does not detract from the royal power; just as the holder of a magnet directs the motion of a needle, so the Lord directs the fruits of actions to the proper persons." (condensed from a lengthy discussion in Śivajñana bhāṣyam , a Tamil commentary of the 18 centuary on Meykaṇḍa Deva's Tamil Sūtras called *Śivañanabodam,* earlier than the 13th century). The Pratyabhijñā schools conceive Maheśvara to create the universe, "by mere force of desire", for he is of "unobstructed power, bliss and independence." This school, therefore, denies causal efficiency to all but the will of Maheśvara.

This difference of starting point has led to a wide divergence of views with regard to the nature and relations of the three metaphysical ultimates that compose the manifested universe.

(1) THE PĀŚUPATA SCHOOL

The three ultimates are called by the followers of this school, the cause, the effect and the defect. The *Sarvadarśanasaṁgraha* quoting from the commentary on the first sūtra of this sect, "Now then we shall expound the rules of Pāśupatayoga of Paśupati," says, "Paśu means the effect, for it depends on something ulterior; Pati means the cause, (Kāraṇa) the Lord, for he is the cause of the world, the Ruler." "The cause is the author of creation, destruction and sustenance (of the world, the effect). On account of differences of quality and action he is subdivided into Pati, Sādhya etc. His Lordship consists in infinite knowledge and power, eternal supremacy, being the First of beings, possession of power, not adventitious, etc." "The Effect (Kārya) is threefold, Vidyā (sentiency), Kalā (the insentient), Paśu (the sentient). Sentiency (Vidyā) is the characteristic of Paśu. it is two fold, according as it is of the nature of Knowledge (bodha), and ignorance (abodha). Knowledge is (again) two fold, according as its procedure is discriminative (viveka) or indiscriminative (aviveka). Discriminative procedure which is based on evidence is called citta. By means of citta, all living beings cognize objects discriminate or indiscriminate when they are illuminated by the light of external objects. Ignorance, again, is either characterized or not by the objects of the Paśu[11]. The insentient (Kalā), while depending upon the sentient, is unconscious. It is, also, two-fold, what is called the effect and what is called the cause. Therein, what is called the effect is ten-fold, the five tattvas, Pṛthvī (earth) etc.; the five qualities, colour etc. What is called the cause is thirteen-fold, the five organs of Cognition, the five organs of action, the triple Antaḥkaraṇa, Buddhi, Ahaṁkāra and Manas having the functions of certitude, self-cognition and desire. Paśu is what is under bondage. It is, also, two-fold, the displayed (Sañjana) and the undisplayed. Of these, the displayed are those that are associated with bodies and organs; the undisplayed are devoid of them." "Mala (defect) is an evil condition pertaining to the soul. It is of five kinds, false conception etc. It is said (by Haradatta) that 'false conception, deviation from duty, attachment, interestedness, and falling (from the path), these five are the root of bondage, to be specially shunned in this system.'" (*Ib.* Chap. vi). Besides the *Paśupati Sūtras,* Mādhava quotes, as authorities of this system, Haradattācārya, and Nakulīśa,[12] the author of *Pañcārthabhāṣ yadīpikā* and *Ādarśa* about whom nothing is known.

(2) THE ŚAIVA SIDDHĀNTA SCHOOL

The doctrines and religious practices of this school are propounded in 28 Śaiva Āgamas, a number of treatises on the Śaiva philosophy and a Bhāṣya by Nīlakaṇṭha on the Vedānta Sūtras on Śaiva lines (usually called Śaiva Viśiṣṭādvaita, besides a voluminous Tamil literature, produced during the last 1,500 years and perhaps more interesting as literature than as philosophy. The cult of Śiva is "the living system which exercises at the persent day......a marvellous power over the minds of the great majority of the Tamil people."[13] It is "the most elaborate, influential, and undoubtedly the most intrinsically valuable of all the religions of India."[14]

The nature and relations of the three ultimates according to this system, are well-explained in the Mṛgendra Āgama,[15] which is the jñānapāda (section dealing with knowledge) of the Kāmika, the first of the Śaiva Āgamas. "Śiva is beginningless, free from defects (mala), the all-doer, the all knower, removes from the individual soul (here called, aṇu, atom, from its limitation), the web of bonds that obscure its nature *(Mṛg. Āg.* ii. 1). The whole Śaiva position is thus "condensed in this one sūtra[16]" *(Ib.* ii.2) Creation, sustenance and destruction of the Universe, obscuration (Tirodhāna), and liberation (of the individual soul), (these five) actions,[17] with their agency and fruit are to be known as His. The creator of the world must be self-existent, otherwise there would be a *regressus ad infinitum* and there will be no final cause of Mokṣa. The essence of consciousness is the act of seeing (caitanyam dṛkkriyārūpam) and it exists in the ātmā at all times and on all sides, for we hear that in the liberated, it is perfect. Though it exists, it does not manifest itself as such (in the unliberated;, hence it is inferred that it is obscured; and it is subject to one whose powers are not obscured (Pati, the Lord), till it reaches liberation. The web of bonds (pāśajālam) is on the whole of four kinds, the enveloping, the will of the Lord, Karma, and the work of Māyā. (Their) names indicate their nature "*(Mṛg. āg.* ii. 3-7).

The Āgama discusses in chap iii. Patilakṣaṇam, the characteristics of the Lord. "As the body and other things are proved to possess the characteristics of products, we must infer that there exists their Maker, different from them. He is everlasting because He is not limited by Time; He is not confined to one locality, because He is all-pervading. He is possessed of powers of creating gradually and simultaneously, because creation is both gradual and simultaneous. He possesses an instrument (Karaṇa), because no action is seen (accomplished) without instruments. This (instrument) must not be taken to be adventitious, because the work has been without a beginning. This instrument is no other than Śakti. Śakti is not unconcious but a concious Being. As objects are infinite, she, (though) one, appears likewise (infinite) both in cognition and in activity. Action (creation etc. does not result from) the seed of preservation, creation etc. (Karma), or from Prakṛti or from the individual soul (aṇu); there only remains the theory that it is the work of the Great Lord, the Free. He is Siva." *(Ib.* iii. 1-5) "Action always proceeds from an embodied actor; in the world we see actions only of persons with bodies. Hence He, too, is like us. (But) the Lord's body is, unlike ours, one of Śakti; Mala etc. cannot attach themselves to it; that body is composed of the five Mantras and subserve His five actions[18] (*Ib.* iii. 8.)." "He is omnicient, because he is the Maker of all: for it is well-proved that one does a thing only when one knows the means, the consituent elements and the results. His knowledge is not veiled in anything, hence does not require any aid to manifest itself, It is without doubts and never at fault." *(Ib.* v. 12,13).

"Śaṅkra's knowledge is not based perception, inference or authority. It shines pure, always, in all things," *(Ib.* v. 15).

The second ultimate is the Paśu , lit. cattle, hence what is owned by, subject to, the Pati, the Lord. "The earth and the rest are effects; the Lord is the cause. They are no use to their Maker; nor to themselves because they are unconscious; nor are they purposeless, for that would be derogatory to their Maker. There only remains the theory that they are for the use of a third, *different* from both, the Kṣetrajña. The Paśu, for whose sake the earth and other things exist, is not the body, for the body is unconscious and hence it follows that itself must be for the use of another. (The body) cannot be a conscious being for it is an object of cognition (bhogya) and liable to changes of state. Such things as cloth etc, which are objects of cognition and liable to changes of state are insentient. If it is said that the body is conscious, because while in the body, there is consciousness of existence (Sadbhāva), (we reply that) as there is no consciousness in a corpse, the body is unconscious. If it is said that consciousness is one of a series of transformations (that the body is subject to) (we reply) that (if so), memory cannot be continuous. But (continuous) memory is well-known. Hence the one that remembers is other than the body. He is not confined (to space), not momentary, not one, not unconscious, no non-actor, possessor of differentiated consciousness, for it is said that, after the destruction of Pāśa, he becomes Śiva "(*Mrg. Āg*.. vi. 1-7) The Paśu , is, in his own nature, "the abode of eternal and omnipresent Cit-Śakti" *(Ib.* vii. 5).

The third ultimate is Pāśa, fetter, bond. It is threefold, (1) Avidyā, ignorance (2) Karma (3) Māyā. Avidyā is otherwise known as Āṇavamala, the defect due to the ātmā thinking that it is but Aṇu (atom), the taint of finiteness. The ātmā who is pure consciousness and Independence imagines himself to be finite, bcunded by his body, of circumscribed knowledge and power. As Kṣemarāja explains, in his commentary on Śiva Sūtras i. 2, "Being infinite consciousness, he thinks, 'I am finite'; being independence, he thinks 'I am the body (Anātmā)". Thus the Āṇava mala is of two kinds, (a) Ignorance of the fact that the Ātmā is consciousness (b) mistaking the body for the Atmā, called respectively Akhyāti and Anayathākhyāti, non-cognition and wrong cognition. This Pāśa is described as a veil over the soul known by a variety of names, Paśutva , bondage, Pāśunihāra, mist round the Paśu, Mṛtyu, death, Mūrcchā, swoon, Mala, defect, Añjana , pigment, Āvṛti, envelope, Ruj , malady, Glāni, depression, Pāpa, evil, Mūla, root, Kṣaya, decay, etc. It is one in all beings, beginningless, dense, great, possessed of numerous powers (Śaktis) residing in every soul and perishing when their time is over. *(Mṛg. Āg.* vii. *6-8)*. The benign Māheśvarī-Śakti, benign, blessing all, is included in the Pāśas, for they act in conformity with them". (*Ib.* 11), The five powers of the Lord are exercised only with reference to Paśus and are hence transformations (pariṇāma) of Avidyā.

For the purpose of bringing about the liberation of the individual soul, the Lord sets the malas evolving; so start the powers of creation sustenance, destruction and obscuration of knowledge (tirodhāna or rodhāśakti); then the Śakti evolves into Anugraha, the power of benediction, in that individual from whom the powers of mala have departed and he becomes liberated. The Lord supports the malas during the whole course of their transmutations for the ultimate good of the Paśus dependent on His Grace. *(Ib.* vii. 11-22). The Second Pāśa or mala, Karma, is described in chapter viii. It is the cause of the conjunction of the conscious soul with the unconscious body. It is local (*i.e.,* not omnipresent), manifold, temporary, associated with individuals, and continuous throughout the births. It is an auxiliary of the first mala, Avidyā. It is called karma, because it is produced by the activities of beings and adṛṣṭa (unseen), because it is subtle (between the ending of the action and the beginning of the phala, the reaction). It is the producer and sustainer of the body, the object of enjoyment. It is threefold (produced by the body, the speech and the mind).

It is good and bad, dharma and adharma, according as it is based on truth or falsehood. It ripens during (cosmic) slumber, prevails during a Kalpa and merges in māyā during pralaya, but is never destroyed without being experienced (viii 1-5).

The third among the malas is Māyā, also called Bheda, difference. This is the Yoni *(Śiva Sūt.* i. 3), the womb of the world, the granthi-pāśa *(Mṛg Āg. ix.* 1), the knot that imprisons the Ātmā in ignorance. "It is single, the cause of misery, the seed of the universe, possessed of many powers and obstructs the individual till the power of its auxiliary (karma) should cease; it is omnipresent and imperishable. For the same reason a creator is inferred from the nature of the universe, it must follow that it has a material cause; for there is no cloth without thread. It is unconscious for its products are known to be so." *(Ib.* ix, 2-4).

The *Pauṣkara Āgama*[19] describes the categories (padārtha) of the Śaiva School as follows:—"Pati, Kuṇḍalinī, Māyā, Paśu, Pāsa, and the causes (kāraka), these are briefly the six categories, in the Śaiva tantras. That category is called Pati whose triple function is destruction, enjoyment and authority, which is unchanging in its nature, and possessed of powers (Śaktis). Kuṇḍalinī (otherwise called, Śuddha Māyā, Pure Māyā) is that whence Pati gets destruction and other functions, by which the Pure Path (Śuddhādhvā) is produced, and she is the form where Śambhu (Śiva) is ever established. Māyā (Aśuddha, impure) is that which produces bodies and organs for making possible, experience and objects; it is associated with men's karma. Paśu is characterized by cognition-action (dṛkkriyā) obstructed by limitation and is threefold, Sakala, Pralayakala, and Vijñānakala.[20] The fifth category, Pāsa, is said to be the totality of principles (tattvas) from kalā to the Earth (kṣiti). Excellent Ṛṣ is,the sixth category is, in the tantras, the supreme action called Initiation (Dīkṣā) whose fruit is experience, liberation and manifestation (of each individual as Śiva)." *(Ib.* i. 2-15).

Śuddha māyā, otherwise, bindu (dot), Kuṇḍalinī (the coiled), Śivaśakti, the Tower of Śiva, is a category intermediate between Śiva that is Pure consciousness and Matter that is unconcious. She is "the Upādhi, the cause of the differentiation of Śiva's function into destruction etc., described above *(Ib.* ii.1.) She is the cause of the bondage of all beings (aṇu) from Ananta (a person next to Śiva) downwards, and also of their release. But she is not the material cause of the world because she is caitanya, conscious being, like Śiva and without transmutation like matter. (*Ib.* ii.2-4). She is the eternal sound,[21] the subtle connecting link between words and concepts (*Ib.* ii. 17). This eternal sound is divided into four kinds, called Vaikharī, Madhyamā, Paśyantī, and Sūkṣmā. Vaikharī is what becomes in the throat the sound that is heard by the ear and takes the shapes of letters. Madhyamā is the form of objects mentally apprehended before they are associated with sounds. Paśyantī is undifferentiated like the yolk within the *egg*. Sūkṣmā[22] is the pure Jñāna Śakti. (*Ib.* ii 19-24). These are called four forms of Vāk (lit. Voice, sound), one objective, the others subjective, and all produce states of consciousness of the Paśu. (*Ib.* ii. 25-26) The individual souls identify themselves with these forms of Vāk and thus result the three Malas (defects) which obscure cognition and action. (*Ib.* ii. 28-29). Kṣemarāja defines the three bonds to be the three cognitions, like 'I am finite', 'I am thin or fat', 'I am the sacrificer etc', respectively illustrative of Āṇava, Māyā and Karma Malas.[23] These fundamental cognitions of limitation, of identity with the body, and of actorship exist in the mind either in the form of words (Vaikharī), or of images (Madhyamā), or of vague states of consciousness not yet differentiated into clear-cut images (Paśyantī) or, again, the mere possibility of such limited consciousness (Sūkuṣmā). Vāk, Sound in its four forms thus marks all the stages of limitation of the individual soul. The names of the Śaktis (goddesses, energies of Śīva) that preside over these and the mantras indicating them are also combinations of Vāk. Hence Śuddhamāyā, the mother of the universe is supreme Vāk, the eternal sound; this is the doctrine of Nāda, 'voice of the silence', which is the basis of the Śaiva and Śākta disciplines.

Paśus (Individual souls) are "of three classes, (i) Sakala (2) Pralayākala (3) Vijñānakala. Listen to their characteristics in order. Sakala is one whose powers of cognition and action are obstructed by (Aṇava) mala, are associated (by Māyāmala) with Kala and other Tattvas[24] for the evolution (of limited, human powers) and bound up with Karma (mala) for experiencing (pleasure and pain). Pralayākala is one who, like the preceding, has cognitive and active energies obstructed, but is released from contact with Kalā etc. as his Karma has been experienced (and done with), though it is possible for him to be again brought under its influence" *(Ib.* iv. 2-5). The Pralayakala is one who is devoid of Karmamala and dissociated from Kalā etc. during Pralaya. "He is called Vijñanakevala in the Tantra, whose cognition and action, being obstructed by (āṇava) mala are almost non-existent." (*Ib.* iv. 5-6). Thus these three classes are respectively under the sway of one, two and three Malas. Their paths are called Śuddhādhva, (pure path), Miśrādhva (mixed path) and Aśuddhādhva (impure path) "The Sūkṣmā Vāk pertains to the śuddhādhva, the grosser (Paśyantī and Madhyamā) to the Miśrādhva, and the grossest, (Vaikharī) to the Aśuddhādhva." (*Ib.* ii. 30.) The doctrine of Vāk more properly belongs to the Śākta school, but the Śaiva and Śākta schools coalesce with each other in most points and, at times, it is almost impossible to differentiate one from another.

A later development of the Śaiva cult is that of the Liṅgāyatas or Jaṅgamas, founded by Basava, about the middle of the XII century in the reign of the Kalacūrya king, Bijjala. Its chief characteristic is a great revolt against the Brāhman supremacy and the abolition of caste. Curious enough Basava, himself, was a Brāhman. His successor, Chennabasava, was his nephew, son of his virgin sister, Nāgalāmbikā. Like all reformers from Buddha onwards, Basava preached in the vernacular. Śrīkara made the movement orthodox by writing a Bhāṣya[25] of the Vedānta Sūtras in Sanskrit in the lines of this Liṅgāyata or Vīraśaiva sect. His fundamental position is indicated in the following extract. "Brahma is never nirviśeṣa (devoid of attributes). He is always bodied (mūrta) as well as unbodied......He is said to be one (only) before creation. The old teachers of the Vedas, Reṇuka, Dāruka, Śaṅkha-karṇa, Gokarṇa, Revanāsiddha, Marulusiddha, etc. have taught that the advaita texts of Brahmā (*i.e.* of the Vedas) refer to the stage before creation, as, then, the world manifested or unmanifested does not exist...The declaration that all knowledge (flows) from the knowledge of one, as in the illustration of earth *(Chh. Up.* vi. 1-4) is due to the identity of cause and effect. If Prakṛti, the substratum of the world exist before creation, how then could there be oneness ? To this, we reply, Prakṛti, being but the Śakti of Īśvara, is not different from him, like the attractive power of magnet, or the burning of fire. Hence those that desire mokṣa do not accept the theory of the falsity of the world."[26] A detailed account of the opinions of this sect is scarcely necessary, as it was but a social reform movement with a veneer of philosophy put on later to gain an orthodox standing.

The Brāhmans have as usual sapped the vitality of this movement by reintroducing caste into the sect. Thus, though the Liṅgāyata reformation started like the Buddhist with a vigorous protest against the caste system, there are now Liṅgāyata Brāhmans, Liṅgāyata Śūdras, etc. The modern Liṅgāyata is marked by his fierce hatred of Viṣṇu and his constantly wearing a liṅga encased in a silver box.[27]

The history of the fortunes of Śiva is more obscure than that of Viṣṇu. The Ṛg-Veda does not even mention him; but speaks of Rudra, sometimes as one God, at other times, as many, and of the Maruts as Rudra's sons. In the other Vedas Rudra gradually rose to first rank and in the age of the composition of the *Rāmāyaṇa* and the *Mahābhārata,* he became identified with Śiva or Mahādeva and later on, became the last person of the Trimūrti. The phallic character of Śiva and his unlovely surroundings indicate the fact that he must have been the God of the aborigines amidst whom the invading Āryan settled and whose gods he had to adopt into his pantheon. The only possible reference to phallic worship in the Vedas is the scornful phrase Śiśna-devas,[28] applied to the enemies of the Āryans, either demons or dasyus. But these aboriginal races have had an ample revenge. Mahāśepha, (a huge membrum virile) is the God of a large majority of modern Indians. It is worshipped in temples[29], in wayside shrines and worn round the necks of the devotees of the 'Great God,' not merely for luck as in modern Italy !

(3) THE PRATYABHIJÑĀ SCHOOL

The Pratyabhijñā School was founded in Kashmir in the eighth century A. D. by Vasugupta, who "discovered" the *"Śiva Sūtras"* and taught them to Kallaṭa. Besides the *Śiva Sūtras,* the chief works of this School are the *Spanda Kārika* composed by Vasugupta or Kallaṭa, *Śivadṛṣṭi* by Somānandanātha (900 A. D.), *Pratyabhijñā Sūtra* by Utpala, son of Udayākara, (930 A. D.), commentaries (Vimarśiṇī) on the previous by Abhinava Gupta (993-1015 A. D.), and commentaries on the first work by Kṣemarāja[30] (1030 A. D.). Būhler, who has fixed the dates[31] of these works in his *"Tour in search of Sanskṛt Mss."* wrongly divides the Kashmir Śaiva philosophical works into two schools, (1) *Spanda-Śāstra* of Vasugupta (2) *Pratyabhijñā-Śāstra* of Somānandanātha and Utpala, because the word spanda occurs frequently in the names of the earlier works and pratyabhijñā in those of the later. But there is not enough difference between the teachings of these two sets of works to justify their being regarded as belonging to two different schools. Spanda is the ultimate principle of the universe—that of the spontaneous *vibration* accompanied by consciousness which underlies all cosmic processes and pratyabhijñā is the discipline prescribed by this school, which consists in the unbroken *recognition* of man's essential identity with Śiva and the falsity of every thing else. The earlier writers naturally treated the discipline as esoteric and the later ones, seeing that the tradition was getting lost, emphasized the pratyabhijñā discipline and did not treat much of Spanda which the earlier ones had amply discussed.

This Kāshmīr school regards all the Śaiva āgamas and the numerous books based thereon as authoritative and similarly, the writers of the Śaiva Siddhānta school quote all the Kāshmīr writers as authoritative; in fact, the analysis of the universe into the categories and tattvas of the previous section is accepted, *in toto,* by the Pratyabhijñādarśana. The chief difference between the two so far as metaphysics is concerned, is (1) the greater insistence on the spanda (active aspect of the ātmā (2) the unreality of a substratum of the universe *apart from* Śiva.

Śiva, spanda, caitanya, the one basis of the universe, is characterized by infinite consciousness which knows no limitations of Time and Space and by unrestricted independence (svacchanda). "Complete independence in connection with conciousness is caitanya. It exists only in the Lord Parma Śiva" (Kṣemarāja's) *Śivasūtravimarśiṇī,* i. 1.) "Though He possesses endless characteristics (Dharma), like Nityatva (eternality), Omnipresence, Formlessness, etc., yet nityatva etc., belong (also) to other beings (than He); hence Independence, which is not found in others, has to be described prominently (as His characteristic)" (*Ib.*) "From whence this objective universe and this group of organs (body), and manas, the internal organ, unconcious, yet simulating concious being, attain the functions of creation, maintenance and destruction, that tattva must be diligently examined, whose Independence is always unobstructed" *(Spanda Kārikā,* 6-7). "As the Jīva (the experiencer, the individual) is the self of all, the source of all (his) experiences, the object, attains identity with him by being experienced by him. Hence nothing other than Śiva exists, in the enquiry regarding word and object. The experiencer always and everywhere is seated as the experienced" *(Ib.* 28-29).

Cognition is a unique act, a fusion of subject and object. Of these two factors, the reality of the subject does not require proof; for in the words of Kṣemarāja, "all proofs depend for their validity on self-luminous consciousness". The other factor—the object—attains the appearance of real existence only when cognized by the subject. "So long as these (Jīvas) do not cognize, how can there be the known, O dear one ? The knower and the known are one Tattva." (*Śuṣmabhairava,* quoted by Kṣemarāja). Hence the only reality of the Universe is Śiva. "As the consciousness on which all this effected world is established, whence it issues, is free in its nature, it cannot be restricted anywhere. As it moves in the differentiated states of Jāgrata etc., (waking, dreaming and sleeping), identifying itself with them, it never falls from its true nature of the Knower. The thoughts, 'I am glad,' 'I am sorry,' 'I am desirous,' manifest themsevles in a place different (from Spanda), wherein the states of pleasure etc., are strong. Where there is no pleasure, no pain, no known or knower, nor again unconsciousness, that alone really exsists "(*Sp. Kār* 2-5)."

From this point of view it follows that a second Reality, independent of Śiva, as the basis of the universe is unnecessary for explaining the cosmos. The cosmos is the projection outside of the experience of the inner organ, Antaḥkaraṇa.

"The illumination of objects as being present, really exists inside but is made to appear outside" *Īśvarapratyabhijñā Sūtras,* V. i). "The Lord, of the form of Cit, (individual), being under the influence of desire, causes the totality of objects to shine as if existing outside, (though) without a substratum, like a Yogī" *(Ib.* V. 6). The (part of the) cognition (Adhyavasā), 'this is a pot,' that transcends name and form, the Śakti of Pareśa, is like the Ātmā and does not shine by objectivity (Idaṁtā),"[32] *(Ib.* V. 17). The theory of perception that underlies this the metaphysical position will be discussed in the Chapter on Psychology.

The active śakti of the other schools is a relatively unimportant person in this school. "She is Mātrika, the basis of knowledge" *(Śiva Sūt.* 1.4). Mātṛka is the alphabet, treated as the mother of the universe, who associates human experiences with the words that describe them and whose body is formed by the mantras which are themselves made up of letters. She is thus but the power behind mantras. Of the three śaktis, jñāna, kriyā, and icchā, the first two are attached in this school direct to the ātmā, so that the mother of the universe loses her predominance. *Śiva Sūtras,* i. 13. says "Icchā śakti is Umā, the girl." As Kṣemarāja explains, in the case of the Yogī who has attained the highest state, his desire is invincible and the power of his desire is the virgin Umā.

Thus, from more than one side, the metaphysical position of the Pratyabhijñā school approximates to that of Śaṅkara. As the Pratyabhijñā is professedly based on the Śākta and Śaiva Āgamas, it raises a presumption that Śaṅkara and his Prācārya, Gauḍapāda[33] must have derived their philosophy from the Āgama schools. According to tradition both were Śāktas. Śakti worship is the chief one followed in the Advaita Mutts which are presided over by those who claim today to be the pontifical successors of Śaṅkara.[34] Gauḍapāda is believed to have been author of *Subhagodaya* and Śaṅkara of *Saundaryalaharī,* both poems in praise of Śakti. They practised the Śrīvidyā—the famous śākta discipline. So it may well be that the source of the advaita, like the source of all other modern Hindu sects, has to be sought for in the Śākta Āgamas. Till the Āgama literature is edited, published and translated, the history of the development of the Hindu religion during the last 2,000 years cannot be written. Būhler records a Kashmiri tradition that Śaṅkara was vanquished in argument by Abhinavagupta who lived three centuries later. No conclusion can be based on vague legends carried down the stream of uncritical tradition.

(iii) The Vaiṣṇava Āgama

The Vaiṣṇava Āgamas are said to be in number, very few of which have been printed. They seem to be developments of the Bhāgavata, the Pāñcarātra and the Sāttvata schools which are mentioned in the *Mahābhārata.* The differentiation into schools seems to have originally depended on the specific mantra, which was the shibboleth of each school. Thus it appears that the Bhāgavatas adopted the 12- lettered Mantra, the Pāñcarātras, the eight-lettered one (Om namo nārāyaṇāya). The Bhāgavatas are, at present, an insignificant community scattered in the Telugu[35] and Maharatta country and have, so far as could be ascertained, forgotten the fact of the importance of their cult in the history of religion in India, their fundamental ideas and practices having been adopted by the Rāmānujīyas and Mādhvas and the later schools of Bhakti. Rāmānuja treats Bhāgavata, Pāñcarātra, and Sattvata practically as synonymous terms in his *Bhāṣya* on *Vedānta Sūtras,* II. ii. 40-43, perhaps because their doctrines were similar, while their mantras differed. The 108 Āgamas already referred to are all called Pañcarātra Āgamas.

The *Pādma Saṁhitā* gives their names; but judging from the contents, some of them e. g. *Bhāradvāja,* are quite modern and hence very much later than the *Pādma Saṁhitā* itself. This raises the presumption that some of these were lost and new ones written up to take the place of the lost ones. Indeed Vedānta Deśika, writing in the XIV century says that in his time many of them could not be found. Moreover as they were kept secret there was plenty of room for forgery. But the *Pādma Saṁhitā* and *Lakṣmī tantra* are decidedly very old. Their tenets are much nearer the Śākta and Śaiva teachings than the post-Rāmānujīya Vaiṣṇava doctrines discussed later on in this section.

The word Pāñcarātra is explained in *Pādma Saṁhitā* (I. i. 73) to be that which turns the other five śāstras into night (rātri) these other Śāstras being the Śaiva, Yoga, Śāṅkhyayoga, Bauddha and Ārhata promulgated respectively by Śiva, Brahmā, Kapila, Buddha and Arhata. This derivation is, on the face of it, fanciful. The *Pādma Saṁhitā* also speaks of four schools of Pāñca-rātra (1) Mantra Siddhānta, accepting one Form (of God), (Ekamūrti) (2) Āgama Siddhānta, accepting four Forms, (3) Tantra Siddhānta, accepting nine Forms, and (4) Tantrāntara Siddhānta, accepting four-headed or three-headed Form. *(Ib.* I. i. 80-83). Of these four schools, the *Pādma Saṁhitā* claims to belong to the Tantra Siddhānta. The fundamental doctrines of the earlier schools of the Vaiṣṇava Āgamas are explained in the following quotations.

"Brahmā is characterized by bliss (ānanda); (he is) the beginning, changeless, always undifferentiated, self-knowing, faultless, superlatively subtle, self-determined, the ruler, self-luminous, spotless, infinite, indestructible, tranquil, invisible, capable of evolving (the world), unchangeable, one full of conciousness of bliss (Cidānanda), the essence of consciousness (cidrūpa), omnipresent, supreme, devoid of past and future, the Lord called Vāsudeva, the source of all beings, Īśvara, the Supreme Puruṣa, of a stainless nature, eternal, without waves, without disturbance, boundless, beyond the guṇas, with guṇas,[36] the giver of all desires (I. v. 29-34).[37]

"His form has been described to be threefold, gross, subtle, and supreme. The gross is called Sakala (divided); the subtle, Sakala-niṣkala; the supreme (form) of Him is Niṣkala (undivided), O, lotus-born. The thousand-headed[38] and other forms are the sakala form of the Paramātmā; the form which has feet etc. and is made of light is sakala-niṣkala; the first form of Śaccidānanda[39] is called Niṣkala." *(Ib.* I. vi. 30-40). The Paramātmā has two natures, Prakṛti and Vikṛti. Prakṛti is the synthesis of Sattva and other guṇas; Vikṛti is Puruṣa, called Paramātmā. She (Prakṛti), the woman who has the three guṇas as her essence, in whom the individual beings (chetana) are established creates the whole world. By His command she sustains it all" *(Ib.* I. vi. 41-43).

In the *Lakṣmītantra* Lakṣmī describes her Lord and herself in clear terms. "Paramātmā is characterized by absence of pain (nirdukha) and enjoyment of boundless bliss . . . They call Him the Path, the end of the Path, Paramātmā . That which is understood by the word ego is called the Ātmā. The ego whose nature is unlimited is called Paramātmā. That is called ego, Paramātmā, the eternal, by whom all this, moving and motionless, is embraced. He is Vāsudeva, the Blessed, considered the supreme Kṣetrajña. He is called Viṣṇu, Nārāyaṇa,

Viśva (The All), Viśvarūpa, (having the Universe as His form). All this world is enveloped by His Ahantā (egoity). Truly that is not, which is not enveloped by Ahantā. He is everywhere tranquil (śānta), changeless (nirvikāra), eternal, Infinite, devoid of limitations of space, time, etc. He is called Mahāvibhūti (Infinite Glory), because he extends infinitely. He is Brahma, the Supreme abode, the Light without a substratum; of six qualities[40] similar to the ocean of immortality (amṛta), waveless, shining. He is one, undifferentiated conciousness (cidghana), tranquil, free from rising or setting. He is called Brahmā, the secondless, being possessed of śakti, which is not different from Him" (*Lakṣmītantra,* II. 1-10).

"The Blessed one, Vāsudeva, of the nature of consciousness, not limited by space, time, etc, is Param Brahma, devoid of (the three) guṇas, spotless, blissful, always the same, with the six guṇas, without old age or death. I am His supreme Śakti, Ahantā, eternal, unchanging. My activity is of the nature of desire to create. I create of my own independent power, by means of a myriad myriadth part of a myriad myriadth part (of myself). I become two kinds of beings—the knower and the known, (cetyam, and cetanī), citśakti being the enlightener of both. Saṁvit, that is my nature, attains the states of the knower and the known. My nature of Saṁvit is pure, independent, full. Like the juice of the sugarcane, it attains solidity by Yoga. Hence the said knower (cetya) attains cit-tva (the state of an individual jīva). As firewood, embraced by fire, becomes fiery (tanmaya), so cetya, embraced by saṁvit becomes cinmaya (filled with the light of consciousness). The nature of cit is undifferentiated as blue or yellow, pleasure or pain. It is differentiated by changes due to manifold upādhis. Of its own power, a huge form (the manifested world) is built out of (a) small (one). The cidrūpa that is differentiated into subject and object is spotless, supreme, neither objective nor subjective." (*Ib.* xiv. 1-10).

In another passage, Lakṣmī clearly describes the relations of the three categories, Paramātmā, Śakti, and Jīva. "He is the

Ātmā of all beings, their ego, called Hari; I am the Ahantā (egoity) of all beings, the eternal. By whatever bhava (form) Vāsudeva, the eternal, is imagined (bhavataḥ), that bhāva I am called. Thence, Brahma the eternal goal, is of the nature of Bhavatbhāva. Bhavat is the God Nārāyaṇa; I, the supreme Lakṣmī, am Bhāva. Hence Brahma, the eternal, is called Lakṣmī-nārāyaṇa[41] Only when enveloped by Ahantā is it possible to cognize 'ego'; what is cognized as 'I' is Ahantā. Know that the connection, the identity of nature (tādātmya) between me and my Lord is due to Avinā-bhāva (unbroken association) and Samanvaya (immediate connection). Without Ahantā 'Ego' becomes indescribable and uncognizable. Ahantā without the cognition of 'Ego' is baseless (nirādhāra), and uncognizable. The Bhavatbhāva perceptible as Samastha (synthesis) and Vyastha (analysis) is conceived in the world as parokṣa and aparokṣa, that which can be (objectively) realized or not. When Brahma is not awake, she, Ahantā, Parameśvarī is not awake, and remains with all the world taken into her lap: What is called his waking (unmeśa), like moonrise on the ocean, that is I, Nārāyaṇī Śakti, of the nature of desire to create (Sisṛkṣā), What is called the winking (nimeṣa)of the Paramātmā, during annihilation, that am I, Narāyaṇī śakti known as suṣuptā, desirous of sleeping. Aiśvarya, indestructible, unlimited, develops in me, the Sisṛkṣā, who rise from God, the Lord of Lakṣmī. That Supreme Brahma is consciousness (Jñāna), all-seer, faultless. Ahantā is, of the nature of consciousness (jñānātmikā), all knower, all-seer. The supreme form of both of us, Brahma and me, is of the nature of consciousness. The rest, Aiśvarya, Vīrya, etc., are eternal qualities (dharma) of Jñāna. The inner form, Ego, is called Jñānarūpa, the form of light like crystal...The indestructible supreme Aiśvarya of mine when I rise (out of Nārāyaṇa) is called Icchā (desire), in the various tattvaṭāstras by the learned. Being the Prakṛti (essence) of the world, (I am) called Śakti. My effortlessness when I create is regarded as Bala; (also) my filling all the created world is called Bala; though I am always Prakṛti, my being devoid of change is Vīrya. Milk gives up its nature (of milk) when curd is formed out of it; such change is never (produced) in me when I become the (manifested) universe. Hence knowers of tattva (reality,) regard Vīrya as absence of change. Vīrya, (also) called Vikrama is (by some) regarded as a part of Aiśvarya. My independence of assistance in doing all works is called Tejas, the sixth Guṇa, by the knowers of tattvas. Tejas is defined by some as the power of defeating others. Some tattva-knowers regard this as (part of) Aiśvarya, These five Guṇas are regarded as flowing from (the first guṇa) Jñāna. The six guṇas, Jñāna and the rest, are my body. *(Ib.* II. 12-35). "Nārāyaṇa, the God, is the eternal Paramātmā, always the ocean of jñāna, bala, Āiśvarya, vīrya, Śakti and ojas. He is beginning-less, not limited by space, time and form. I am his supreme Goddess, shining supreme with the six guṇas, the Śakti (goddess, power) that causes all effects, eternal, called Ahantā. My nature (svarūpa) is saṁvit (conciousness), Pure, Free, Full. All jīvas are established in me; all of them are in me. I make manifest all the world, of my own free will (svechchhayā), on Ātmā as the substratum; in me the world is reflected as birds in water. Of my own free will, independent (of extraneous help) I start manifestation, I, the author of the Five Actions.[42] The author of manifestation am I, called citśakti. My contracted form, (*i. e.* the jīvātmā), he is Pure, Free, undifferentiated conciousness (cidghana). In me does the world shine as the mountain in a mirror. Like a diamond-stone, he (the jīva) shines everywhere pure. His characteristic (dharma) is caitānya, like the stainless radiance of the Sun. By it does shine the jīva, with (the light) suitable (to him) of his own accord. The jīva, too, always does the Five Actions. His activity as in blue, yellow, etc., (differentiated objects) is called creation by the wise. (His) attachment to objects is called sustenance (sthiti). His giving up an object grasped on account of the desire to grasp a new one, is called destruction (samhṛti) by those that know the tattvaśāstras. Its vāsanā (deposits in the mind) is tirobhāva, its dissolution, anugraha. His characteristic is grasping and enjoyment always destroying (what he enjoys) like fire. The Jīva always feeds little by little my brightness" [43] *(Ib.* xiii. 18-29).

In the later Vaiṣṇava schools, namely the Viśiṣṭādvaita and the DvaitaVedānta, though to a large extent based on the Pañcarātra Āgamas, Lakṣmī, the really active factor of the cosmos is degraded to an obscure position. One subsect regards Lakṣmī as a sort of intermediary in the matter of the grace that leads to Mokṣa; in another, she is inferior even to the Ācarya. The earlier Pāñcarātra Āgamas are utilized much more by the rival Śaiva school than by the modern Vaiṣṇavas.[44] In another point have the modern Vaiṣṇava schools gone away from the position of the Āgamas. The relation between the individual soul, called Kṣetrajña (as in the *Bhagavad Gītā),* and the Paramātmā, is much nearer the Advaita position than would be palatable to the modern Viśiṣṭādvaitīs and Dvaitīs who regard this work as authoritative. "It is taught in the śruti that the Ātmā of the Para and the Kṣetrajña is one. The limitation of the Kṣetrajña is known to be due to the difference of bodies, as one image is differentiated into many in many mirrors. Kṣetra (the body) is made of the five,[45] (gross) elements (bhūta) etc.; the jīva is established in it; the wise sūris[46] (Gods) by their eyes of wisdom know him, the kṣetrajña, to be the supreme, which cannot be reached by Buddhi, untouched, transcending the manifested, beyond the supreme, Viṣṇu" *(Ib.* I. vi. 15-18). "As the Akāśa in a pot moves when the pot is moved, truly there is no difference between the Para and the Jīva" *(Ib.* I. vi.20).

The modern Viśiṣṭādvaita is a school of eclecticism, blending the Rāmānujīya Vedānta philosophy and Āgama cosmogony and practices. Rāmānuja, himself, though the Ācārya, *par excellence,* of this sect, and though he pleaded for the orthodoxy of the Pāñcarātra books, expounds only the Vedānta philosophy and discipline. But his followers have neglected Rāmānuja's philosophy and brought into greater prominence Āgama doctrines and practices. The modern Viśiṣṭādvaita is clearly expounded in Pillai Lokācārya's *Tattva-*

trayam, a Tamil work of the age of Sāyaṇa. This work is much read by the Srīvaiṣṇavas, who are a fairly widespread sect in Southern India. The *Tattvatrayam* is an exposition of the three ultimates—Īśvara, Cit and Acit. "Cit is Ātmā . The nature of Ātmā is (being) other than body, sense-organ, Manas, Prāṇa, Buddhi which are each superior to the one preceding it; (Ātmā is) not-unconscious, blissful, eternal, infinitely small, imperceptible, inconceivable, indivisible, immutable, the seat of knowledge; (He is) inspired, supported and disposable by Īśvara (*Tattvatrayam.* i. 3-4). "His size is but atomic (minute); his characteristic is the union of knowledge and bliss; of the dimensions of a trasareṇu (mote) and shining with millions of rays" (*Viṣvaksena Saṁhitā* quot. in Maṇavāla's comment, on *Ib. i* 14). Whereas cit is aṇu, Īśvara is Vibhu, infinite and this constitutes an eternal difference between the two. The individual Soul resides in the heart. "He is a knower and hence an agent and an enjoyer" (*Ib* i. 29) "Cit is the seat of knowledge. If he were knowledge merely, we should say 'I am knowledge' and not 'I know'." (*Ib.* i. 27, 28.) This relation between the Soul and consciousness as substratum and quality (dharmadharmibhāva) differentiates Vīśiṣṭādvaita from Sāṅkhya and Advaita and approximates it to Nyāya and Vaiśeṣika. This school like the last, also admits that the Ātmā is the actor and the enjoyer, unlike the Sāṅkhya and the Advaita which conceive of action and enjoyment as belonging to matter. The individual souls are of three classes, baddha, mukta, and nitya, those who are in bondage, those who are emancipated, and those who were never bound. *(Ib.* i. 42).

"Acit is the unconscious, and the seat of vikāra (phenomenality). It is of three kinds, śuddhasattva (pure sattva), miśrasattva (mixed sattva) and sattvaśūnya (devoid of sattva). Śuddhasattva is a rarefied state of matter, pure Sattva, without the admixture of Rajas and Tamas, eternal, productive of knowledge and bliss, capable of modification not by Karma but by divine will into chariots, towers, pavilions, palaces etc.

(in Vaikuṇṭha) of infinite brilliance, and difficult to be measured by the eternally emancipated and by Īśvara himself. This (state of matter) is regarded by some to be unconscious and by others conscious." *(Ibid.* ii. 1-6.) Though this superlatively refined state of matter is by some regarded as conscious it is different from the individual soul and from knowledge. "Miśrasattva is that species of Acit which is compounded of Sattva, Rajas and Tamas, causes the destruction of the knowledge and bliss of souls in bondage, produces false knowledge, is eternal, affords a field for Īśvara's sport (*i. e* creation etc.,) evolves into similar and dissimilar forms by differences of place and time and is called Prakṛti, Avidyā and Māy. It is called Prakṛti because it causes changes (vikāra); it is called Avidyā, because it destroys knowledge; it is called Māyā, because it has wonderful creative power" *(Ib.* ii. 9-10).

"Sattva Śūnya is Time. It is the cause of the evolution of Prakṛti and material objects; itself changes as Kalā, Kāṣṭā (small periods of time), is eternal, the field of Īśvara 's sport and His body. The other two classes of Acit are (I) fit to be experienced (Bhogya) by Īśvara and Ātmā, (2) means and fields of (their) enjoyment. '(Those) Fit to be experienced' (Bhogya) are objects; 'means of enjoyment' are organs like eyes etc, 'fields of enjoyment' are the four places and all bodies. Of these, the first Acit (superfine matter) is bounded below and unbounded around and above; the middle Acit (ordinary matter) is bounded above but unbounded below and around. Time (the last Acit) is the same everywhere. Time is Nitya (eternal) in Paramapada (the supreme abode of Īśvara), and here (in the manifested worlds*),* anitya (finite)." *(Ib. 43-48).* 'Eternal Time' is called Akhaṇḍa, unbroken into finite periods, infinite duration undifferentiated by the rate of flow of changing states of consciousness. Finite Time is Khaṇḍa, consisting of periods divided as seconds minutes etc. These two are called Time and No. Time in *Mait. Up. VI.*

Īśvara, the third tattva, "is opposed to all evil, infinite, self-illumined, blissful, shining with hosts of auspicious qualities like Jñāna, Śakti etc. the cause of the creation, maintenance and destruction of all universes, the Refuge of the four kinds of men, 'the afflicted, the enquiring, the solicitous and the sage' (*Bhagvad Gītā* vii. 16) the giver of the four kinds of fruits— virtue, objects love and release, of a splendid form, and the Lord of Lakṣmī, Nīlā and Bhūmī". (*Ib.* iii.1).

Lakṣmī and the other two are Goddesses manifesting the three Śaktis of knowledge, action, and inertia. The auspicious qnalities referred to are wisdom, power, forbearance, mercy, love, activity, righteousness, friendship, gentleness, and accessibility. (*Ib.* iii. 10)

"His 'splendid form" is infinitely superior to forms (like Ānandamaya) and qualities, worthy of Him alone, eternal, one, constituted of Śuddhasattva, not obstructive of wisdom like human bodies, illmunative of His Divine nature which therein is like the gold placed in a ruby cup, the treasury of His hosts of qualities like delicacy etc, of infinite brilliancy, fit to be meditated on by Yogīs, dazzling all beings, generative of all enjoyments and dispassion, always delightfully beheld by the eternally free beings, quenching the afflictions of all like a lotus tank, the root of all avatāras protecting all, the substratum of all, and ornamented by implements and ornaments." *(Ibid.* iii. 40.) The 'implements and ornaments' are various symbols of the divine attributes conceived as existing in physical shapes in his Divine Form.

The fortunes of Viṣṇu, among the gods of India, have been the most varied. In the earliest Vedic age, he was the highest,'[47] being placed in the sky and the 'last', [48] in the series of Gods to whom a portion of the sacrificial food was to be offered. He was the friend of Indra and the supporter of the world. In the age of the Brāhmaṇas, he became the 'sacrifice', the supreme Puruṣa, whom the Gods stretched on the sacrificial altar. The Nirukta tried to explain him away as the sun. In the early Āgamas, he became the Param Brahma and his cosmic duties were discharged by "his goddess", Lakṣmi. Finally in the Purāṇas and in the popular imagination of modern India, he is the second person of the Trinity, always sleeping stretched leisurely in his couch (of Ādiśeṣa the cosmic serpent) and comforted by three wives, Śrī, Bhū, and Nīlā, on the ocean of milk which extends through all space and interfering with the affairs of the world as an avatāra, only when his help is invoked by his colleague and son, Brahmā. The śālagrāma a fossil ammonite shell of Tertiary times is his favorite haunt and is treasured in the homes of his devotees and the modern Vaiṣṇava sips the water in which the fossil ammonite is washed to the chanting of the Puruṣa sūkta,[49] for disinfecting his inside of the bacillus of sin !

SECTION IV

The Vaiśeṣika and the Nyāya

These schools were based on the logical processes of Definition and Deduction. They were uncompromisingly anti-monistic in their aim. Even the Sāṅkhya, while admitting each Puruṣa to exist absolutely apart from other conscious beings, conceives all unconscious substances from Buddhi downwards to be successive transformations of one substratum—matter, but these schools do not attempt to derive one kind of substance from another. They divide objects into genera and species, define them by these marks, but refuse to be attracted by the eternal mocking mirage of monism that has produced so much bad metaphysics and worse science even in our days. The earliest Vaiśeṣika book we have is the Sūtras of Kaṇāda, and the earliest Nyāya book, the Sūtras of Gautama and these are not much later than the age of Buddha, while the Vaiśeṣika-Nyāya system, the ancient rival of the Sāṅkhya-Yoga system, and also of the Vedānta system, must be older. Praśastapāda, who lived not much later than the Ist century A. D. wrote a *Bhāṣya* on the Sūtras of Kaṇāda. This Bhāṣya is not a commentary but a systematic restatement and amplification of the Vaiśeṣika system, utilizing where possible the words of Kaṇāda. Vātsyāyana, was the first commentator on the *Nyāya Sūtras* and he lived sometime before the 6th cent. A. D. In later days the Vaiśeṣika and Nyāya schools got very much mixed up, so that in modern works on Tarka (Logic) so-called, the part contributed by the Vaiśeṣika school could scarcely be disentangled from that contributed by the Nyāya school. Similarly the Sāṅkhya and Yoga are one and the Vedānta and Āgama have in modern times become inextricably one, making it extremely difficult to discover the historical development of each philosophical idea.

(A) Vaiśeṣika

The Vaiśeṣika school analyses padārthas into six. Padārtha literally means the meaning of a word, the thing which corresponds to a word and is generally translated category. It is more properly, a fundamental general concept under which can be subsumed what are indicated by words. These are six according to the early Vaiśeṣika—substance (Dravya), quality (Guṇa), action (Karma), Sāmānya, (the relation of a thing to its genus), Viśeṣa (differentia) and Samavāya (coinherence). (*Vais. Sūt.* I. i. 4). Kaṇāda restricts the word Artha to the first three (*Vaiś. Sūt.* VIII. ii. 3) and Praśastapada extended it to the others also.[50] In later days a seventh category, Abhāva (non-existence), was added to the list and the total Padārthas acknowledged today are thus seven.

The characteristics of substance are that it serves as a substrate of qualities and actions and is a coinherent cause. (*Ib.* I. i. 15). Qualities like colour, and actions like expansion, cannot exist *in vacuo* but require substance as their Ādhāra (substrate). "A substance is not destroyed either by its effect or by its cause." (*Ib.* I. i. 12). Thus the threads are not destroyed when they become woven into cloth, but coinhere in the cloth: But "qualities (are destroyed) in both ways." *(Ib.* I. i. 12); when one taste is produced by a combination of a number of others, each of these latter loses its individuality. "An action is destroyed by its effect" (*Ib* I. i. 14); the tension of a bow is destroyed when disjunction of the arrow from the bow is produced. The characteristics of quality are that it inheres in a substance, it is without qualities, and is not a cause of (or) is concerned with conjunctions and disjunctions." *(Ib.* I. i. 16) "The characteristics of action are that it inheres in one substance, it is without qualities and is the sole cause of conjunctions and disjunctions" (*Ib.* I. i. 17,30). Kaṇāda also discusses sāmānya (nature of genus), viśeṣa (nature of species) and samavāya, (coinherence), though he does not include them in the categories, for they are not objects (artha) of perception. "Generality and speciality are buddhyapekṣam, conceptual. (*Ib.* I. ii. 3). The *Summum Genus,* "that which is a genus (without being a species) is B h ā v a (existence), for it is the most extensive concept." *(Ib.* I. ii. 4). "Substantiality (dravyatva), qualitativeness (guṇatva) and activity (karmatva) are both general and specific. (And so all others) except ultimate species, (the atoms etc.)" *(Ib.* I. ii. 5-6.) In the later Vaiśeṣika, the word viśeṣa (difference) has been restricted to what is called here, antyaviśeṣa, ultimate species, the detailed description of which gave the name Vaiśeṣika to this school.

The last padārtha, according to Praśastapāda is coinherence, Samavāya. Kaṇāda defines coinherence to be "that by which (we speak) of cause and effect, that the one is in the other" (*Ib.* VII. ii. 26). Praśastapāda discusses Samavāya fully. "The connection of what are inseparably connected and are in the relation of substrate and accessory which causes the cognition 'here' is Samavāya. From the cognitions, 'Here, in the threads(is) the cloth,' 'Here, in the grass (is) the mat (woven from the grass), 'Here, in Dravya (are) Dravya, Guṇa and Karma,' Here in Dravya, Guṇa and Karma (is) Sattā, 'Here, in Dravya (substance) is Dravya-tvam (substantiality),' 'Here in Guṇa (quality), is gunatvam (qualitativeness),' 'Here, karma (action) is Karmatvam (activity),' 'Here in eternal (atoms) are the ultimate species (antyavi-śeṣāh),' we can understand there is some connection between the members of these (pairs). This (connection) is not Saṁyoga (conjunction like that between a pot and the milk placed in it)" (*Vaiś. Dars.* Mumbai Ed. p.

66). Of these padārthas, the first three, Dravya, Guṇa and Karma possess Sattā. Sattā is defined thus:—"Whence we say of Dravya, Guṇa and Karma that they *are*—that is Sattā. Sattā is anartha (a thing) different from substance, quality and action. (*Ib.* I. ii. 7-8). "Existence is one, for 'to be' is no specific mark (of things) nor has it specific marks of its own." *(Ib.* I. ii. 17.) "Existence is uncaused and eternal" (*Ib.* IV. i. 1). Thus the Sattā of the Vaiśeṣikas is a general concept and other than Dravya, Guṇa and Karma, and hence is not a noumenon, a reality behind phenomena, like the Prakṛti of the Sāṅkhyas. Praśastapāda notes that the other three padārthas, Sāmānya, Viśeṣa and Samavāya are characterized by Svātmasatva, which Udayana explains as being devoid of Sattā (*Praśastapada bhāṣya* p. 30.)

The first of these padārthas has been described as substance. The ultimate substances are uncaused and eternal. They are of two classes, aṇu and vibhu, atomic and pervasive. The idea of an atom is derived from the consideration of the divisibility, or as it is called avayavovayavīprasaṅga, the relation of the constituent parts and the constituted whole. The divisibility of matter must end somewhere; if not, there would be no differencc of size between Mount Meru and a grain of mustard, for both would be made up of an infinity of parts. Matter of the size of a trasareṇu, a mote in the sunbeam, contains three dvayaṇukas, double atoms. Each dvayaṇuka is made up of two paramāṇus atoms. Five are atomic substances, earth, water, air, fire and manas. Four are pervasive substances, time, space, ākāśa and ātmā.

Of these nine eternal, ultimate substances the most important is Ātmā, by which all other substances are cognized.

"The objects of sense are universally known. The universal cognition of the objects of sense proves that there is a substance other than (those) objects of sense (which cognizes them). It is an invalid argument (which says that cognition is a quality of the body or the senses), because of the unconsciousness of the causes of the sensation and consciousness of the effects *i. e.* the cognition. " (*Ib.* III, i. 1-5). "The (cognition in the) term 'I' being characteristically different (from every other cognition) no scriptural testimony is required" to prove the existence of the soul (*Ib.* III. ii. 9). On the contrary, 'the cognition of the Ego is an immediate intuition of an entity other (than the body), because it applies to the soul that reflects on itself and nothing else" (*Ib.* III ii. 14).

This rejection of scriptural testimony for the existence of the ātmā is in direct contradiction to the Vedānta, which admits scripture *i.e.* testimony, of either supersensuous beings or teachers (gurus) who have gained an experience not attained by ordinary men as the only evidence of the existence of the ātmā, for Vedānta asserts the existence of a universal Ātmā, which is not given in ordinary human consciousness. That 'I am' every one will admit. That I am more than I am now' is the fundamental position of the Vedānta and this can but be a matter of faith till that greater I is actually experienced. The Sāṅkhya and the Vaiśeṣika which are essentially rationalistic cannot help being schools of individualism.

The soul is "manifold, because of the distinctness" of one man's experiences from every other (man's) *(Ib.* III. ii. 21). Moreover "the activity and inactivity observed in one's own soul are marks (to prove the existence of different souls) in others." (*Ib.* III. i 19). As Śaṅkara Miśra, a commentator on the Sūtras says, "Activity and inactivity produced by desire and aversion are (two) species of effort. From them are born bodily functions called muscular actions having for their object the attainment of pleasure and avoidance of pain. Hence, when we see muscular action in a body other (than our own), we infer (the existence of) another soul for this muscular action is born from effort, because it is a muscular action like our own muscular action and that effort is born from some soul or based on some soul because it is an effort like our own effort."

"The marks of the (presence of the) soul (in a body) are

the outgoing and in going breath, the opening and closing of the eyes, vitality (that builds up tissue), the motion of manas, affection of the other sense-organs, pleasure, pain, desire, aversion and volitional effort" (*Ib.* III. ii-4).

The play of breath in a body is the result of a constant effort of the soul to keep up the life of the body exerted as much during sleep as during waking moments. This is called 'the conation that is the basis of vitality (jīvanayoni prayatna); winking and the anabolic processes are also due to the same conation. The movements of manas in bringing the Ātmā and the organs of sense into conjunction to produce perception depend upon desire and effort both of which reside in the ātmā. Pleasure and pain reside in the Ātmā which is their substratum. Thus the Ātmā of the Vaiśeṣikas comes nearest to the Western conception of the soul. As in European philosophy, desires, conations and preceptions are conceived as qualities of the soul, and not as processes of subtle forms of matter, the object; but the Vaiśeṣika school clearly separates conciousness from these, which it does not regard as modifications of consciousness as is held in the West. Consciousness is separate from them and can and does exist apart from them.

Time is another ultimate substance. The marks of its existence are "the notions of later, simultaneous, slow and quick." *(Vaiś. Sūt.* II. ii. *6).* "It is called a cause as it does not exist in eternal things and exists in non-eternal things." *(Ib.* II. ii. 9). Dik, space is another substance whence (rises) the notion "this is (so far) from here." (*Ib.* II. ii. 10). Time and space are substances, because they do not inhere in any other substance and possess actions and qualities and are eternal. (*Ib.* II. ii 7.11 Time is one and so is Space though they appear manifold, on account of accidental qualities added to them. *(Ib* II, ii. 8, 12) The division of time into minutes, hours, etc. and into past, present and future and of space into East, West, etc, are not due to their inherent qualities but to the course or position of the Sun. The conception of time as past, present or future is due to the distinction of the states of objects into antecedent non-existence, present existence and subsequent non-existence. These distinctions being transferred to Time lead to its division into past, present and future, though it is really one. Like the soul, these two substances are vibhu, pervasive and infinite and not aṇu, atomic. It must be noted here that Space is called Dik, which literally means, direction. It is the distance between two objects measured along a straight line. Modern Hindūs use Akāśa for space, whereas Akāśa, being the substrate of sound is a definite substance with qualities attached thereto. The idea of infinite space does not seem to be discussed in Hindu books. The Upaniṣads speak of 'Ākāśam Brahma'; this can but be the manifestation of Brahma as 'subtle sound', not mere infinity of extension, devoid of any extended thing, which is the modern conception of infinite space.

Manas is another eternal substance. It is the organ that brings into contact the soul and the objects of sense through the sense-organs. "The proof (of the existence) of Manas are existence and non-existence of cognition on the proximity of the soul and sense-objects (according as Manas serves as their medium of contact or no). (*lb.* III. ii. 1). It is atomic (indivisible and invisible) because it can be in contact with only one sense-organ at a time whereas if it were all-pervading it could be in contact with all sense-organs and we could have a number of sensations at the same time. As we cannot imagine it to be constituted by constituted parts it follows that it is eternal. It is an ultimate substance because on it as substratum takes place the conjunction with sense-organs to produce cognitions.

In the substances are 'Earth ', 'Water', 'Fire', 'Air' and Ākāśa. Of these the first four are aṇu, atomic and the last is vibhu, pervasive. The sensation of sound is a quality which inheres in in Ākāśa. The sensation of touch inheres in the atoms of 'air.' 'Fire' has two qualities, colour and touch, 'Water' has three qualities, colour, taste and touch. 'Earth' has four colour, taste, smell and touch. Thus these four represent four hypothetical elementary substances, which combine and produce the perishable objects of the universe. The latter are kārya or effects which derive their qualities on account of the Samavāya or coinherence in them of their causes—the eternal substances. In the words of the Sūtras, "the nature of the effect (is derived) from the nature of the cause." *(Ib.* IV. i. 3.) These effected (objects) are also distinguished by being avayavī, complex, consisting of body, organ and object. (*Ib.* IV. ii.1).

Kaṇāda does not mention a God or Supreme Creator among his ultimate substances. When the Vaiśeṣika philosophy in much later days chiefly under the influence of the Śaiva cult developed the notion of a personal creator, the commentators attempted to derive the notion of a Supreme God from a misinterpretation of one sūtra. This sūtra (I. i. 3) runs thus:—'Tadvacanādāmnāyasya pramāṇyam'; it means 'The authority of the scriptures (is due) to (their) describing it. 'It' refers to Niḥśreyasa (highest good) in the previous sūtra, where Niḥśreyasa is said to be derived from Dharma and hence this sūtra points out that the Veda is authoritative because it points out the way to the highest good. The later commentators have tried to wrench this passage out of its context and understand by 'Tad' the absolute Brahma of the Vedānta. This sūtra recurs again as the last of the work (X. ii. 9), and there, again, the reference is not to Brahma but to the unseen effect of vedic ceremonial. Another sūtra is also wrongly explained to refer to God. It is II. i. 18. and runs, 'saṁjñākarmatvasmadviśiṣṭānām liṅgam'. This means 'The action of naming' (a substance) by Beings higher than ourselves, is the mark of (the existence of) that substance", because, as the next sūtra says, "they name substances on account of direct vision of them" (II. i. 19). Their vision being developed by Yoga, they see substances invisible to us, like air, or Ākāśa and then name them. Hence the fact of their naming a substance is a proof of its existence. This sūtra occurs amidst the proofs of invisible substances beginning with Vāyu and has absolutely no reference to God.

(B) Nyāya

The Nyāya and the Vaiśeṣika agree in fundamental points; the Vaiśeṣika being a school of Metaphysics tinged with Logic and the Nyāya, being a school of Logic tinged with Metaphysics. The Nyāya, therefore, does not analyse the universe into its constituent parts. It discusses Metaphysical questions only casually. It does not define Padārtha or Dravya, but Prameya, what is to be proved. The Prameyas are twelve, Ātmā, body, sense-organs, sense-objects, cognition, manas, activity, fault, transmigration, fruit, pain, and beatitude (*Ny. Sū t.* I. 9.) The five Elements, Time and Space are introduced incidentally.

The existence of the Ātmā is proved first by the consideration that a sense cannot be the soul, "because, through both sight and touch, we apprehend a single object" (*Ib.* III. i), which would be impossible unless something other than those sense-organs synthesised those sensations into an object. The body is not the soul, because "when the body is burnt up (after death) sin would become non-existent," for there would be none to suffer for the sin (*Ib.* III. 4.). It might be held (by some) that the mind is the soul, "because the argument that establishes (the existence of) the Ātmā apply (also) to the mind." (*Ib.* III. 16). Not so, "since there is a knower and an organ of knowledge" (*Ib.* III. 17.) This Ātmā is eternal "because to him that is born there occur joy, fear and grief by relation to his memory of previous experience" (*Ib.* III. 18.) "because of his desire for the (mother' s) breast from his habit of eating before death (*Ib.* III. 22) and because we do not see any birth devoid of desire" (*Ib.* III 25).

The five "elements are earth, water, fire, air, and Ākāśa." (*Ib.* 1. 13). "Of odour, taste, colour, touch and sound, those ending with Touch (are qualities) of Earth; rejecting each preceding one in succession they belong to water, fire and air; the last belongs to Ākaśa." (*Ib.* III. 61). The elements are found both in the objects of sense and in the sense-organs, "because only what have the qualities can be the organs (which can perceive them) (*Ib.* III. 6).

The Nyāya, like the Vaiśeṣika, believes in the eternal existence of atoms. "As the atoms have real existence, no pralaya (destroys them). What are beyond being cut are atoms. '(If it is said that) it is impossible (for such a thing to exist), because the Ākāśa must (pervade) and divide (the atom, for otherwise) Ākāśa would not be all-pervasive, (we reply that) the words 'within' and 'without' apply to effects and do not exist in what are not effects because they refer to what are other than causes." (*Ib*. IV. 81-85). (If it is argued that the atoms) must have real parts, because all bodies having form must have a collection of parts and (also) all bodies that conjoin (with others), (we reply that) the atoms cannot be given up because it would occasion a *regressus ad infinitum* and because a *regressus ad infinitum* is not proper " (*Ib.* IV. 88-90).

As the Yoga added to the Sāṅkhya the conception of an Īśvara, so the Nyāya to the Vaiśeṣika. But the Īśvara of the Nyāya Sūtras is concerned only with the adjustment of fruits of action. Some actions are followed by consequences immediate and visible; but others are not. This is adjusted by a Supreme Being called Īśvara. "Īśvara is a cause, for we do not see (all) the fruits of action. (If it said), this can not be, for in the absence of (the individual's) action, fruits cannot come forth, (we reply) action is not the (whole] cause, for (it is) caused by Him." (*Ib.* IV. 19-21), The later Nyāya developed the notion of God, the creator. Udayana's *Kusumāñjaḷi* is devoted to this one question. Its main arguments will be summarised in the next chapter.

The Nyāya ranged itself against idealism and affirmed the existence of the external world, independent of the cognizing mind, thus opposing certain schools of Buddhism and, in later days, the Pratyabhijñā school and the more degenerate forms of the Advaita. "If it is said that Real existence cannot be perceived because things are known only by means of cognition, just as the existence of a cloth cannot be perceived when the threads are removed (*i. e.* cognition is a part of real existence and objects cannot exist independent of cognition), (we say, no,) for this is no argument on account of the falsehood of the assertion in the analogy. The threads and the cloth are different entities, (though) they are not perceived separately because of the inherence (of the thread in the cloth)", *(Ib.* IV. 91-93). "(The theories that] the relation of cognizer and cognised is like the relation [of man) to things (experienced) in a dream, or like jugglery or the city of the Gandharvas or a mirage cannot be proved, because of the absence of any proof" *(Ib.* IV. 96-98).

It is noteworthy how each school of thought has used a different name for the man other than his bodies, the study of whose nature is the starting part of all philosophy. The Sāṅkhya calls him Puruṣa, a word of uncertain etymology[51] but originally meaning 'male,' a very curious designation of the inactive witness of the dance of Prakṛti. The Draṣṭā of the Yoga is a very appropriate term. The Āgama schools prefer Cit or Caitanya, which in later Sanskṛt at least, means active and thus denotes the Āgama conception fairly accurately. The Vedānta popularized the word Ātmā, which means, self, nature, essence, in accordance with its tendency to regard the whole world as being rooted in one noumenon, Brahmā, that which grows into or that which fills the Universe. The Vaiśeṣika and Nyāya schools also accepted the word, perhaps because they felt it to be a non-committal term. They attributed so many functions to 'the soul' that they avoided words like Puruṣa, or Caitanya which had definite connotations attached to them and preferred the vaguer word Ātmā. It must not be forgotten that these words, though in later philosophical discussions treated as synonymous, have definite meanings depending upon their derivation and their definition in each School.

Thus though the Sāṅkhya, the Yoga, the Vaiśeṣika and the Nyāya are all schools of individualism, yet we see that there is a great difference between the Puruṣa of the former two and the Ātmā of the latter two. 'Puruṣa'is pure citiśakti (power of conciousness, of illumination) and nothing more. But in the Nyāya-Vaiśeṣika systems the Ātmā is the substratum of a number of qualities—involuntary vital action, voluntary action, desire, aversion, cognition, pleasure, pain, etc.,—in fact, all that is described by the Sāṅkhya, as the modifications of the internal organ; this difference is due to the difference of the darśana, the original view-point and the consequent difference of the line of investigation adopted. The Sāṅkhya-Yoga schools base their metaphysical and psychological theories on their realization of Pure Being (Kaivalya) as the result of the discrimination of mutable Prakṛti from immutable Puruṣa. Conciousness of Pure Being is described as 'the conclusive, incontrovertible absolute and pure knowledge 'I am not I', nought is mine, I am not' (*Sāṅkh. Kār.* lxiv). A sense of being with the consciousness of Ego dissolved and the consciousness of non-ego ignored, is best called Kaivalya, aloneness, as the Sāṅkhya has named it. To one who experiences Kaivalya, all change, mutability, all phenomenality cannot but be regarded as outside, objective; hence Prakṛti, the changeable, in his view includes all that is not Puruṣa; and the mental functions of knowledge, action and desire which the ordinary man regards as belonging to the world of self and not to the outside world, is but Prakṛti to the Sāṅkhya. But the Vaiśeṣika or the Naiyāyika has as his goal the abolition of pain consequent on birth in physical bodies which is caused by desires for objects. He therefore sets about analysing the composition of objects and when he learns to estimate them at their proper value, he ceases to hanker for them, thereby abolishing birth and pain. His aim being the cessation of the pain of compulsory incarnation of the soul, when this point is reached his analysis of the world stops. Hence he regards the ātmā as possessing all the qualities which cannot be explained by the seven substances—earth water, fire, air, ākāśa, time and space—which are outside man. These qualities of the ātmā are involuntary vital action, voluntary action, desire, aversion, cognition, and control of the organs of sense (jñanendryas) and the organ of attention (manas). The realization of the ātmā as possessed of these qualities is as legitimate a goal of life and a release (mokṣa) as that realized by any other discipline; and hence the Vaiśeṣika explanation of the cosmos is as valid as any other.

It is not a philosophy subservient to or leading up to any other but one solution of the riddle of the universe, self-consistent and final and as true as any other. The monists of India, on account of the fancied superiority of their metaphysics to the atomic theories of the Vaiśeṣikas and the Naiyāikas superciliously turned the names of the founders of these schools, Kaṇāda and Gautama, to ridicule. The former name is by them paraphrased as Kaṇabhuk, eater of atoms and the Utter is as Akṣapāda, he who has eyes in his feet, to help him in his search of atoms. But the atomic theory is by no means a less valid explanation than any other.

SECTION V

Pūrvamīmāṁsā

The Vedic literature consists of various strata of different ages mixed up in almost hopeless confusion. First of all, there are the very ancient hymns belonging to the age when the ritual was yet simple and the Ṛṣis[52] sang hymns in praise of Indra and Viṣṇu, Mitra and Varuṇa as occasion arose for them and propitiated them with meat and soma to avert a calamity that immediately threatened them in their individual or tribal lives or to gain some urgent desire of their hearts,[53] There are, again, other hymns which show that the sacrificial ritual had already become highly complicated and which refer to the various functionaries therein.[54]

When the age of inspiration ended, the work of compilation of the hymns floating in the memory of the people began. Between the *composition* of the hymns (Ṛks) and prose formulae (Yajus) and their *compilation* as the Vedas there must have elapsed a period long enough to cause the original purposes and occasions of the mantras to be largely forgotten. The whole literature was now the holy Śruti and had to be used for recitation during sacrifices so that no part of the precious revelation might be wasted. Even in this early age, the sentences of the hymns were dislocated from their context and used as Mantras and not understood as literature. There is a tradition referred to in the *Viṣṇu Purāṇa* (III. iv. 11), that at first the Veda was one and called the Yajur Veda and Vyāsa[55] separated it into four, each part being a collection of the mantras to be recited by one class of priests officiating at the sacrifices. The Adhvaryu was the actual performer of the sacrifices and for his use was compiled the *Yajur Veda* which contains the Mantras (poetical or Ṛk and prose or Yajus), with which he was to accompany each detail of the ceremonies from the simple Darśapūrṇamāsa iṣṭi (new and full moon sacrifices) to the highly complicated Aśvamedha and Puruṣamedha (Horse-sacrifice and human sacrifice).[56] The *Yajur Veda* is the most complicated, because it is the Veda of the Adhvaryu who performs the actual work of the sacrifice and hence it follows closely the order of the various ceremonies. We can therefore understand why it was the first to be compiled. The Hotā invited the Gods to the sacrifice and praised them by reciting hymns, in a sense he represented the ancient Ṛṣis who composed the hymns, for his function was to invoke the Gods by praise. His recitations were long and not generally correlated to definite acts as in the case of the Adhvaryu. Hence in the Veda compiled for him was included many of the original hymns in the form in which they were composed, *i. e.* without detaching individual verses from their context. Hence it happens that the *Ṛg-Veda* contains so many connected compositions—a fact which has led some European scholars to think that it was compiled earlier than the *Yajur-Veda* while others go so far as to regard it as a 'historical' work. The Udgātā was the singer of select hymns during the sacrifices and for his benefit the *Sāma-Veda* was compiled. Thus was constituted the *Trayīvidyā,* which contained what may be called the national or rather tribal religious ceremonial of the ancient Hindus. The domestic ceremonial, which affected home life and embodied the wishes and aspirations of the ordinary folk, was in the earliest times the office of the Atharvaṇa, the family 'medicineman' and the hymns used by him were collected in his Veda. Even the Ṛg Veda, as it is, contains bits absolutely like the Atharva Veda as when *R.*

V. VIII. 91-5 refers to the desire of a maiden for a peculiar hirsute decoration and the necessary ritual to secure that growth. Later on, when the increasing complexity of the sacrificial ritual required a supreme director of ceremonies called Brahmā and a distinct house ritual, called Gṛhya,[57] nominally based on the Trayī (the three Vedas) was evolved, the Atharva Veda was technically associated with the Brahmā and actually fell into comparative oblivion. From the earliest times the Trayīvidyā, the imposing ritual of the sacrifices loomed large in the imagination of the Hindus and from the frequent references to it and its constant glorification in the early literature, have resulted two misconceptions (1) that the Atharva Veda is later than the others, (2) that it deals with black magic and is somewhat disreputable. The Atharva Veda contains a great number of Sūktas also found in the Ṛg Veda; but this does not mean that the former borrowed from the latter. They were compiled for different purposes and tapped the same original source. Just because it was at least as old and as sacred as the rest that it was assigned to the Brahmā when that office was invented. The magic of the Yajur-Veda is as primitive as that of the others. The Adhvaryu regards everything he touches or uses, stones, grass, fire, as a fetish and flatters the spirit behind it so that he may not harm him, just as the Atharvaṇa charms neualgia away from a man by praising the spirit that causes it. The following extract from the *Āpastamba Śrauta Sūtras* with the mantras referred to there proves the magic of the Vedic Yajñas to be as crude as any other magic.

"Having heated the Sānnāyya vessels on the Gārhapatya fire with the invocation, 'may the Rākṣasas be burned, may those intent on mischief be burned,' taken the Upaveṣa with 'you are bold, give me the Brahma' *(Tait. Sam;* I. 1-7), taken out from the north side of the Gārhapatya fire a live coal with 'May quarrel and fear be removed, may the army that comes (against us) be removed,' he (the Adhvaryu) places the pot on it (the live coal) with 'Thou art the milk-kettle of Mātariśva, thou art Heaven, thou art Earth, thou art the bearer of all, be firm (in your place on the coal), by (your) transcendent power; do not fall down, (*Ib.* I.i.3). Or (he places the pot on the coal) with, 'O, two cooking pots. I place (you) on (the fire) for avoiding the miscarriage of the Yajña. May (you) hold, for Indra's sake the boiled (milk), yielded by the cows, and the curd. (*Tait. Brāh. III.* vii. 4. 34.). Having placed fire round the pot, from right to left with 'Become heated by the tapas of Bhṛgu and Aṅgiras' (*Tait. Sam.* I. i. 7), he places the Śākhāpavitrainit (the pot) with the tips to the East with 'you are the pavitra of the Vasus hundred fold, you are the pavitra of the Vasus, thousandfold, (*Tait. Saṁ* I. i. 3). He places the Śakhāpavitra (with the tips) to the North in the morning. Having grasped the pot from behind, he is silent. Or he is (so), holding the pavitra. [Having thus made the pot ready for boiling the milk, he proceeds to milk the cow]. He grasps the ropes (for tying the calf, before milking), with 'Thou art the rope of Aditi.' The Yajamāna consecrates (the rope) which is being grasped with, 'Thou art of thirty-three threads. Come with holiness. May this rope for tying the calf serve the calf well (not hurt it).' (*Tait. Brāh.* III. vii. 4. 33). He (the Adhvaryu) ties the calf (to a post) with 'Thou art Pūṣā, (*Tait. Brāh.* III. vii. 4. 39). He invites (the milker) with 'Tell me (when the calf, has been) taken (to its) mother.' (The milker) calls (the Adhvaryu) with 'I take (the calf to its mother).' He takes the calf with 'I take (O cows, your) calves to you who are without disease and are the increase of wealth' *(Tait. Brah.* III. vii. 4. 40.) The Adhvaryu commands, 'Do not walk between the cows to whom the calves have been taken and the Vihāra (the place of the three sacred fires).' If (any one, goes between the (calves) taken (to the cows) and the Vihāra, he shall say. 'Do not carry off the Sānnāyya.' (The milker) says 'sit.' The milker sits with, 'I admit calves to you, who are without disease and are the increase of wealth. I, who live, sit near you who are living, who are overflowing with strength-giving milk and ghī' (*Tait. brāḥ.* III vii. 4. 40). A Śūdra shall not milk or shall milk. He milks into a wooden pot. The Yajamāna accompanies the admitted (calf), the milked (cow), the sound of the streaming (milk) with, 'I admit calves to you, who are without disease and are the increase of wealth, 'May Dyāvāpṛthvī milk for this yajña. May Dhātā, Soma, Vāyu and Vāta, may they give wealth to the Yajamāna (*Tait. Brāḥ.* III. vii. 4. 41)." Except that the magic[58] here is more complicated than in the Atharva veda, there is nothing to distinguish it from the latter. The four *Saṁhitās* suffixed the needs of a fairly long period of time.

After this period there must have occured a break of culture, long enough to allow of the language of the *Saṁhitā* to become obscure to a later generation. The language changed during this period to that of the *Brāhmaṇas,* which is midway between Vedic and classical Sanskṛt. The meanings of the hymns having become obscure, they began to be applied indiscriminately for sacrificial purposes and interpreted in fanciful ways. Discussions frequently arose in the assemblies of the priests about details of the rituals, applications of mantras, etc. To settle such questions, whai were called Nyāyas were frequently utilized.[59] The Nyāyas are analogies, or inferences or proverbs which make statements, probable or acceptable and are even now largely used for purposes of argumentation. The Ahikuṇḍala Nyāya (the analogy of the snake and its coils being one and yet more than one), Sthālīpulāka Nyāya (judging of the state of rice in the cooking-pot by examining one grain) are illustrations of the humble beginnings of Logic. Such Nyāyas form the backbone of all bhāṣyas of all the modern sects. Decisions on *considerations like these and* cruder ones too are scattered throughout the Brāhmaṇas, which contain besides, traditions, real or imaginary, regarding the composition of particular mantras, cosmogonic speculations, etc.

In time the Brāhmaṇas, too were added to the holy canon and became fixed as a part of the revealed Veda. With the extension of the Scripture to include "the Mantra and Brāhmaṇa," the task of the exegete became more difficult and complicated. The work of explaining the various discrepancies of the Veda and solving the various difficulties of the ritual became a profession and the scheme of Nyāyas[60] was developed into the Mīmāṁsā Śāstra. A collection of such is the *Sūtras* of Jaimini. On them Upavarṣa is said to have commented and Sahara wrote his Bhāṣya. Jaimini is referred to and his opinions controverted by Bādarāyaṇa in his *Brahma Mīmāṁsā Sūtras* and could not have lived very much later than the 6th century B. C. when Vedic sacrifices were so rampant as to evoke the Buddhist reaction headed by Gautama Siddhārtha. The object of Jaimini's *Sūtras* is to expound Dharma. 'Now, then, the investigation of Dharma (duty). Dharma has for its purpose what follows from a scriptural injunction. Now (commences) the examination of its origin. When there is a connection between Puruṣa and Indriyas, Buddhi[61] (perception) is produced. Such perception is not the origin (of duty), for it deals with what exists (at the time of perception while duty does not then exist" *(Pūr. Mim. Sūt.* I. i. 1.4).

Thus according to Jaimini, the sanction of Law must be from what transcends perception, human or superhuman. Even the highest Puruṣa is limited by his organs of perception and is hence incompetent to prescribe duty with authority. The authoritativeness of the Vedic injunctions is derived from the fact that they deal with objects beyond the reach of experience of man or of the Devas. Hence there is no room for an Īśvara in the Mīmāṁsā system. The Karma Kāṇḍa of the Vedas, *i. e.,* the Vedas *minus* the Upaniṣads had not worked out except vaguely and that in the latest passages the idea of Brahmā being the noumenon of the universe. Even the doctrine of the Ātmā, man's continued existence apart from those he lives in the various bodies he inhabits seemed to have been an open question for a very long time as is proved by Naciketās' second question to Yama about the continuity of man's postmortem life with that before death and by Yama's remark that the Gods themselves were in doubt (*Kath. Up.* i. 20-22). The question was, in Gautama Buddha's time, still so fluid that he could ignore it while preaching his special displine. Similarly the original mīmāṁsā let these questions severely alone and contented itself with establishing the authority of the Veda and the binding nature of the Vedic rites. The only possible way of proving this authority without invoking the sanction of a personal being, high or low, was to argue that the Veda existed from all eternity. This could be only if the words of the Veda were uncreate, *i. e.* if the connection between a word and the object that the word names were itself eternal. The Mīmāṁsā Sūtras therefore, say:—

"Because the connection of sound and sense is unborn. Hence it conveys unerring knowledge with regard to matters which cannot be reached (by perception and inference). This is the authority accepted by Bādarāyaṇa, because it requires no further proof." (*Ib.* I, i. 5). Like Jaimini, Bādarāyaṇa has to rely entirely on the final authority of the Veda to prove the existence of conscious Brahma, as the noumenon of the universe, for this cannot be proved "by perception and inference" *(Ved. Sut.* I. i.5). He therefore generally accepts the position of Jaiminl that the Vedas are eternal, though the Devas and the world are not so, because of the identity of names and forms before and after Pralaya (*Ib. iii. 28* 30).

Jaimini gives the following reasons to prove the eternity of sounds. (1) Sound is eternal because it serves to convey meaning. The object referred to by a name always rests, as it were, upon the name, (*Mīm. Sūt.* I. i-18). (2) It is recognised by all simultaneously. How could this be possible if it were a vanishing thing? (*Ib.* I. i-19.) (3) It is incommensurable. One sound repeated ten times is not ten sounds, as it would be if sound were a mutable substance. (*Ib* I. i.20). (4) There are no grounds for expecting its destruction. *(Ib.* I. i-21). (5) (If sound were a modification of some other substance,) there would be no appropriate object to be perceived by the organ of 'hearing Each sense-organ corresponds to an elementary substance in the world. Hence sound is an elementary substance and not a merevikāra (mode) of another. *(Ib.* I. 1-22). (6) It is seen that the Veda also proclaims the eternity of sound (*Ib.* I. i. 23).

The objections of the Naiyāyikas to the theories of the eternity of sound are summarised in *Ib.* I. i. 6-11, as follows—

Sound is a product because (1) We see it produced. (2) It dies. (3) We use the phrase 'he makes a sound'. (4) It is perceived at once by different persons far and near. Therefore it cannot be one and immutable. (5) It is susceptible of prakṛti-vikṛti. Sounds change from one to another in sandhi. Thus dadhiatra becomes dadhyatra. *(6)* It is augmented by the number of those that make it. These objections are met in *Sūtras* I. i. 12.17. It is admitted by both schools that the perception of sound is momentary. But the non-perception of sound which is always existent is due to the want of union of the hearer and the sound, the object of hearing. Sound exists always but becomes manifested as nāda, (noise), conjunctions and disjunctions of air, when uttered by a man. These vibrations of air serve to connect the pre-existing sound with the auditorium of the hearer. The phrase 'makes a sound' means the starting of these vibrations, which of course are transitory. The fact that many persons hear the same sound at the same time does not prove that it is not one and immutable. Herein it resembles the sun, which being one and immutable, is still seen by men remote from one another at the same time. In Sandhi one sound does not change into another, but the second sound (in the illustration) is substituted for the first. Lastly when there is an increase of sound, it is the manifesting nāda (air-vibrations) that is increased, not the original substance, Śabda.

If we remember that in Indian philosophy, mental states are modifications of matter, it is not difficult to understand this Mīmāṁsaka theory that the connection between sound and sense is eternal. A mental concept of an object being a modification of subtle matter is permanently attached to the substratum of the name of the object in the same grade of matter. An uttered name is nāda, which is a temporary manifestation of the eternal sound; this latter is a permanent modification of that Ākāśa which is also the material of the organ of thought. Hence a thought exists permanently attached to its name; in other words nāma and rūpa are one; the thought and the name rise together in consciousness. This explanation also helps us to understand why manifestation is always called nāmarūpa in Hindu books, and why Uddālaka in trying to illustrate to Śvetaketu the knowledge that makes us hear what cannot be heard and perceived what cannot be perceived says, "As, my dear, by one clod of clay all that is made of clay is known, the change is a *mere matter of words, nothing but a name* (vācārambhaṇam vikāronāmadheyam)" (*Chānd. Up,* vi. I. 3.)

This idea of the eternity of the meaning of a word is not so ridiculously old-fashioned as some people think it is. Sir Oliver Lodge writes in *Life and Matter,* which may better be entitled, 'the metaphysics of a physicist', "The connection between soul and body or more generally between spiritual and material, has been illustrated by the connection between the meaning of a sentence and the written or spoken word conveying that meaning. The writing or the speaking may be regarded as an incarnation of the meaning, a mode of stating or exhibiting its essence. As delivered, the sentence must have time relations; it has a beginning, middle and end; it may be repeated, and the same general meaning may be expressed in other words; but the intrinsic meaning of the sentence itself need have no time relations, it may be true *always,* it may exist as an eternal "now," though it may be perceived and expressed by humanity with varying clearness from time to time." (p. 115) Max Müller remarks on this Mīmāṁsaka doctrine that the philosophers of India understood that the study of language was an integral part of philosophy.

"They had evidently perceived that language is the only phenomenal form of thought, and that, as human beings possess no means of perceiving the thoughts of others, nay even their own thoughts, except in the form of words, it was the duty of a student of thought to inquire into the nature of words before he approached or analysed the nature of what we mean by thought, naked thought, nay skinned thought, as it has been truly called, when divested of its natural integuments, the word. They understood what even modern philosophers have failed to understand, that there is a difference between *Vorstellung* (presentation or percept) and *Begriff* (concept), and that true thought has to do with conceptual words only, nay, that the two, word and thought, are inseparable, and perish when separated" *(Six Systems of Indian philosophy,* p. 526).

After establishing to his satisfaction the eternity and consequent authority of the Veda, Jaimini proceeds to consider the inconvenient questions of the rationalists of his age with regard to those numerous passages of the Veda which have nothing to do with the Dharm a of Yajña, but deal with ordinary worldly matters. To explain this was invented the theory of Arthavāda, subsidiary, explanatory statement. Whatever in the Veda was not a commandment was explained away as an explanatory statement. In the schools of the Mīmāṁsā, this fruitful suggestion of separating the sentences of the Veda into various classes was worked till ultimately was elaborated the division of Vedic sentences into five classes *viz.*, Vidhi, Mantra, Nāmadheya, Niṣedha, and Arthavāda. A Vidhi is an injunction occuring in the Veda and is of four kinds, (1) Utpatti-vidhi, an injunction that originates others (2) Viniyoga vidhi, one in which the auxiliaries of sacrifice are mentioned (3) Prayoga-vidhi, injunction of the main sacrificial action (4) Adhikāra vidhi, which deals with the position one enjoys as the result of a sacrifice.[62] A Mantra is a sentence that serves to remind one of matters connected with sacrifices. Those Mantras that do not serve this purpose contribute in some unknown way to the success of the sacrifice. [63] Nāmadheya includes specific names of special kinds of sacrifices, like Udbhid, Citra etc. Niṣedha refers to sentences prohibiting certain actions. Lastly, Arthavāda passages are those that are subsidiary to vidhi or niṣeda and contain either praise or blame. It is of three classes (1) Guṇa-vāda is the statement of a quality contrary to ordinary perception, *e.g.* 'the sun is the sacrificial post'; (2) Anuvāda is a statement agreeing with human experience, *e.g.* 'fire is a remedy against cold'; (3) Bhūtārthavāda is a statement which is not related to other means of proof, *e.g,* "Indra raised the thunderbolt against Vṛtra".[64] Gradually the word Arthavāda acquired the meaning of what may be neglected and every inconvenient passage became an arthavāda.

Besides the question of the eternity of the connection between sound and meaning, another metaphysical question was worked out in the schools of the Mīmāṁsā—that of Apūrva or potential energy. Sacrificial acts are not followed by visible (dṛṣṭa) fruits. The question, then, rises, how can it act so as to produce a result in the future; 'action at a distance' of time being inconceivable. Therefore it was conceived that sacrifices produced an unseen change (saṁskāra) which when the time came operated to bring about the fruit of the sacrifice. This idea is expounded by Jaimini in a brief sūtra (II. i. 5), "codanā, again, ārambha" which is thus commented on by Śabara. "By codanā we understand Apūrva. 'Apūrva, again' (exists, for) 'Ārambha' is ordained, as in 'Let one desirous of svarga, sacrifice.' Otherwise, the ordinance becomes fruitless, as the sacrifice ends (and is not continued till the fruit is seen). If the sacrifice ends without producing anything else, the fruit cannot be (produced) in the absence of anything. Hence it produces (something). It cannot be said that it (the Yāga) does not itself die, because its fruit is declared; (for) we cannot find any form of (the persistence) of Karma (other than Apūrva). That is said to be Karma which takes its substratum (from one place) to another place; it cannot inhere in the Ātmā, for Ātmā is everywhere.

Ātmā's action (knowledge) being everywhere is evidence of its being everywhere and not of its going (to one place) from another place for the absence of motion does not contradict (the causality of the Ātmā). (Moreover) the material with which sacrifice was associated (ghī etc.) is also destroyed (burnt up); as the material is destroyed, it is inferred, the sacrifice, too, is destroyed. The material is destroyed because its ashes are perceived. If it is said that though it is burnt, it still exists, (we reply) that while the existing things (ashes etc.,) are seen, it is not seen. If it is said that the fructification is evidence (of the existence of the material), one must explain why it is not perceived. If it is thought that (its not being perceived) is due to any one of the causes of invisibility, subtility etc, [65] it becomes speculative predication. Then it becomes a question whether Apūrva should be predicated or that (cause). It is more reasonable to predicate a new substance and to, predicate a new property (of the material). If it is said that the Karma has no substratum, that, too, can be disproved similarly. Though a new property is predicated of it, it cannot obtain motion. Hence (it is concluded) that the sacrifice is destroyed; as it is destroyed, there exists Apūrva." This Apūrva, then, is the unseen substance in which inheres the fruit of the many sacrifices of the Veda.

Jaimini's sūtras are, of course, highly disappointing viewed at from the standpoint of the philosopher, but we must remember that Jaimini does not contemplate the analysis of the universe from any special philosophic standpoint. Nor was it possible for him to do so, weighted as he was with an extraordinary load of ritual to be gone through, teeming with a crop of questions of exegesis, whose solutions did not require anything more than grammar and logic. But his followers feeling that his darśana could hold its own against its rivals only if it discussed the current questions of philosophy included the means of proof (Pramāṇas), the padārthas of the Universe and many other philosophical questions in their discussions of Mīmāṁsā. They are divided into two schools--the Gurumata of Prabhākara and the Bhāṭṭa of Bhaṭṭa Kumārila.

The following reference to the views of the first of these two schools is taken from the *Sarva-Siddhānta rahasya* attributed to Śaṅkarācārya[66] "Dravya, Guṇa, Karma, Sāmānya, and Paratantratā[67] (dependence) are five categories; with Śakti, Sādṛśya (similarity) and Sāṅkhya (number), they are eight. Viśeṣa and Abhāva are not (categories), separate from the earth and other objects in which they inhere. *(Ib. Chap.* IX). Ātmā is other than Buddhi, Indriya, and Śariras. It is not limited by space (vibbu), eternal. It becomes manifold in various bodies. It manifests itself in the cognition of objects. In the cognition, 'I know the pot,' there are three things at the same time; the pot as object; the subject enters in it as 'I', knowledge manifests itself as self-luminous." *(Ib.)*. A fairly complete metaphysical system was evolved by Bhaṭṭa Kumārila who lived a little before Śaṅkara's time, in his voluminous *vārttika* on Śabara's Bhāṣya, divided into three parts are called *Śloka vārttika, Tanttavārttika* and *Ṭupṭika*.

The doctrine of the eternity of Śabda was violently attacked by the Nyāya, Vaiśeṣika and Sāṅkhya schools, who all the while pretended the Vedā to be authoritative[68] Patañjali, the author of *Mahābhāṣya* modified the theory by regarding the substance of the Veda to be eternal, but the words not so. He says, "It is said 'the Vedas are not created (things); the Vedas are eternal'; their sense is eternal, but the order of letters (words etc.) is not eternal, through their difference are produced the versions of the Kaṭhas, Kalāpas, Mudakas, Pippalādakas, etc." *(Mahābhāṣya* IV. iii. 101).

Bhartṛhari, the famous writer of the 7th century A. D., expounds the doctrine of the sphoṭa in his Kārikā called *Vākyapadīya*. "Those that know sound know that there are two sounds in the words that we speak; one, the cause of sound; the other is used for indicating an object." (*Vākyapadīya* I.*44)*. The two sounds referred to are, first, what exists in the mind before the word is actually pronounced, and, second, the pronounced word. "Some of those that follow the ancient path say that these two are different in nature. Others say, we divide in two by our thought what is really one. Just as the light (potential) in the fire-stick (araṇi) is the cause of other lights being produced, so the sound (sphoṭa) in the mind (buddhi) is the cause of the various sounds heard (nāda). It is first thought out by the mind, then associated with some meaning and then is grasped (by the hearer) as sound. Nāda is produced in succession (in time); but sphoṭa is not before or after (*i. e,* produced in succession). What is not successively produced appears as if gradually made and thus appears divided. As a reflection seems to take on the motion of the water in which it is seen (lit. exists), being under the influence of the action of the water, that is the relation of sphoṭa and nāda." *(Ib.* i. 45-49). Sphoṭa is, thus, the potential word which exists in the mind *i.e.* the mental antecedent that is revealed by the uttered word, as water reveals the moon reflected in it. Kumārila, attacks this sphoṭa theory in his *Śloka Vārttika* on behalf of the Pūrva Mimāṁsā and Śaṅkara, in his *Bhāṣya,* (*Ved. Sūt.* iii. 29) on behalf of the Uttara Mīmāṁsā.

The theory of the eternity of sound, like most other theories developed in India, has its roots in the Ṛg Veda, in various hymns of which Vāgdevī is praised. She is often the Gāyatri metre personified; She is called Sarasvatī, Sāvitrī, Satarūpā etc. In the Brāhmaṇas she became the solitary companion of the First Born (Brahmā the creator) and co-operated with him in the work of evolving Name and Form. In (*Śat. Brāh.* X. vi. 5.4), it is said, 'his mind entered into union with speech' and in the same place she is identified with Aditi. As she represents the power of the Mantras, she later became identical with the Śakti of the Āgamas. In the schools of the Śaiva cult, where the goddess loses her predominance, the conception reappears *(Mait. Up.* vi. 22) as the Śabda Brahma, first mentioned in the Bhartṛhari, expounds the doctrine in the *Vākyapadīya* from the standpoint of the philosophy of grammar.

Vijñāna Bhikṣu (who lived in the XVI century), in his *Yogasāra-Saṅgraha* claims the Sphoṭa theory as belonging to the Yoga school and gives a clear exposition of the theory. "Sound is of three kinds. (1) the object of the organs of speech (2) the object of the sense of hearing and (3) the object of Buddhi alone. Of these the sound marked off (as belonging to) the throat, palate and other places is the object of the organs of speech, as produced by them, the sound produced by the sound in the ear and different from the organs of speech, is the object of the sense of hearing, as being perceived by it.[69] Words, like 'pot,' etc., however, are the objects of Buddhi alone, for they are grasped by the Buddhi alone, as will be explained. These words manifest meanings, and are hence called Sphoṭa (manifester). That word is other than the letters which are pronounced one by one by the organ of speech, for each letter dies very soon (after it is uttered) and cannot unite (to form a word) and hence one (whole) word (for the ear to deal with) cannot exist and there will be nothing to denote the meaning (if we except the Sphoṭa). The cause of this Sphoṭa is a specific effort. If it were due to pronunciation by means of many distinct efforts, it will not be possible to regard it as one word, and to refer to one meaning. The discloser of this sphoṭa is the cognition of the last letter preceded by a series of letters. To Buddhi alone belongs the perception of Sphoṭa, for as Buddhi alone can cognize a succession (of letters) it is simpler to attribute the disclosure of the Sphoṭa to the cognition of this succession than to anything else, because they coexist.

Hence the sphoṭa cannot be cognized by the ear, for it is impossible for the ear to grasp a succession (of sounds), as *gha* followed by *ṭa;* moreover, sounds (of single letters) which die in the instant (they are made) cannot unite (with succeeding sounds); hence, as the impression of the letters already pronounced and their memory reside in the antaḥkaraṇa, the antaḥkaraṇa, alone can properly be the auxiliary (of the perception of sphoṭa)" (*Ib.* iv).

SECTION VI

The Bhagavad Gītā

It has been already pointed out that the *Bhagavadgītā*[70] was an early attempt to weld together the Vedānta, the Sāṅkhya and the Āgama points of view.[71] Two passages have already been quoted (p. 72-3) describing the conscious supreme Brahma—the one real cosmic ultimate of the Vedāntīs. In other passages Kṛṣnaa propounds the sharp distinction between Puruṣa and Prakṛti deliberately using the Sāṅkhya technical terms.

"Know Prakṛti and also Puruṣa to be both without a beginning; know that changes of form and guṇas spring from Prakṛti. The origin of the making of causes and effects is Prakṛti; Puruṣa is the experience, of pleasure and pain. Puruṣa, established in Prakṛti, experiences the qualities. born of Prakṛti; his attachment to guṇas is the cause (of his birth) in good and bad wombs. Onlooker and permitter, lord, experiencer, the great lord, and the supreme self (paramātmā), too, is he called, Puruṣa, who is supreme here (in this body)". (xiii. 19-22) "O mighty-armed, learn from me the five causes declared in the Sāṅkhya system (as necessary) for the accomplishment of all actions; the body, the agent, the several organs, the various kinds of several activities, and the presiding deities, the fifth; whatever action man does by his body, speech and mind, right or wrong these five are the causes thereof. That being so, he who from imperfect understanding sees the lone self to be the actor, verily that fool sees not' (xviii. 13-16).

The Āgama analysis of the Universe into three factors is also expounded. "Īśvara dwells in the heart-region of all beings, O Arjuna, causing, by his wonder-working power, all beings to revolve as if mounted on a machine" (xviii. 61.) "Another, indeed, is the Supreme Puruṣa, called Paramātma, who, having entered the three worlds[72] sustains (them), the changeless Īśvara." (xv. 17).

In various passages Kṛṣṇa claims to be that Īśvara. "I am unborn, the changeless Ātmā, the lord of beings" (iv. 6), "I am the origin and the end of the whole universe. Nothing exists higher than I, O Dhanañjaya. All this is strung on me as rows of gems on a thread." (vii. 6-7). The other two tattvas are the two Prakṛtis of Īśvara. "The discrete Prakṛti, that is mine, is eight-fold, Earth, water, fire, Vāyu, Akāśa, Manas, Buddhi and Ahaṅkāra" vii. 4). "The great elements, Ahaṅkāra, Buddhi, Avyakta, the organs ten and one, the five ranges of the (sense) organs, desire, hate, pleasure, pain, the (bodily) whole, intelligence, constancy, this is the field (kṣetra) described briefly along with its modifications" (xiii. 5.6). This is the lower

Prakṛti, corresponding to the Idaṁtā of the Śāktas, Aśuddhamāyā of the Śaivas, Acit of the Vaiṣṇavas. "Know my other Prakṛti, higher than this, who becomes living (Jīva), O mighty-armed, (and) by whom this Universe is upheld." (vii. 5). "Being a portion of myself, it becomes in the world of the living an eternal living being and attracts to itself the sense-organs of which Manas is the sixth", (xv. 7.) This category is called in the Āgamas Tejas or Ojas and these words occur in xv. 12-14. "What Tejas (light-energy) in the sun brightens up the world, what in the moon, and what in fire, that Tejas know to be mine. I enter the Earth and support life by my Ojas (energy); becoming Soma, the essence, I nourish all plants. Becoming Vaiśvānara (the fire of life), I enter the bodies of breathing beings and united with Prāṇa and Apāna (two kinds of winds on which the vital fire is carried), digest the four kinds of food."

These three systems Kṛṣṇa, in other passages, tries to transcend and he indicates a Supreme Reality, higher than the conscious One Brahma of the Vedāntīs, the dual Puruṣa and Prakṛti of the Sāṅkhyas and the triple Īśvara, Cit and Acit of the Āgamikas. This is called 'Brahmā-tat' (vii. 29), 'Akṣaram Brahma paramam' (viii. 3), 'my supreme abode' (viii. 21.), 'the supreme seat' (viii. 28). Kṛṣṇa calls himself 'the pratiṣṭhā of Brahma, the undying, the changeless, the eternal, the Dharma, the unending bliss" (xiv. 27). Pratiṣṭhā means pedestal, and hence vehicle. As Kṛṣṇa's acknowleging a higher entity than himself goes against the grain of all schools of Vedānta, every commentator, from Śaṅkara onwards has expended a good deal of ingenuity in explaining away the obvious meaning of this passage.[73]

This 'supreme abode' which Kṛṣṇa differentiates so carefully from himself, the Puruṣottama, and also from a Puruṣa, higher than himself, whom he seems to refer to by the adjectives Kavi, Purāṇa, etc. in viii-9., and by the name Ādi Puruṣa in xv. 4, is frequently called 1 *Padam*' or, *Gait,* path. " Verily there exists higher than that Avyakta (*i. e.* Mūlaprakṛti) another Avyakta (undifferentiated, noumenon) eternal, which is not destroyed, when all beings are destroyed. It is called Avyakta (the absolute), Akṣara (the unchanging); they call it the Supreme Path. Having reached it, no one returns. That is my Supreme abode." (viii. 20-21). "There[74] the sun does not shine, nor the moon, nor fire; having gone there they return not; that is my Supreme abode." (xv. 6.) In this "Supreme abode" the author of the *Bhagavad Gītā* finds the one noumenon into which the ultimate tattvas of the other schools merge. This is the foundation of all that is; on which are established Puruṣas from the lowest to the highest, out of which rise all the elements of the evolved world. It is not conscious being nor is it unconscious being but "that beyond," 'the knower and the known and the Supreme fixed dwelling place' (xi. 38).

This Supreme Reality as Kṛṣṇa conceives it is different from the Nirguṇa Brahma of Śaṅkara. This latter is the Saguṇa Brahma or conscious Universal Being shorn of 'name and form' used for purposes of meditation; when these distinctions are negatived, it is the higher. (*Ved. Sūt. Bhāṣ,* iv. iii. 4.) Beginningless Avidyā (ignorance) according to Śaṅkara leads us to attribute 'name and form' to that which is not thus limited and this, according to Śaṅkara, is the Param (higher) Brahma, which is Sat, and opposed to Avidyā which is Asat. This doctrine of Avidyā being the cause of ' name and form' is not found in the *Bhagavad Gītā;* nor again the doctrine of Māyā, which Śaṅkara's later followers have elaborated, by which they conceived that the Param Brahma, the one without attributes, who is Sat, Cit, and Ānanda becomes in some inexplicable way entangled in Māyā which is neither existent nor non-existent and thus evolves or rather degenerates into the Saguṇa Brahma or Īśvara and begins to weave the universe out of nothing. This doctrine is a travesty of the attempt of the early thinkers to find the common noumenon of Sat and Asat.

Rāmānuja on the other hand tries to whittle down all the passages where Kṛṣṇa describes this supreme noumenon, "whence speech returns along with mind, being unable to reach" this high level thought. He interprets paramdhāma as a locality, a region of space which Nārāyaṇa has delimited as his special province where he holds his court seated on his serpent throne, the hoods of the serpent acting as his royal umbrella and to which he admits his 'elect' as a matter of favour!

The teachings of the *Bhagavad Gītā* have suffered more than those of any other Indian book from the hands of the Commentator.[75] It is not cryptic in style like the Sūtras; but yet, from the great veneration paid to it on account of its supposed authorship and on account of its real superiority to every other scripture, Indian or non-Indian, so many Bhāṣya-kāras have attempted to use it for buttressing up their special theories and expended their tender mercies on it. Its teachings and its locutions, technical or otherwise have been violently tampered with by the commentators who did not possess what we call a 'literary conscience'. The commentator did not aim to discover what exactly his author thought or attempted to express, but used the text for supporting his own special theories. If any passages were inconveniently opposed to the commentators theories, they were to be explained away by utilizing grammatical and etymological tricks. Thus the *Śvetāṣ vatara Upaniṣad* is indispensable to the Vaiṣṇavas; but it sings the praises of Rudra and not Viṣṇu. Hence Rudra is explained by Raṅgarāmānuja,[76] as *Saṁsāta rujo drāvayati,* who drives away the disease of saṁsāra. *(Śvet. Up. Bhāṣ.* iii. 2). In the *Chāndogya Upaniṣad,* Janaṣruti who learns the Samvarga Vidyā from Raikva is called a Śūdra (*Ib.* iv. 2. 3), Since the Śudra is unfit for Brahma Vidyā, Śaṅkara explains that the word Śūdra *can* be etymologised as Śucādravaṇa, the rushing of grief. *(Ved. Sūt.Bhāṣ.* I. iii. 4.). *Bhagavad Gītā* xiv. *27* is explained in two possible ways by Śaṅkara. Everywhere it is a case of how inconvenient passages can be explained away and not what the original author thought. The more ingenuity displayed by the commentator, though in violation of what we nowadays regard as laws of evidence, the greater is the admiration of the devout follower. Even European scholars have quietly succumbed to the spell of Śaṅkara's verbal gymnastics so much so that Max

Muller, Deussen and Gough in translating passages from the Upaniṣads put into them matter found not in the text but only in *Śaṅkara Bhāṣya*. No interpreter of other people's thoughts, especially the thoughts of the ancients can escape reading some of his own thoughts into his author's book, but we might at least honestly strive to minimize this tendency and strenuously avoid reading a third man's thoughts also therein.

Besides this one fruitful source of confusion, another more potent one has also been operative. These different schools of Vedānta have in modern India all become orthodox revealed religion. The Vedānta being orthodox, it was felt that the other schools ought to be assimilated to it and hence the commentator has felt it necessary to furnish the Sāṅkhya, Pūrva Mīmāṁsā and Vaiśeṣika schools with God for whom Kapila, Jaimini and Kaṇāda had no place or need in their systems; to mix up the Īśvara of Yoga, the Paramātma of Nyāya and Brahma of Vedānta; to confuse the non-committal word Puruṣa of Sāṅkhya with the Jīvātmā of the *Upaniṣad;* to identify Brahma, Paramātmā, Puruṣottama and Īśvara wherever they occur in the *Bhagavad Gītā*.

This spirit has in recent times been further complicated by the necessity for extolling the Advaita at the expense of the other schools. Hence has been invented the extraordinary theory of the temporary validity of the other schools as steps leading to the Advaita, which Madhusūdana Sarasvati propounded in his *Prasthāna bheda* and Vijñāna Bhikṣu in his *Sāṅkhya Pravacana Bhāṣya*. (*Vide* Muir's Original Sanskṛt texts iii. Pp. 194-202). The immediate reality of which every one can be certain is the momentary experiences of changing states of conciousness, the kaleidoscopic changes of Cittavṛtti, Metaphysics is the attempt to classify them, pigeon-hole them under general categories which will systematize them, reduce the chaos of immediate experience into an intelligible cosmos. These cosmic ultimates must necessarily be concepts of the mind and not objective realities independent of the mind. The mind analyses its own experiences for the purpose of guiding its own function in ordered ways, so as not to be a helpless way in the buffeting of the waves of experiences and memories. The fact that different minds are attracted by different methods of metaphyshical analysis indicates that minds themselves are coloured by different temperaments and hence each self-consistent metaphysical system, if it explains all the experiences of the inquiring mind is as valid as the others. Cosmic ultimates are not material, objective realities that can be reached or acquired. There cannot possibly be any merit in devoutly believing in the 'correctness' or orthodoxy of any particular system. But each mind has to find out what system attracts it, what method of analysis appeals to it an following that method, analyse its experiences, train to distinguish its place in the cosmos, so that the enlightening consciousness bound up with it might 'free' itself from the mind in which it is involved and soar to its own levels wherefrom there is no return to bondage.

References

1. The words Sāṅkhya yoga and Karma yoga as used by Kṛṣṇa are generally misunderstood. The former not only means intellectual discipline, but also includes the Yoga of Patañjali, whereas the latter includes what are understood as the religion of humanity and as theism in Europe.
2. It is unfortunate that the word Vedānta means different things to different Indians. In this book it is invariably used to mean the doctrines of the *Upaniṣads*, the *Bhagavad Gītā* and the *Sūtras* irrespective of the sectarian differences found in the Bhāṣyas.
3. A MS. work loaned to me by Mr. Govind Dās of Benares.
4. Upaniṣad means literally 'sittinig near by.' As the sitting posture (Āsana) is absolutely necessary for the practice of most vidyās (*Ved. Sut.* IV. i. 7-10), the word Upaniṣad came to mean a-vidya or a collection of vidyās,
5. The horrible images and bloody rituals of the Nature-goddesses of the Dravidians were also adopted in this worship.
6. Innumerable Vedic passaages prove that Agni coalesced with Śiva

and Indra and Sūrya with Upendra, Viṣṇu. Kṛṣṇa's defeat of Indra might refer to this latter incident. Brahma corresponds to Vāyu as he is cosmic Prāṇa. He is identified with the atmosphere...the region of Vāyu in *Atharva Sam.* X ii. 25.

7. A Sūtra is ordinarily a series of extremely brief prose aphorisms, generally unintelligible without a Commentary. A Kārikā gives the substance of a Sūtra in verse form and is also terse. A Bhāṣya is the exposition of the supposed teachings of a Sūtra but really the teachings of the Bhāṣyakāra supported by a great wealth of argument and quotation. A Vṛtti is a further exposition of the same. A Bhaṣyakāra always strikes out an original line of thought and twists the Sūtra as he likes; but a Vṛttikāra is supposed to follow the lines of a Bhāṣya. A Vārttika is generally a Vṛtti in verse form. A Tippaṇi contains brief explanations on a Sūtra, on the lines of some Bhāṣya.

8. For fuller details regarding these works, Vide Lakṣmīdhara's comments on Saundaryalaharī, Sl. 31.

9. A Bhāṣya by Kṣemarāja. a writer of the 11th Century, A. D. on the Śiva Sūtras, supposed to have been discovered or perhaps composed in the 10th Century by Vasugupta the founder of the Īśvara Pratyabhijña system of Cashmere. This work has been edited and translated by me and published by the Theosophical Publishing Co., Adyar, Chennai.

10. A Mss. copy of this work, also called *Nityāṣoḍasikārṇavam* (the Ocean of the 16 *Nitya* goddesses) and its commentary, by Bhāskararāya, called *Setubandham* (the building of the bridge) has been kindly placed at my disposal by Dr. O. Schrader of the Adyar Library. This work is divided into two parts called *Pūrvacatuśśatī* and *Uttaracatuśśatī*. Lakṣmīdhara, a commentator on *Saundaryalaharī* says that the Vamakeśvara Tantra is a part of the *Āgama* called Bhairava yāmala. (Vide page 17 Mysore Edition of *Saundaryalaharī*.)

11. The reading of these two sentences is corrupt and the translation is unsatisfactory.

12. The proper form of this name is Lakulīśa, synonymous with Daṇḍāyudha, changed into Nakulīśa, in Eastern and Southern India.

13. Pope's Tiru-Vāśagam, p. ix.

14. *Ibid.*, p. lxxiv.

15. This and a few other Śaiva Āgamas, have been printed with Tamil commentaries in Chennai. The Mrigendra is being edited and transtated by Mr. M. Nārāyaṇaswāmi Iyer, Chennai, who kindly furnished me with advance proofs of the first xi chapters.

16. It is curious that Śaiva writers give the name Sūtra to ślokas. The *Īśvara Pratyabhijñā Sūtras* are a mixture of ślokas and Sûtras as we ordinarily understand them.

17. The five functions are in the Śakti Sūtras, of course, attributed to Her and called Ābhāsa (illumination), Rakti (coloration), Vimarśana (Examination), Bījāvasthāna (sowing the seed) and Vilāpanata (lamentation.)

18. The five mantras. *Tait. Araṇ.* x. 43. 47, called Sadyojāta, Vāmadeva, Aghora, Tatpuruṣa, and Īśāna, respectively corresponding to the five functions of creation, preservation, destruction, obscuration and liberation, are the forehead, the mouth, the heart, the guhya and the feet of Śiva.

19. The Jñāna pada of this work has been published in Channai with a Tamil commentary.

20. More commonly, Vijñānakevala, For a description of these three, *vide infra*.

21. As opposed to the rudiment of sound, Śabdatanmātra which is a product.

22. More commonly called Para.

23. Com. *Siv-Sut*. i-4.

24. The phrases 'kalā, etc', 'from kala to the earth (Kṣiti)', mean 'throughout the manifested universe'.

25. I have been able to get a mss. of the first Adhyāya of this work in Ganjam Dt.

26. *Śrīkara*'s *Bhaṣya* on *Ved Sūt*. I. i. i.

27. Each sect relies upon an unconscionable misinterpretation of some vedic text or other for legitimizing some un-vedic practice which has grown upon it. The Liṅgāyatas quote 'amṛtasyadeva

dhāraṇobhūyāsam' [*Tait. Up.* 1, 4-1] 'O God, may I possess wisdom' and interpret it to mean, 'may I wear the God'. The Śaivas besmear their body with burnt dung and support the practice by quoting, 'Bhūtyai na pramaditavyam' [*Ib.* I. ii. 1], 'Do not neglect greatness' and twisting its meaning into, 'Do not forget to besmear yourself with burnt dung'. The Vaiṣṇavas quote a phrase 'charanampavitram', meaning 'holy feet' and interpret it as referring to sacramental painting with clay and to branding. They have besides 'discovered' a whole Upaniṣad, *Gopīcandana Upaniṣad,* to uphold their elaborate painting of the body, similar to the *Bhasma Jābāla Upaniṣad* 'found' by the Śaivas.

28. *R. V.* VII 21. 5., X. 99. 3 The word has been variously interpreted, but the most probable meaning is, 'those who have śiśna for their God', or 'tailed demons'.

29. The oldest Liṅgam so far known in one discovered by my friend, Mr. T. A. Gopinatha Row in the North Arcot District. I am indebted to him for a description of this superlatively realistic idol which must be much older than he is willing to allow. He has also sent me a photograph of Liṅgam, which for obvious reasons cannot be published here.

"The temple of Paraśurāmeśvara in which the strangely realistic Phallus (Lingam) is set up, is situated in the village of Gudimallam six miles north of Renigunta, a station on the Chennai Railway line. One of the inscriptions belonging to the temple informs us that it was completely reconstructed in the 9th year of the reign of Vikrama Coladeva (1126 A. D.). The present structure is not after the common model of the period to which it belongs. Tho Vimāna [dome over the idol] has the so-called Gajapṛṣṭhakṛti. A close study of the plan and sections whereof, hereunder given, would warrant the conclusion that the architect had distinctly in view the shape of the Liṅga and hence the vimāna might be better styled the Liṅga kṛti-vimāna."

"Again the Liṅga of this temple is, as has been already stated, a most remarkable one in that it is an exact copy of the *phallus* and has the various portions shaped very accurately. It has been made out of a hard igneous rock of a dark brown colour, samples of which are found near the Tirumala hills. The Liṅga and the image of Śiva carved on its front side are very highly polished. Unlike the later representation, the image of Siva has been made with only a pair of hands, the right carrying a ram by its hind legs and the left holding a water-vessel. A battle-axe rests on his left shoulder (from which perhaps he derives his name of Paraśurāmeśvara) and there is the usual matted and twisted hair (Jata) on his head. He is standing on the shoulders of a rākṣasa, whom the sculptor has represented with a pair of animal ears. The Liṅga is the only one of its kind in Southern India and from its sculpture it might be set down to about the 2nd or 3rd century A. D. Compare this image with the picture of a yakṣa given on page 36 of Grunwedel's "Buddhist Art in India" as translated by Gibbson and Burgess. The face, the ears and ear-ornaments, the arms and the ornaments on them, the necklace, the arrangement of drapery, particularly the big folds that descend between the two legs—all these are identically similar in both the image of Śiva of Gudimallam and the Yakṣa of the book referred to above.

"The temple has several old inscriptions the earliest of which is dated the last quarter of the 8th century. All of these inscriptions call the place in which the temple is situated, Tiruvir-Piramapeḍu, and is said to be in the Śilaināḍu belonging to the Tiruveṅgaḍakkoṭam, a province of the Western Vaḍuga country ruled over by the Mahābali- Bāṇarayas, the powerful feudatories of the Pallavas of Kāñci. Guḍimallam now belongs to the Kālahasti Zamindari and is a petty village."

30. For fuller details of this work, see my introduction to my English translation of it.

31. The following scheme of dates of the writers of the Kashmir school and Guruparamparā, indicated by vertical lines, is mostly based on Buhler's investigation.

Vasugupta, discovered *Śiva Sūtras,* 8th cent. A. D.

↓

Śa, contemp. of Avantivarman, 854 A. D.

↓

Somānandanātha, cir. 900 A. D.

↓

1. Utpala, cir. 930 A. D.

↓

2. Nārāyaṇa, Trivikrama (?)

↓

Lakṣmaṛuṇa Gupta, cir. 950 A. D.

↓

Abhinava Gupta, 993-1015 A. D.

↓

Kṣemarāja 1030 A. D.

(Sometimes called Kṣemendra, to be distinguished from contemporary, Kṣemendra Vyāsadāsa, author of works on Alaṅkāra, some Tales and other works.)

Bhāskara. Rāmakaṇṭha.

32. This word 'idamtā' can be compared with 'haecceitas' of Duns Scotus.

33. It is noteworthy that Gauḍapāda is scarcely a proper name; it is a descriptive epithet, the reverend Gauḍa.

34. Even in Kālidāsa's time the Āgamas were so prevalent that he complains of their manifoldness. V. *Raghuvaṁśa*. X.26.

35. Where they are called Karaṇakamma.

36. He transcends the three guṇas of matter but is the possessor of six guṇas explained *infra*.

37. This passage and the succeeding verses not quoted here show a striking resembance in ideas and phraseology to the description of Param Brahma in *Bhagavadgīta* Chap, xiii, showing that both are derived from the same original Āgama source.

38. Described in the *Puruṣa Sūkta*.

39. It is noteworthy that the word saccidānanda, so frequently used in the postśaṅkara advaita schools as the description of Param Brahma occurs in this Āgama text and, so far as I have been able to search, *not* found in the *Śaṅkara Bhāṣya* on Bādrayaṇa's Sūtras. This shows that advaita, like viśiṣṭādvaita, derived a fresh accession of doctrines and ideas from the Āgamas, after it passed from the founder to the later teachers. Among the Upaniṣads, this expression first occurs in the *Nṛsiṁha Tāpanī* and *Rāma*

Tāpanī, which are, apparently earlier than the time of Vidyāraṇya and later than that of Rāmānuja.

40. The six Guṇas, to be Carefully distinguished from the three Guṇas of matter, are Jñāna, Bala, Aiśvarya, Vīrya, Śakti and Tejas or Ojas and will be presently discussed.

41. These lines are a little obscure. The relation between Viṣṇu and Lakṣmī is that between noumenon and phenomenon or abstract and concrete, corresponding to the Prakāśa and Vimarśa of the Śākta schools.

42. Sṛṣṭi sthiti saṁhṛti tirobhāva, anugraha.

43. Each act of concious life is a manifestation of my power,

44. Compare the quotations in the *Spandapradīpikā* with those in the *Tattvatrayam.*

45. (1) Gross elements (2) subtle elements (3) jñānendriyas (4) Karmendriyas (5) antaḥkaraṇa.

46. In the Vaiṣṇava tradition, the sūris are beings who were never bound.

47. *R.V.I.* 22. 20. *Ait Brāḥ.* I. i. i.

48. *Āśval.-Śr. Sūt.* iv. 2.

49. The Puruṣa Sūkta and the Gāyatrī, which every orthodox Hindu recites daily in his worship were also used in ancient times in the Puruṣamedha, when the human victim was bound and about to be immolated. *Śat. Brāh. XIII.* 6. 2, 9,2.

The following chronological note has been furnished by Mr. Gopinatha Row.

That side of the Viṣṇu-cult which concerned itself with temple worship became popular in Southern India in the age of the 12 Ālvārs, Vaiṣṇava saints [of assorted castes] who lived between the 6th and 9th cent. A. D. and produced Tamil literature collected as the four thousand verses *(Nālāyira prabandham)* and fixed as the sacred Tamil Vaiṣṇava canon by Nātha-Muni, who lived in the reign of Rājarāja I and the earlier Rājendra-Coladeva I (985-1030 A. D.) His grandson, Ālavandār, otherwise, Yāmuna wrote the *Siddhi-trayam,* the first exposition of the fundamental ideas of the Viśiṣṭādvaita Vedānta, as well as *āgama-*

prāmāṇyam and thus paved the way for the amalgamation of the Vaiṣṇava Āgama and the Vedānta teachings. Rāmānuja lived from 1055-1137 A. D. Pūrṇa-prajña, otherwise Mādhva is said to have been born in 1206 A.D. The third in descent from him was Narahari-tīrtha, Dewan Regent of Kaliṅga, (Orissa) during the minority of Vīra Nārasimha Deva. His successor, Akṣobhyatīrtha was a contemporary of Vidyāraṇya, like the two well-known expounders of Rāmānuja, Vedānta Deśika and Pillai Lokācārya. Akṣobhya's disciple, Jayatīrtha is the greatest among the expounders of the Mādhva cult. From Akṣobhya there arose a branch, the first member of which was Kṛṣṇa Caitanya, the prophet of Bengal. Vallabha, the founder of the Kṛṣṇa-Bhakti cult, a Telugu Brahman of the Nellore District, was a contemporary of Kṛṣṇa Davarāya of the Vijayanagaram dynasty (1500-1527 A. D.) and a contemporary of a late Mādhva teacher, Vyāsatīrtha.

The Śaiva temple-cult spread among the Tamils more extensively than the corresponding Viṣṇu-cult and gave birth to a more extensive Tamil literature. The Tamil Śaiva saints, Śivanaḍiyārs, were 63 in number. The greatest of them was Tiruñana Sambandha, who converted the powerful Pāṇḍya King, Kūn Pāṇḍya from the Jaina to the Śaiva cult. Śaṅkarācārya, who lived in the later half of the 8th. century refers to Sambandha as Draviḍa ṣiṣu *(Saundaryalaharī,* sl. 75). Hence Saṁbandha and his very militant friend, Appar, (or Vāgīśar) who conducted a vigorus crusade against the Jaina religion must have lived and worked about 650 A. D. Another famous Śaiva teacher, Sundaramūrti lived about 850 A. D. He was a protege of Narasinga Munaiyaraiyan of Naḍu Nāḍu (in the South Arcot Dt.). The Tamil songs of these a Śiva Saints are called *Tevāram.* About 100 years later lived Mānikka vā śagar, author of *Tirurāśagam,* edited and translated by Dr. G. U. Pope. Nīlakaṇṭha wrote a Bhāṣya of the Vedāntasūtras to suit the tenets of the Śaiva Siddhānta, and it is called Śaiva Viśiṣṭādvaita Bhāṣya. Meikaṇḍa, (1236 A D.) and Umāpati Śivācārya, (1313 A. D.) wrote voluminous Tamil works expounding the same.

The following note has been furnished by my friend Mr V. Venkayya, Govt. Epigraphist, Ootacamund.

The Nānaghāta inscription begins with invocations to Indra Saṅkarṣaṇa, Vāsudeva, Yama, Varuṇa and Kubera.

The worship of Bhagavat Saṅkarṣaṇa and Vāsudeva and a Vaiṣṇava temple are mentioned in a still earlier inscription. *Ind. Ant.* Vol. XVIII, p. 190.

That the worship of Śiva is more ancient than the time of the founder of Buddhism is rendered probable by the tradition that the Śākyas were worshippers of Śiva. The Chinese pilgrim Hiouen Tsang was shown near the eastern gate of Kapilavastu the old temple of Īśvara, where the infant Siddhār that was taken by his father, because "the Śākya children who here seek divine protection always obtain what they ask. According to the legend the stone image then raised itself and saluted the prince. That this legend is very ancient is proved by the fact that the scene is represented on the Amarāvati stūpa *(Ep. Ind.* V. 3.) which has probably to be assigned to the Maurya Period.

50. Bodas, in his introduction to the *Tarka Saṁgraha* p. 30-31 has proved that *Vaiś. Sūt.* I. i. 4. is an interpolation made later than the age of Śrīdhara, the author of *Nyāya Kandali* (991 A. D).

51. The Vedic etymology, he who bides (-ī) in this strong hold (pur) *(Śat. Brāh.* xiii. 6. 2.1.) is fanciful.

52. The Ṛṣis were originally 'rune-masters'.

53. *e. g. R. V. X.* 103-8-12.

54. *e. g., R. V. I.* 162, 3.

55. Dattātreya is also said to have done the same work perhaps in another age. *Māgha* xiv. 79.

56. Probably the first *Yajurveda* referred to in the *Viṣṇu Purāṇa* contained the Mantras of the other priests till Vyāsa compiled separate manuals for the different classes of priests. Even now the *lack Yajur Veda* is a confused mass of Saṁhitā and Brāhmaṇa, which Yājñavalkya separated into the *Vājasaneya Saṁhitā* and *Śatapatha Brāhmaṇa* which together form the *WhiteYajur Veda.*

57. The elaborate series of house rites, from Garbhādhānam to Sapiṇḍīkaraṇam, which are the chief relics of Vedic ceremonies still fairly common among the 'twice-born' form the so-called

Smārta Karma, while the Yajñas are the Śrauta, though the Mantras accompanying both belong to the same age. The Mantras of the former, collected in groups called Mantrapāṭha or Mantrapraśna were floating hymns from ancient times and, of course, never formed part of the Trayī which was compiled for purposes of Yajña, and are hence generally regarded as Khila, fragments of a supposed lost canon.

58. Well does this explain Krishna's stinging description of the followers of the veda as 'avipaścita,' uninspired *(Bh. Gītā.* ii. 42). Milking a cow and plating a pot on fire required so much adulation of the Gods and abject fear of them!

59. Col Jacob has published a collection of them under the name *Laukika nyayāñjali.*

60. Mīmāṁsā, both Pūrva and Uttara is still called Nyāya. Mādhava speaks of Jaiminiya Nyāyamālā and Vaiyāsika Nyāyamālā. The Nyāya of Gotama is a development of the same humble and popular Nyāyas but on rationalistic lines.

61. Buddhi, intellection, is a function and not an organ according to Mīmāṁsakas and Naiyāyikas.

62. Another classification of Vidhis is (1) Apūrva Vidhi referring to what is unknown, e. g. 'One desirous of heaven should sacrifice' (2) Niyama Vidhi referring to what is only partially explained, *e. g.* 'he beats the paddy,' meaning, hunks it. (3) Parisaṁkhyā Vidhi, excluding one of two alternatives This classification has nothing to do with the four main classes of Vidhis mentioned in the text.

63. It is noteworthy how the relation between Mantras and Brāhamaṇas became reversed in the time of Jaimini, thus showing the enormous antiquity of the Mantras. Jaimini's conception of the Veda as primarily dealing with Dharma can apply only to stray sentences in the Brāhmaṇa and not at all to the mantras. Hence amantra is degraded to the position of a sentence which cleverly described a sacrificial action or serves to remind one of it *(Mim, Sūt. II. i. 31-32).* Instead of the Brāhmaṇa being an adjunct to the Mantra, it is the reverse; the Mantras exist so as to a contrast to the ancient view of the Mantras as a force impelling the Gods,

making the Gods themselves grow in strength *(R.V.* vi. 17 13, vi. 44-1 3) !

64. For further discussion of these terms the reader is referred to Dr. Thibaut's edition of the *Arthasaṅgraha,* of which the above it a condensation.

65. Of. *Saṅkh Kār,* vii. The fact that Saukṣmyāt is placed at the head of the list of the causes of invisibity herd shows that Sabara does not quite from Īśvara Kṛṣṇa but from Sāṅkhya Sūtra now unknown.

66. An incomplete mss. copy of this work with Śeṣa Govinda's commentary thereon was kindly placed at my disposal by Mr. Paravastu Raṅganāthasvami proprietor of the Ārṣa Library, Vizagapatam.

67. Explained by Śeṣa Govinda to be the Samavāya of the Vaiśeṣikas. "It has beginning and ending. No sensible man will hold that when the material is either destroyed or not produced, the relation can remain independent of the material." Herein the Prābhākaras differ from the Vaiśeṣikas.

68. *Ny, Sūt.* ii. 81 ff. *Vai. Sū.* vi. 1. 1; *Sāṇ. Sūt. v.* 4. ff.

69. The motion of the organs of speech is what is here called the sound that is the object of the organs of speech. The sound hoard in the ear is the round that is the object of the sense of hearing.

70. This name has been translated 'the song celestial', 'the Lord's song', etc., though there is absolutely no lyrical touch in it. This translation is perhaps due to reminiscences of 'the song of Solomon', and the early life of the boy Kṛṣna and his flute-playing described in the *Bhāgavata purāṇa* and the *Gītagovinda.* The *Bhagavad Gītā* is the 'divine poem'; or rather 'the proclamation, in verse, by the Lord.'

71. Hence it has lent itself to the tortures of the Bhāṣyakāras who have commented on it each from only one point of view. All existing translations, too, have been done consciously or unconsciously only from the point of view of one the three great modern sects—- Śaṅkara, Rāmānujīya and Mādhva.

72. In the previous Stanza, Kṛṣṇa has been speaking of the mortal and immortal Puruṣas, "loke," which word may mean either "in

this world," or as in xv. 18, in the Śāstras not based on the Veda, as the rationalistic Yoga or Nyāya.

73. The various interpretations of this śloka are discussed in my forthcoming *Study of the Bhagavad Gītā.*

74. In opposition to the world supported by the Īśvara referred to in xv. 12.

75. e. g., ii. 16. has been so done to death that it is impossible to discover what its author meant thereby.

76. A recent Vaiṣṇava commentator of the Upaniṣad who slavishly follows Śaṅkara, except where Viśiṣṭādvaita points have to be driven in Rāmānuja did not comment on the Upaniṣads.

CHAPTER - III

THE WORLD-PROCESS

The question of the nature of the world-process, what kind of change in the material of the universe underlies its endless Becoming has also been variously answered. The material of which any substance is made is called Upādāna Kāraṇam; we have seen in the last chapter that the material of the world is held by the Nyāya-Vaiśeṣika school to be heterogeneous— nine different substances going to make up the cosmos. All the other schools teach that the material cause of the world is homogeneous, the Sāṅkhya-Yoga regarding it as unconscious matter and the rest as conscious Brahma. Hence have arisen two opposed theories, called the Ārambha-vāda, the theory of atomic combination and the Pariṇāmavāda, the theory of transmutation. The former theory holds the atoms of matter, *i. e.* of elemental earth, water, fire and air to be Ārambha Upādānam, lit. originating material, material which originates all objects of the world without losing each its own specific nature, just as yarn, when woven into cloth still retains its own character as yarn. In the other theory the cause of the world is Pariṇāma Upādānam, material which undergoes transmutation, *i. e.,* loses its distinctive character when evolving into objects, just as milk loses its character as milk when it becomes curd, as the flower is no more the flower when it becomes the fruit.

This divergence of theory with regard to the nature of the world-process necessarily led to a difference of view with regard to the relation of cause and effect. The Nyāya-Vaiśeṣikas hold the Asatkāryavāda, the theory of the non-existence of the cause in the effect, and the other schools hold the opposite theory—the Satkāryavāda, the identity of cause and effect, the potential pre-existence of the effect in the cause.

(A) ĀRAMBHA VĀDA

Kaṇāda, in *Vaiś*. *Sūt*. VII. ii. 7. says, "causal and effected substances are not one and identical, because unity and identity are not cognized between them." Yarn is the cause of the cloth into which it is woven but we cognize yarn as different from cloth. The connection of cause and effect is hence one of coinherence, Samavāya. "That is coinherence whence (we say) of cause and effect, this is here." *Ib.* VII. ii. 26. The con-junction of a thread and a pot on which it lies is accidental, but that of a mat and the grass blades of which it is constituted in Samavāya coinherence. "A substance is said to be a cause on account of its inhering in its effects." *Ib. X.* ii, 1. The ultimate substances of the universe are the causes of all objects, which are produced by their conjunctions. These constituent substances preserve each its own qualities but yet combine to produce objects with qualities previously non-existent. "An effect is non-existent previous (to its being produced) because actions and qualities cannot be predicated of it." *Ib.* IX. i. 1.

The same subject is referred to by Gautama in the *Nyāya Sūtras* IV. 48-50. The first of these Sūtras explains the opponent's view, (Pūrvapakṣam) and the succeeding two, the view of the author of the Sūtras (Sīddhāntam). They run as follows:—

(The effect, before it is produced,) is neither non-entity, nor entity, nor again entity-non-entity because entity and non-entity are incongruous." *Ny. Sūt* IV. 48. On this Vātsyāyana comments thus:—"Before (an effect is) produced, the effect to be produced cannot be a non-entity, because of the necessity of the material, *i.e.*, a particular material is used for producing a particular object; all materials do not produce all objects. Hence it cannot be held to be a non-entity. It is not an entity; because it is not admissible to predicate existence of that which is produced, before its production. It is not an entity-non-entity, because entity and non-entity are incompatible with each other, for entity is the admission of an object and non-entity is the denial of an object. These two are opposed to each other and not the same". This argument is refuted by Gautama in the next two sūtras. "That which is produced is truly a non-entity before its production, because both its production and destruction are witnessed by us" (*Ib.* 49). "(Though the effect before its production) is a non-entity, it is determined by the mind.", *i. e.* conceived by the mind. (*Ib.* 50).

This fundamental position of the Vaiśeṣika and the Nyāya Schools was forced on them by their scientific (as opposed to metaphysical) temper. When we deal with the actual objects of the universe, analyse and reconstruct them, we find that qualities which do not exist in the constituents appear when an object is constituted out of them and that therefore the Asatkāryavāda rests on a solid basis of experimental fact. That in the later developments of Indian philosophy, this theory was eclipsed by the rival one of the Satkāryavāda was due to the fact that the foundations of science laid by the Vaiśeṣikas and Naiyāyikas of old were overlaid with a load of verbal gymnastics and dull dialectics, just as in Europe, the science of ancient Greece was choked out of life by the logic of the Schoolmen. But that the Asatkāryavāda itself is a valid concept, accepted by modern science is proved by the following extracts from Sir Oliver Lodge's *Life and Matter.* " A property can be possessed by an aggregation of atoms which no atom possesses in the slightest degree." (*Ib.* p,. 91) "It must not be thought that aggregation only produces quantitative change and leaves quality unaltered. Fresh qualities altogether are liable to be introduced or to make their appearance at certain stages—critical stages—in the building up of a complex mass." (*Ib.* p. 186.) "It may be said that a sun differs from a dark planet only in size; for it is just the fact of great size which enables its gravitative shrinkage and earthquake-subsidence to generate an immense quantity of heat and to maintain the mass for eons at an excessively high temperature, thereby fitting it to become the centre of light and life to a number of worlds. The blaze of the sun is a property which is the outcome of its great mass. A small permanent sun is an impossibility. Wherefore, properties can be possessed by an aggregate or assemblage of particles which in the particles themselves did not in the slightest degree exist" (*Ib.* pp. 72-3).

The Nyāya-Vaiśeṣika theory of the production of the cosmos by perpetual conjunctions and disjunctions of atomic as well as non-atomic substances is called Arambha-vāda. The basic axiom of the *Vaiśeṣika Sūtras* is "Dravyāṇi dravyāntaram ārabhante" (*Ib.* I. i. 10), substances originate other substances, without themselves being destroyed. Probably as Rāmānuja points out in his *Śrī Bhāṣya,* II. i. 15, the word ārabh is ā + labh, to touch, to grasp and the Vaiśeṣika conception of the essential cosmic process is that the elementary substances embrace one another to form objects and while such a conjunction lasts, a new property is produced; when an object is destroyed, the atoms are disjoined, that property disappears and the atoms are free to form fresh conjunctions. This conception is the same as the picture of the behaviour of atoms in the atomic theory of modern chemistry.

The atoms were conceived as "round, extremely minute, invisible, incapable of division, eternal in themselves but not in their aggregate forms" (Davies, *Hindu Philosophy,* p. 128). They were called aṇu (atom) or paramāṇu (ultimate atom). The combination of two atoms constitues a dvyaṇuka, (two-atom), or molecule. Molecules combine into objects.

The formation and destruction of the various objects of the universe is due to the conjunctions and disjunctions of the four kinds of atoms. The following account of the evolution of a red baked claypot out of a black unbaked one is taken from *Siddhānta Muktāvalī* and given as a specimen of the degeneration to which the valid Vaiśeṣika ideas attained for want pursuing them with the help of 'the experimental method of modern science. 'From conjunction with fire an action (is produced) in the ultimate atoms which exist combined as dvayaṇukas, molecules, (of the unbaked pot); thence a disjunction of the ultimate atoms from each other; thence the destruction of the conjunction which had produced (the molecule); thence the destruction of the molecule; thence the destruction of the blackness (of the ultimate atom); then the origination of red etc. (in the ultimate atom); thence the action auxiliary to the production (ārambha) of a (new) object; thence disjunction (of the atom from the space it occupied temporarily); thence the destruction of the previous conjunction (with space soon after its reduction to the state of ultimate atoms); thence the conjunction (of the atoms) to produce (the red baked pot;) thence the production of molecules (dvayaṇukas); thence the origin of red etc. (in the molecule)". This maze of words constructed by unrestricted ingenuity satisfies the cravings of the modern Hindu Nyāya- Vaiśeṣika philosopher and does duty for physics in his studies. Endless disputations displaying a diabolical ingenuity beguile his tedium and satisfy his instinct for physical research!

Who started this complicated dance of the atoms? It has been pointed out in the last chapter that the Sūtras of Kaṇāda do not contemplate a supreme creator. The question then arises, who first set the atoms in motion and started the world process. Kaṇāda occupies an agnostic position with regard to this. He proves the existence of an adṛṣṭā, unseen, cause of some actions. These are actions other than that due to an impulse (*e. g.*, the action of fire on a bamboo), an impact (e. g., the action of an axe), or a conjunction (*e. g.*, of a harness with a horse). These latter three actions are explicable, referable to a known agency. There are actions other than these, caused by an unseen cause. (*Vaiś Sūt*. V. ii. 2), like circulation of sap in trees, (*Ib*. 7). "The upward flaming of fire, the sideward motion of wind, the first action of atoms and of manas are due to an unseen cause". (*Ib*. 13.) Kaṇāda thus deliberately avoids predicating a cause of creation. Praśastapāda teaches the orthodox modern Hindu theory of creation by Brahmā and destruct by Śiva. "At the end of one hundred years of the measure of Brahmā, He reaches the time of his release. Then Maheśvara, the Lord of all the worlds desires to destroy (all beings) so that all living beings that are troubled in saṁsāra may enjoy a night's rest. Then cease the functions of all the adṛṣṭā (unseen, potential result of acts) of all beings, that causes the bodies, sense-organs and great elements. Then, by the action of the desire of Maheśvara and the union of Ātmā and the atoms, is produced a disjunction of the atoms that produce the body and the sense-organs. Hence their union ceases and they become destroyed and sink back into Paramāṇus (ultimate atoms). Similarly, of the great elements—Earth, water, fire and air, by the same cause, each is destroyed and absorbed into the following one. Then the disjoined ultimate atoms alone remain. Then Ātmās remain with the potential deposit of their good and bad deeds attached to them. Afterwards, for the experience of the living beings, (is born) the desire of Maheśvara to create. Then the adṛṣṭā resumes its functions in all Ātmās. By the support of this adṛṣṭā and the union of Ātmā and atoms, an action is produced in the ultimate atoms of Air. They become mutually conjoined into a molecule of two-atoms etc., in proper order. Thus is produced a great wind which moves in the Ākāśa. Then therein similarly a great ocean of water is produced by the atoms of water and it flows in a great flood. Then in that very ocean by the ultimate atoms of earth, conjoining in the regular order into molecules etc., a great earth is produced and remains firm. Then in that very ocean by the atoms of fire is produced in the order of molecules etc. a great collection of rays of fire which remains burning. When these four great elements are thus born, by the mere will of the Supreme Īśvara, a huge sphere is born from the atoms of fire supported by the atoms of Earth. Therein He creates Brahmā, with four lotus-faces the grandfather of all the universe as well as the worlds and commands Him to create all beings. Being commanded by Maheśvara, Brahmā possessed of wonderful knowledge, dispassion and power knows the fruits of the acts of all beings and creates his sons—the mind-born

Prajāpatis, Manu, the Devas, the Ṛṣis and the pitṛs, the four castes from his face, arms thighs and feet, and all other beings high and low, each endowed with knowledge, enjoyment and length of life according to their Karma. He endows them with virtue, knowledge, dispassion and power, each according to his desire" (*Praśast. Bhā.* Mumbai Edn., p. 18-19).

It was also pointed out in the last chapter that the Nyāya Sūtras conceive of God as the cause of the distribution of the fruits of action, because such fruits are not always visible soon after the action. A definite refutation of all atheistic systems was undertaken by Udayana, the great teacher of Nyāya, in his *Kusumāñjali,* probably written in the 12th century. This book is remarkable in that it is the only Sanskrit theological book solely and directly dealing with the question of the existence of God, like the numerous European books on the subject, by the Schoolmen and by Protestant theologians, it is divided into five chapters, each chapter being regarded a cluster of Kusuma flowers. In the first chapter Udayana establishes that there is an adṛṣṭa, an unseen cause of events of the world. Thus far Kaṇāda went but Udayana goes one step further, by blending the Nyāya with the Vaiśeṣika position and pointing out that adṛṣṭāa cannot operate as a cause, except by means of the concurrent energy of Īśvara *(Kusumāñjali* i. 18. 19). He, then, demolishes the atheism of the Mīmāṁsā by pointing out that as right knowledge of the Veda requires an external source, since even the Veda is destroyed during pralaya and it has to be repromulgated at creation, Īśvara is proved to be the source of traditional knowledge. *(Ib.* ii. 1). He then meets the arguments that are generally used to prove the non-existence of God from the six methods of testimony, perception (pratyakṣa), inference (anumāna), analogy (upanāna), tradition (śabda), presumption (arthāpatti), and non-perception (anupalabdhi). The general trend of the argument here is that as the various methods of proof themselves depend on Him for their validity they are paralysed by "looking into His face" and though they are unable to prove His existence, they are enough to disprove arguments against it. (*Ib.* III. 23.) Udayana then disproves the Mīmāṁsā argument that even if God existed, he could not be a source of right knowledge, for this consists in knowing what was not known before. He rebuts this by defining right knowledge to be intuitive unerring perception. *(Ib.* IV. 6.) Finally Udayana offers eight positive arguments. "From effects[1], combination, sustenance, traditional arts, traditional knowledge, Śruti, texts and number (underlying creation), can be proved an omniscient, eternal Being". (*Ib.* V. 1) Thus was the Nyāya-Vaiśeṣika once for all wedded to theism and it continues to affect modern Indian thought chiefly through the Śaiva and Vaiṣṇava sects.

(B) PARIṆĀMA VĀDA

The Sāṅkhya, the Yoga, the Vedānta, and the Āgama schools conceive of the relation of cause and effect differently. They maintain the Satkāryavāda, the theory that the effect exists in an unmanifested form in the cause. The following five arguments are given in the *Sāṅkhya Kārikā* ix, to uphold the theory that the effect exists antecedent to its manifestation, (1) A non-existent thing cannot be produced. Oil cannot be pressed out of sand. (2) To produce every effect we take an appropriate material. For making curd we take milk, not water. (3) Any effect does not result from any cause. (4) An agent does only what it is able to do. (5) The effect has the same nature as the cause. Cloth has the same nature as the threads of which it is woven. The Sāṅkhya thus reverses the Vaiśeṣika view. The latter holds that the thread coinheres in the cloth; therefore the cloth which did not exist before its production, has been originated by its cause, the thread. The former holds that the cloth inheres in the thread in an unmanifested form before its production and its production is therefore but the manifestation of a latent object.

The *Vedānta Sūtras* devote a section (adhikaraṇa) to the Satkāryavāda, the doctrine of the identity of cause and effect. "That they (cause and effect) are not different (is to be inferred) from the words "*Origin,* etc." (*lb* II. i. 14). The word *'origin'* is found in *Ch. Up.* VI, i. 4., "As my dear, by one lump of clay all that is made of clay is known, the change being a name having *its 'origin'* in speech." The next Sūtras (15-16) give further reasons. "From perception (of the cause) when (the effect) exists"[2]. "From the later existing (in the original cause)"; in the sentence 'This, my dear, in the beginning was but Sat', *(Ch. Up.* VI. ii. i.), it is said that this evolved world was in the beginning merely the causal entity, in other words, the effect was concealed in the cause. The Āgama schools also accept the Satkāryavāda generally; though they seldom discuss this fundamental question of philosophy.

The Satkāryavāda—the concept of the "persistence of the really existent", underlies all philosophy, ancient and modern. "Whatever really and fundamentally *exists* must, so far as bare existence is concerned, be independent of time. It may go through many changes, and thus have a history; that is to say, must have definite time-relations, so far as changes are concerned; but it can hardly be thought of as either going out of existence, or as coming into existence, at any given period, though it may completely change its form and accidents; every thing basal must have a past and a future of some kind or other, though any special concatenation or arrangement may have a date of origin and of destruction..............The thing that *is,* both *was* and *shall be"* (Lodge. *Life and Matter,* pp. 101-3).

Both the Satkāryavāda and the Asat kāryavada, though opposed to each other as theories are not necessarily mutually exclusive when used for explaining the cosmos. Explanation is a mental attempt to form a picture of what is outside the mind. An explanation must be self-consistent; otherwise it fails; but a self-consistent explanation should not be imagined to include *the whole of the facts* of the cosmos we try to understand.

It is noteworthy that this old world dispute between the Satkāryavāda and Asatkāryavāda rages to-day in an acute form among the biologists. Are variations that underlie evolution due to innate causes, but manifestations of latent qualities? Or do they arise from something like a chemical combination of the germ and the sperm plasms? Do they evolve as response to environment? Or are they due to spontaneous impulsion? How far are the characteristics due to heredity? What are the limits of educability? All these questions are being discussed on the basis of one assumption or the other.

From the Satkāryavāda it follows that the world material becomes gradually transmuted into various forms to produce the succession of phenomena that forms the evolution of the world. This theory is called the Pariṇāmavāda, the theory of evolution or transmutation, for the noumenon of the object is Pariṇāma Upādānam, material that changes form and not Arambha Upādānam, originating material.

1. SAṄKHYA

The material that according to the Sāṅkhya (and the Yoga) undergoes transformation to produce the world is homogeneous Pradhāna or Mūlaprakṛti. The impulse that sets Pradhāna in motion cannot be a supreme Person; "because an intelligent person engages in actions either for his own gain or on account of benevolence; these (motives) cannot apply to the creation of the world which therefore cannot be due to an intelligent person. God, who can have no desires unfulfilled, can desire to gain nothing from the creation of the world. Nor can his engaging himself in creation be due to benevolence; for, before creation, jīvas have no sense-organs, bodies, objects (and hence cannot experience pain); in the absence of pain, how can there be a benevolent desire to remove it? If (we say that) benevolence rises on observing pain after creation, (we commit) the fault of arguing in a circle, (inferring) creation from benevolence and benevolence from creation" (Vācaspati Miśra, *Tattva Kaumudī,* 255). Therefore the impulse to creation is a blind, unintelligent impulse. "As the unconscious milk flows (of itself from the cow) for the nourishment of the calf, so Pradhāna begins to evolve for the release of Puruṣa (*Saṅ. Kār.* lvi). The mere contiguity of the cow and the calf is enough to set the milk flowing from the cow: so the mere contiguity of Puruṣa and Prakṛti causes a movement in the latter. Then there results "a union of both, like that of a lame man (mounted on the back of) a blind man. Hence starts creation." *(Ib.* xxi.). Puruṣa is lame, having no powers of action : Pradhāna is blind as it does not possess the illumination of consciousness. When they are united, "thence, on account of that union, the unconscious seems to be characterized by consciousness; though the guṇas act, the inactive (Puruṣa) becomes as if he were an actor." (*Ib.* xx.). The first result of the union is the disturbance of the inert condition in which the three guṇas subsist during Pralaya when matter is avyakta, unmanifest. They blend with each other in varying proportions and thus the course of evolution (Sañcara) is started. This evolution runs in three parallel lines—the cosmic, the individual and the objective or the adhidaivata, the adhyātma and adhibhūta.

The first product (vikāra) of Pradhāna from its union with Puruṣa is Buddhi, cosmic or individual. It is the first result of the reflection of the intelligence of the Puruṣa on unintelligent Pradhāna, of the first cancellation of the contrast and distinction between pure subjectivity and pure objectivity. It is the certitude (adhyavasāya) caused by the identification of the subject with the object which underlies all mental processes. "In cognition in a single act the contrast is virtually superseded as regards both the one-sidedness of subjectivity and the one-sidedness of objectivity. At first, however, the supersession of the contrast is but implicit. The process as such is in consequence immediately infected with the finitude of this sphere, and splits into the two-fold movement of the instinct of reason, presented as two different movements. On the one hand it supersedes the one-sidedness of the Idea's subjectivity by receiving the existing world into itself, into subjective conception and thought, and with this objectivity which is thus taken to be real and true for its content it fills up the abstract certitude of itself. On the other hand, it supersedes the one sidedness of the objective world, which is now, on the contrary, estimated as only a mere semblance, a collection of contingencies and shapes at bottom visionary. It modifies and informs that world by the inward nature of the subjective, which is here taken to be the genuine objective. The former is the instinct after truth, cognition properly so called: the theoretical action of the idea. The latter is the instinct of the Good to fulfil the same, the practical activity of the idea or volition." (*Logic of Hegel, Wall.*, p. 363). Buddhi, thus, is the root of the universe and cosmic Buddhi, Brahmā[3] is the world-creator. Kṛṣṇa speaking in the *Bhagavadgītā* as the cosmic Puruṣa says "To me, Mahat-Brahmā is the Yoni; therein I set the germ; thence the birth of all beings, O Bhārata. Of the beings of all forms arising in all wombs, O Kaunteya, Brahma-mahat is the Yoni, I the father, giver of the seed" (XIV. 2-3).

From Buddhi is evolved, Ahaṁkāra, the organ of self-consciousness and (necessarily) of other-consciousness. After the first faint glimmering of differentiated consciousness comes the stage when the individual identifies himself with the definite portion of space occupied by his body (gross or subtle) and says, 'this is I', 'that is not-I'. Now Ahaṁkāra is developed; the relative consciousness which alone all of us are familiar with, becomes possible. This Ahaṁkāra is a function of matter, for till the Puruṣa identifies himself with a portion of matter and regards other portions of matter as outside himself, the cognitions of I and of Not-I cannot be experienced. This is true as much of the cosmic Gods as of the individual man and of the hosts of animals which stand below man in their evolution. Cosmic Ahaṁkāra is Rudra. The highest development of self-consciousness in man is union with Rudra. Hence Śaṅkarācārya makes the refrain of most of his Śiva Stotras, "Śivoham," (I am Śiva), "Śivaḥkevaloham", (I am pure Śiva), "Pratyagātmā Śivoham", (I am Śiva, the ego of introspective meditation).

From the Ahaṁkāra develop the eleven organs in the Adhyātma (individual) and the corresponding deities in the Adhidaiva and also the Adhibhūta (objective universe). The Taijasa (bright) Ahaṁkāra develops into the deities. The Sāttvic or Vaikhārika Ahaṁkāra acted on by Rajas produces the Manas, the five sense-organs, and the five action organs, making up the eleven organs. The Tāmasa Ahaṁkāra, dark egoism, becomes transformed into the five tanmātras (*Ib.* xxiv, xxv). Thus is started the triple line of evolution the whole scheme of which is given below in tabular form.

	Adhyātma (individual)	**adhidaiva (cosmic)**	**adhibhūta (objective)**
1.	Buddhi	Brahmā	Certitude
2.	Ahaṁkāra	Rudra	Egoism
3.	Manas	Candra	Saṅkalpa
4.	Ear	Ākāśa	Sound
5.	Skin	Vāyu	Touch
6.	Eye	Āditya	Sight
7.	Tongue	Varuṇa	Taste
8.	Nose	Earth	Smell
9.	Voice	Agni	Utterance
10.	Hands	Indra	Grasping
11.	Feet	Viṣṇu	Walking
12.	Organ of Pāyu	Mitra	Excretion
13.	Upastha	Prajāpati	Ānanda.

Of these the first three are organs of knowledge and action; the five next are organs of knowledge; the five last are organs of action. These thirteen Karaṇas (instruments) with the five Prāṇas, five Mahābhūtas, Pradhāna, and Puruṣa make up the twenty five tattvas (principles) of the cosmos the enumeration of which gave the name of Sāṅkhya (counting) to this school.

The word tanmātra means 'that merely', the pure essence of a sensation conceived as a modification of subtle matter. The illuminated (Sāttva) aspect of it becomes the fundament of a sense organ; the dark (tāmasa) aspect of it becomes the rudiment of the corresponding sense-object—Sūkṣmabhūta.

The conception that the organ of a sensation and the object that possesses and produces that sensation are modifications of the same material essence is in keeping with the idealism that underlies Hindu philosophy. Western science has led philosophy into an *impasse* by generalising the objective causes of sensations into vibrations of material particles which philosophy by no stretch of imagination can assimilate with anything like sensations. The Sāṅkhya regards the tanmātras, *i. e.,* pure sound etc. to exist inside the perceiving sense-organ and in the world as well. To form a sense-organ it is acted on by sattva, it takes an illuminated form; to form a sūkṣmabhūta, subtle, (ultimate) element, it takes a tāmasa, dark, resisting form; and when there is a contact between these two forms, the sense organ and the sense object, sensation results by the illumination of the object by the sense organ.

This concept that sensation is not a mode, a function, of intellect but an element, a constituent of matter, perhaps looks paradoxical but is not so difficult to conceive as it looks. All admit that smell exists as infinitesimally small particles of matter shot off from odorous substances. According to modern physical notions light is but a case of electricity and all matter is but electricity. Hence "atoms of light" are infinitesimally small particles of matter. Extending this to the other three sensations it is not impossible to conceive the five sensations to be the five (metaphysical) elements of matter out of which objects and the sense-organs which perceive them are evolved. Physics attempts to form a picture of the universe by making or conceiving mechanical models of the action of the complex objects of the universe. Such models are extremely helpful in what is called scientific explanation. So far the formation of scientific hypotheses is valid. But when one steps beyond and says that the plan of the universe is a copy of the many mechanical models conceived by the scientific man, it is but the intrusion of bad metaphysics into good science. The only valid metaphysical explanation of the universe is the analysis of it into five elementary sensations or tanmātras as the Hindu calls them.

These tanmātras are Aviśeṣa, (lit. un-specific), perceptible only to the Gods whose bodies and sense organs are subtle. When they become Viśeṣa, specific, differentiated, they give rise to subtle bodies, to the bodies that spring from a father and mother and the Mahābhūtas (empirical elements). (*Ib.* xxxviii). The tanmātras first evolve into empirical elements called Mahābhūtas, or Sthūlabhūtas (gross elements). From Śabda tanmātra is evolved Sthūla Ākāśa; this mixed with Vāyutanmātra becomes Sthūla vāyu, and so on, each 'gross element' (mahābhūta) containing the properties of all the elements above it and serving as the basis of their differentiation. This process of differentiation is called Pañcīkaraṇa—quintuplication. These gross elements thus evolved constitute on the one hand the objects of the physical universe and on the other the physical bodies (with the physical sense organs) which form the habitat of the incarnating Puruṣas. The creation of these bodies is called liṅgākhya Sarga, evolution of bodies, related to Bhāvākhya Sarga, evolution of characteristics. (*Ib.* lii). These bodies are of fourteen kinds, of which eight are divine, *i. e.* subtle, namely, (1) Brāhma, that of Brahmā; (2) Prājāpatya, those of the creating hierarchies, of Manus, and of Ṛṣis, (3) Saumya, those of the lunar beings; (4) Aindra, those of Gods of the rank of Indra; (5) Gāndharva, those of the attendants on Indra and beings of that order; (6) Rākṣasa; (7) Yākṣa; (8) Pāiśāca, those of three classes of demons. The ninth class of bodies is that of man; the other five are infra-human —domestic animals, wild beasts, birds, creeping animals and immovables (vegetables and minerals). These three groups of bodies, divine, human, and infra-human are respectively characterised by Sattva, Rajas, and Tamas . (*Ib.* liii, liv). Hence the Gods lead a life of indolent pleasure; man, one of activity and the beings below man are enveloped by ignorance; but all beings—high or low act not out of any imaginary principle of free will but all action in the manifested universe is the mechanical result of the play of Sattva, Rajas and Tamas. These three kinds of bodies are also called Ūrddhvasrotas, Arvāk-srotas and Tiryagsrotas, *i, e.* those whose vital energy flows upwards, downwards and horizontally (*Viṣ. Pur.* V).

This completes the evolutionary process and provides a large variety of bodies in which Puruṣas may reside and experience the pain arising from decay and death till, (on attaining Mokṣa) they are released from connection with the Liṅga-deha. *(Śāṅkh. Kār.* lv).

2. YOGA

The Yoga school accepts *in toto* the scheme of the past evolution of the Universe as taught by the Sāṅkhyas; but its especial concern is more with the future release of the soul that is bound and the means of securing that desirable consummation. The Satkāryavāda is accepted in *Yoga Sūtras iv.* 12. "The past and the future (forms of things) exist is their essence, the cause (of development of various) properties is due to change (of time, place etc.)". The substratum contains in it all forms in latency and they manifest themselves in due time. "They are (either) visible or subtile and are of the nature (of modifications) of the Guṇas." *(Ib.* iv. 14). These suble and visible forms of objects start their course of evolution on account on the contiguity of the seer and for his sake. "Though variegated by innumerable impressions (mental deposits of souls associated with the objects) they exist for another (*i. e.* the seer) because they operate on account of association (with him)" *(Ib.* iv. 23).

The stages of evolution are four. "The stages (of the evolution) of the Guṇas are the specific, (viśeṣa), non-specific (aviśeṣa) the liṅgamātra and the a liṅga. (*Ib.* ii. 19). The "specific' (viśeṣa) or complex comprises the objects of the world. The 'non-specific' are the simple pure sensations (tan-mātra) of which all objects are compounded and the Ahaṁkāra —the foundation of the cognition of I and not-I. The liṅgamātra, the mere characteristic, the touch of matter that colours the pure consciousness of the Puruṣa and characterizes him as bound soul, is Buddhi. The aliṅga is the characterless, homogeneous Pradhāna.

After all objects are evolved they continue in a state of constant flux, for flux is life. This flux is of three kinds, Dharma, Lakṣaṇa and Avasthā. *(Ib.* iii. 13). This triple flux affects objects and the organs of perception and the action by means of which we contact them. *(Ib.)* Dharma is change of characteristic. Thus when a pot is made of a lump of clay, the (material) clay gives up the characteristics of a lump and takes on the characteristics of a pot. This is the flux of Dharma, affecting the Dharmī (material), clay. This flux—change of characteristic—consists of two moments, (1) the rise of the new characteristic (of the pot), (2) the destruction the old characteristic (of the lump). Dharma is thus the flux of form while the Dharmī, material, is permanent; the various characteristics, the outgoing and the incoming ones are both existent, only when the former is held in check (nirodha) the latter manifests itself. Thus when the *lumpincss* (piṇḍatva) of clay is held in check, its *pothood* (ghaṭ atva) is in manifestation (vyutthāna). Dharma itself, is subject to a triple flux, called Lakṣaṇa, the flux of time. The form of a pot is a Dharma of clay. This form has three states with reference to time—future, present and past. So long as the pot is not made, but is only as it were immanent in the clay, it is *prospective pot-hood* (anāgata ghaṭatvam). This quality of capability of becoming a pot is held in check (nirodha) and *present pot-hood* (vartamāna ghaṭatvam) comes into manifestation (vyutthāna) when a pot takes shape. Similary a statue exists in latency in marble before the sculptor carves it. Carving is the act of keeping the latency under control so that the actual statue may manifest itself. When, finally, the pot is broken, its *present pot-hood is* held in check and its state as a past (atīta) pot is manifested. Thus goes on this procession of each form of each object from a prospective to a present and on to a past state (Lakṣaṇa), each presenting two moments, Nirodha and Vyutthāna, one moment merging and another manifesting itself. The flux of an object with regard to time is thus analysed, so that the fundamental idea of Satkāryavāda, that nothing is created, nothing destroyed, may be consistently followed in explanation of the world-flux. While the triple flux of Lakṣaṇa takes place, Dharma is fixed. The idea of Lakṣaṇa as a procession of temporal states of a form is indicated by each state being called an Adhvā (way). Each adhvā contains a Nirodha and a Vyutthāna one state checked and another manifested. Nirodha and Vyutthāna are always acting. If the former is strong and the latter is weak, a certain state is kept under control; when the latter is strong and the former is weak, manifestation of a state results. Thus Nirodha and Vyutthāna, each has two phases; in Nirodha, Nirodha is strong and Vyutthāna is weak; in Vyutthāna, Vyutthāna is strong and Nirodha is weak. Each of these phases is called an Avasthā. Thus Dharma is the flux (Pariṇāma) of Dharmī, Lakṣaṇa is the flux of Dharma and Avasthā is the flux of Lakṣaṇa. This intricate analysis of the flux of objects taken from Vyāsa's *Commentaries on Yoga Sūtras* III. 13, reminds us of the barren hair-splitting of the Nyāya-Vaiśeṣika School; its only virtue, if it is virtue at all, being a consistent carrying out of the doctrine of *Ex nihilo nihil fit*. Cittavṛtti, the flux of psychoses, is similarly analysed, but this will be discussed elsewhere.

3. VEDĀNTA

So early as in the age when the Ṛks were composed, was the momentous question raised, "what was the wood, what was the tree, out of which they fashioned the heaven and the earth? Inquire mentally, ye sages, what was that on which he took his stand when establishing the worlds?" *(Ṛg Veda,* X. 81. 4). The question was answered in the *Taittirīya Brāhmaṇa,* II. viii. 9. 6., "Brahma was the wood, Brahma the tree from which they shaped the heaven and the earth. Ye sages, I tell you, he stood on Brahmā supporting the worlds." This process of world-shaping is called pariṇāma, the march of forms on an unchanging material substratum, in *Ved-Sūt*. I. iv. "(Brahma is the materical cause of the universe) as it is said He meditated ('may I become many, may I grow forth'), as both (creation and dissolution) are referred in the Veda directly (to Him, as in *Tait. Brāh,* II. viii. 9. 6. above quoted), as (it is said) He Himself made Himself *(Tait. Up*. II. 7.), by pariṇāma"(*Ved. Sūt*. I. iv. 24-27).

The question, then, rises, how can Brahma, who is conscious Being evolve into the forms of unconscious (jaḍa) material objects? This difficulty does not occur in the Sāṅkhya-pariṇāmavāda wherein unconscious material objects evolve out of an unconscious causal proto-matter. The Sāṅkhya therefore objects to the Vedānta appropriating his theory "on account of the differe.1ce of that *(viz*. the world, from Brahma)" *(Ved.Sūt*. II. i. 4). The Vedānta Sūtras meet this objection tersely, "But it is seen" *(Ib*. II. i. 6). that the world presents many instances of things of different nature related as cause and effect, *e. g*. hairs and nails grow out of man, scorpions out of cow dung, worms out of hondey. To this crude way of meeting this difficulty, the Ācāryas add each a clever supplementary argument derived from their sectarian teachings. Śaṅkara argues that evolution of the objects that constitute the world is Illusory (vivarta pariṇāma) and Brahma is but the seeming material (vivarta upādāṇam),[4] "Brahma becomes the substratum of all phenomenal changes like evolution etc., superimposed on him by Avidyā (ignorance); in His real nature he remains beyond all phenomenal changes and untransformed" *(Comm. on Ved. Sūt. II* i. 27). Rāmānuja attributes to Brahma even in his causal state (Kāraṇāvasthā), a subtle body made up of individual souls and the elements of matter that have become absorbed in Him. During the Kāryāvasthā, when the world is in manifestation, it is this *body* of His that evolves, He Himself being the unchangeable, avyakta.

Thus all schools interpose between Brahmā that is Pure Conscious Being and the evolved world, a state of proto-matter which is held to be real or illusory according as consistency with their fundamental metaphysical position requires. The hiatus between Brahma and this proto-matter is the weak point of all Vedānta theories. This original state of proto-matter, Mūlaprakṛti as the Sāṅkhyas call it, is called Asat in the Vedas. "Asat was this at first, from it sprang Sat *(Tait. Up.* II. 7. 1; *Ch. Up. lit.* 19. 1.) "Sat is founded upon Asat. Beings (bhūtas) are founded upon Sat" *(Athar. Ved.* XVII i. 19). From Asat, Manas was created. Manas created Prajāpati. Prajāpati created beings." *(Tait. Brāh* II. ii. 9. 10). "Asat was this at first. They say, 'what is this Asat? The Ṛṣis say that 'At first Asat existed'." *(Śat Brāh* VI. i. 1. 1). By Asat, therefore, is meant a state when distinct objects were not evolved, a state of homogeneity,[5] the chaos of the Greeks. This state is also called Tamas, to be distinguished from Tamas, one of the three guṇas. "Tamas existed, enveloped by Tamas, in the beginning" (*Ṛg- Veda* X. 129. 3), "In the beginning Tamas alone was this." (*Mait, Up.* V. 2). By Tamas. darkness, was symbolized a state when nothing objective is manifested. Another and frequently used symbol of the unmanifested state of matter, is 'water'. "All this was undifferentiated water." *(Ṛg Veda,* X. 129. 3.) "At first all this was water, (nothing) but water." *(Śat. Brāh.* XI. i. 6. 1. 9, *Tait. Sam.* VII. i. 5. 1, *Tait. Brāh.* I. i. 3. 5, *Tait. Āraṇ,* I. 2 3. 1).

Sṛṣṭi, creation, started with an agitation of this primeval matter. Sṛṣṭi is more properly emission, the omission of energy into the waters, which started the work of evolution. This first starting of creative activity is described in the earlier writings as a 'desire'. "Desire (Kāma) first arose in it, this was the seed of mind, that which was first. Wise men, by mental introspection, have found this bridge between Asat and Sat". *(Ṛg-veda* x. 129. 4.) "Being Asat, it desired 'may I become Sat'" *(Tait. Brāh.* II ii. 9. 1). In the theistic Āgama schools, this desire is furnished with a motive, that of leading individual souls to salvation (Mokṣa); but this idea is not found in the early literature. On the contrary, it is said that creation is "not on account of any (special) purpose but is a mere sport (līlä), such as we see in ordinary life (when people play)" (*Ved. Sūt.* II. i.

32-33). The desire that underlies the evolution of the world, the will to manifest is not due to the motive to gain something thereby; nor is it due to constraint, but spontaneous, self-initiated out-flow of energy.

"From Asat came Sat". "From Asat was created Manas". These words Sat, Manas, indicate the earliest beginnings of evolution, the stage when existence could be predicated, when homogeneous proto-matter was streaked with the first marks of differentiation. "It (Sat) developed, it became an egg" (*Ch. Up*. III. xix. 1) "Manas created Prajāpati". This represents the next stage, Prajāpati, on the one hand and the world-egg on the other. The former was the Ādi Puruṣa, the first male, the creator with some elements of personality in him; the latter was the first discrete form of the universe; These are the two lines of evolution.[6] The work of Prajāpati is described variously in various cosmogonic hymns. Most frequently it is described as Tapas (meditation accompanied by austerity). "He desired," may I become many, may I produce children.' He performed tapas; after he performed tapas, he emitted all this; and whatever there is. Having emitted it, he entered into it." (*Tait. Up*. II. 6) "Prajāpati desired, 'may I produce children.' He performed tapas; he became pregnant. He became yellow-brown. Hence a pregnant woman becomes yellow-brown. Being pregnant with a foetus, he became exhausted. Being exhausted, he became black-brown. Hence an exhausted person becomes black-brown." *(Tait. Brāh.* II. iii. 8. 1). Prajāpati's work is also conceived as a sexual act. "The Ātmā, in the form of a Puruṣa, was this at first. Looking around, he saw (there was) none but himself. . . He desired a second. He was as much as a man and woman locked in embrace. He made himself fall asunder in two parts. Thus arose man and wife. He cohabited with her. Thence men were born." (*Śat. Brāh,* XIV. iv. 2. 1). Creation is also described as due to uttering mantras. "With 'Bhūḥ,' Prajāpati generated this; with 'Bhuvaḥ', the intermediate region; with 'svaḥ,' the sky". (*Ib*. VI. i. 4. 11). It is also conceived as a sacrifice. The ritual of the Vedic sacrifice was supposed to be an earthly copy of this sacrifice of creation. Viṣṇu is generally referred to as the sacrificial victim. Lastly, creation is sometimes described as an act of self-sacrifice. "Brahma, the self-existant was in contemplation. He thought, 'there is no infinity in this contemplation. I shall sacrifice myself in beings and beings in myself.' Then sacrificing Himself in all beings and all beings in Himself, he acquired superiority, self-effulgence and lordship" *(Śat. Brāh.* XIII. vii. 1. 20).

The Golden Egg of the universe developed in "the period of a year. It burst in two. The two halves became (one) golden and (the other) silver. The silver (half) is this earth, the golden (half) the sky; the chorion, mountains, the amnion, cloud and mist; the blood-vessels, rivers and the fluid, the ocean" (*Ch. Up*. III. 19. 1-2).

The order in which the various beings were created also varies in different accounts. The *Taittirīya Brāhmaṇa* makes it out to be Asuras, Fathers (Pitṛs), men, Devas (*Ib.* II. iii. 8. 1). The elements were created in the order in which the Sāṅkhya makes them evolve. "From that Ātmā sprang Ākāśa, from Ākāśa air, from air fire, from fire water, from water earth, from earth herbs, from herbs food, from food retas (seed) from retas men" (*Tait. Up*. II. 1). By 'man' here we must here understand his gross body, for in the previous series he appears between the Fathers and the Devas. All this work of evolution is done by the Supreme Brahmā. "The making of names and forms (belongs) to Him who renders (the elements) tripartite, according to the teaching of the Śruti" *(Ved. Sūt.* II. iv. 20). Making the elements 'tripartite' refers to *Chāndogya Up*. vi-2, where tejas āpas and annam (firè, water and food or earth, as usually interpreted) are alone mentioned; from such crude speculations, the Sāṅkhya elaborated its well-thought and finished analysis of the Universe. When this was done, though the Vedānta was directly opposed to the fundamental Sāṅkhya teaching and the author of the Brahma Sūtras devoted two sections of the work to refute the Sāṅkhya heresy, by appealing both to reason and revelation, it accepted the Sāṅkhya scheme of transmutation; its promulgator

Kapila has become an incarnation of Viṣṇu and his philosophy a revelation as unassailable as the self-promulgated Veda.

The Vedānta has elaborated the Vedic scheme of three regions, the earth, the sky, and the intermediate region (antarikṣa) into three cosmic spheres, the Vedānta scheme being perhaps a rival of the Vaiṣṇava scheme. The *Māṇḍūkya Upaniṣad* is the first to propound the scheme. "Brahmā that is this Ātmā is four-footed. The first foot is Vaiśvānara, seated in the waking consciousness, sensing external objects, with seven limbs[7] and nineteen doors', experiencer of the gross (compounded) world. The second foot is Taijasa, seated in the dreaming consciousness, sensing internal objects, with seven limbs and nineteen doors, experiencer of the [8] elementary (subtle) world. Deep sleep (suṣuptam) when the sleeper desires nothing whatsoever, dreams not at all; becoming one with the state of deep sleep a mass of (undifferentiated) consciousness, filled with bliss, the enjoyer of bliss, he is Prājña. the third foot. This is the Lord of all, this the omniscient, this the indweller of all, this the cause of the birth and death of all beings. Not sensing the internal, not sensing the external, not-sensing both, no mass of sentiency, not conscious, not-unconscious, unseen, unusable, untouchable, indefinable, inconceivable, indescribable, the essence of the intuition of the one Ātmā, where the world is not, the unchnaging, the blissful, the one without second, that, which is to be known, is the Ātmā, the fourth (foot)" *(Māṇḍ. Up.* 2.7).

Nṛsiṁha Tāpini Upaniṣad, II. i, is a commentary on the *Māṇḍūkya Upaniṣad* and presents a systematic parallelism between the three states of the individual consciousness and of the cosmic consciousness as follows :—

States	**Individual**	**Cosmic**
Waking	Viśva	Vaiśvānara
Dream	Taijasa	Hiraṇyagarbha
Sleep	Prājña	Īśvara

The worlds and bodies corresponding to these three states of consciousness are called Sthūla Sūkṣma and Kāraṇa, gross, subtle and causal (the fourth, Turīya, being the Absolute). The three worlds are also called Virāṭ, Svarāṭ and Saṁrāṭ

4. ŚAIVA AND ŚĀKTA ĀGAMAS

The Sāṅkhya divided the objective universe into twenty-four tattvas,[9] which with the Puruṣa make up the twenty-five principles that constitute the macrocosm and the microcosm. The Śaivas analyse the universe into thirty-six tattvas. Between Prakṛti and Buddhi they interpolate Guṇa as a tattva separate from either. Thus there are twenty-five tattvas below Puruṣa, who is the twenty-sixth. Above him there are five, called Pañca kañcuka, the five-fold envelope, *viz.*, Niyati, Kāla, Rāga, Vidyā, and Kalā. Above Kalā, there are Māyā, Śuddha Vidyā, Īśvara, Sadāśiva and Śiva tattvas.

These thirty-six tattvas are divided into three classes, the highest, Śivatattva, being a class by itself, the next three, Sadā-Śiva, Īśvara and Śuddhavidyā being the Vidyātattva and the thirty-two beginning from Māyā and ending with the earth being the Ātmātattva.

The first of the Ātmā tattvas is Māyā, not the Śuddha Māyā mentioned in the previous pages Māyā is the root of the universe. It is "eternal, one, pervading, of the form of objects, the substratum in which the potential results of actions (Karma) inhere, impure and common to all Sakalas. It is, during manifestation, the cause of the subtle and gross bodies etc. of the Pralayākalas, which end with pralaya. As the trunk, the leaf, the fruit, etc., latent in the seed grow (therefrom so the universe) from kalā to kṣiti (earth) developed from Māyā)." *(Pauṣ. Ag.* in. 2-4) "It first evolves into the subtle tattvas (Kalā etc.), by manifesting the power of sight (dṛkśakti, power of perception) in the Ātmā; then it evolves into the gross worlds and bodies. The subtle Kalā etc. first bind the man (aṇu); then the gross." (*Ib.* iii. 61, 62). Kala is the first tattva evolved from Māyā. "Kalā overcomes in all ways the malas (impurities) that obstruct the manifestation of caitanya and thus helps caitanya to manifest. Caitanya is of the form of cognition and activity and is the auxiliary of the Ātmā; (when) it is obstructed, Kalā manifests it. Kalā does not manifest the Ātmā in its entirety, but makes the caitanya shine partially, as Kaḷā works in accordance with Karma." *(Ib.* v. 2-5). Vidyā, the next tattva, evolves from Kalā; without it the Ātmā cannot derive experience of pleasure and pain. "That instrument with which the Ātmā who has become an actor sees the oprations of Buddhi is called vidyā in the Śaiva Śāstras." (*Ibid.* v. 9.) Vidyā is different from Citśakti; for the latter shines only when Buddh and other material modifications are destroyed. Cit-Śakti leads to pure knowledge, whereas Vidyā causes the knowledge that is bondage. Vidyā is thus a reflection of the light of consciousness (prakāśa) as kaḷā is a reflection of power, independence (svacchanda). "Rāga inclines to (worldly) experience one who is attached to it; for the one without desire has no enjoyment (of pain and pleasure); nor is there satisfaction for one who is subject to enjoyment of impure (bliss)." (*Ib.* v. 22-23). Rāga is a reflection of cit Śakti or icchāśakti. "Rāga is of two kinds, of the form of images and of the form of latent (desire); of these the former (attaches men) to objects." *(Ib.* v. 37). After Rāga comes Kala, time, which makes manifests the aforesaid tattvas as past, present and future. "Without (the flux of) time, nothing can be born, nothing die; hence time is a cause (of objects) as the wheel is (a cause) of a pot" *(Ib.* v. 50). Time is not eternal; for eternity is being outside time *(Ib.* v. 66). Niyati is the force that attracts a man to the results of his Karma, whether he desires them or not. It also determines what bodies, organs, etc, each man is to get. Karma by itself. has no power to afflict man. Śiva's power has to intervene, in the form of Niyati (*Ib.* v. 83-88). The Puruṣa clothes himself with these 'five envelopes' developed from Māyā being set thereto by Śiva. The name Puruṣa applies only, to the sakalas; they are enveloped by ignorance (avidyā) which comes from Prakṛti; the Vijñanākalas and Pralayakevalas are not called Puruṣas. (*Ib.* vi. 2-4). Prakṛti is also the stuff of which the worlds which the Puruṣa is to experience are made. It is the first of the gross developments of Māyā, Kalā and the other four (pañcakañcuka) being subtle ones. It is also called Avyakta (*Ib.* vi. 18). In it the guṇas are in equilibrium (*Ib.* vi. 21). From Prakṛti evolve the Guṇas; from the Guṇas, Buddhi. The rest of this part of evolution is substantially the same as that taught in the Sāṅkhya school.

The Vidyātattvas (to be distinguished from the tattva called Vidyā, the thirtieth in the series) are three modifications of the highest tattva, that called Śiva. This Śivatattva is niṣkala, undifferentiated, where Śuddhamaya, with all its activity ended, becomes absorbed (reaches laya); from it radiate the powers of consciousness and action; it is indestructible, omnipresent. Eternal, unchanging, omniscient (lit. with face in all directions) (*Pauṣ-Āg.* i. 18-20).

Sadāśiva is the next tattva, the first of the three Vidyātattvas. "When Śuddha-māyā, the Śakti of Śiva begins her life of activity, then Śiva passes to the state of Bhoga Śiva (lit., Śiva that experiences, the first stage of differentiation); he is Sadāśiva, also called Sādākhya, not really separate from Śiva. When Śuddhamāyā is actually active, Bhoga Śiva passes on to the stage of Adhikāra Śiva (lit., Śiva that superintends or rules); he is then Īśvara, not really separate from Sadā Śiva (*Ib.* i. 25-26). The body of five mantras referred to in the previous chapter belongs to Sadāśiva, for the highest, undifferentiated Śivatattva, can scarcely be said to have a body, even one composed of mantras.

Bindu, otherwise Śuddha Māyā, also Śivaśakti, the active counterpart of these three highest tattvas is not counted as a separate tattva; so that the Śākta āgamas give her prominence and throw the Śivas in the background. "The laya and other (two) different states of Śiva already described have Bindu as their substratum; she is the same as Kuṇḍalinī (the globular)." She it is that binds Ananta and the rest to the bondage of their (respective) activities and releases them therefrom. Moreover at the time of creation the world beginning with that of mantras proceed from her and become absorbed in her." *(Ib.* ii. 1-4). "Her activity in manifesting tattvas determines the four (highest tattvas), Śivatattva, Sādākhya tattva, Īśvara tattva, and (śśuddha) Vidyā tattva." *(Ib* ii. 32.33). "Śuddha Vidyā is the cause of true knowledge" (*Ib*. ii. 40).

Besides this line of evolution of the various 'principles' of the Universe, the Śaiva Āgamas also describe the evolution of hosts of beings, succeeding the rise of Māyā. "Then at first he creates eight qualified Kevala souls (aṇus), accompanied by Vāmā and other Śakti's and surrounded by the 7 crores of mantras." *(Mṛg. Ag.* iii. 1). They are here called kevala because they belong to the class already described as Vijñānakevala, those that have Āṇavamla1a sticking on to them but are rid of Karma and Māyā. They are Ananta, Sūkṣma, Śivottama, Ekanetra, Ekarudra, and Śikhaṇḍī, lords of lords (Rājarājas). Then the Lord being manifested Ananta and the rest, creates from Māyā tattva (the knot), the 118 (īśvaras) whose bodies begin from Kalā." *(Ib.* 9). These evidently are subject to two malas.

"Afterwards the Lord enters into those rulers of the worlds (bhuvaneśvaras) who are tainted (with the three malas) from whom all this (universe has arisen) and whose work depends upon (their) karma." *(Ibid.* iii. 10). They are Brahmā, Viṣṇu, Rudra, (the destroyer of a minor universe, to be distinguished from the great Lord), and the rest, who thus are Saka1as. These beings inhabit various spheres, called Bhuvanas into the description of which it is profitless to enter.

The line of separation between the Śaiva and Śākta Āgamas so far as mythology is concerned is generally faint; but the more rigorous Śākta schools, while accepting the Śaiva analysis of the tattvas substitute hierarchies of female divinities for the Śaiva deities. Parāśakti, the Supreme Goddess is always surrounded by hordes of followers, like the queen of the amazons, One hierarchy is that of the 16 Nityās—Mahā Tripura-sundarī, Kāmevarī, Bhagamālinī, etc; another consists of Mantrini,

Daṇḍinī, Nakulī and other Devīs. Their names, functions and the Mantras which appeal to them from the chief subject matter of Śākta books. They are generally distinguished as Īśvarīs when pure Sattva, Rajas and Tamas excluded, forms their essence, and as Yoginīs when they are tainted by Rajas and Tamas. No useful purpose will be served by a more detailed study of these divine charmers.

Varivasyā rahasya expounds the secret teachings with regard to the starting of the process of creation, quaint and interesting. "This is the order of creation. A man, desirous of begetting offspring, on account of the adṛṣṭa (karma) of the son to be born, contemplates his own powers and himself enters, in the form of Śukla, the wife that is the half of his body; . . . then the wife in the form of Śoṇita enters within the Śukla; thence the bindu swells out, like the seed of the banyan and the udumbara; then in the order in which the sprout etc. generate, in process of time, children etc. are generated; when the sun's rays enter a mirror opposite the sun, the sun's rays and rays from the mirror become mixed and start as a bindu of light and fall on a wall. Similarly, on account of the Adṛṣṭa (karma) of (all) beings, Brahmā who is Prakāśa, becomes desirous of creating the world which had been absorbed in himself, turns to see his Śakti, enters her in the form of a bindu of light and becomes a bindu of Śukla. Thence Śakti, becomes Śoṇita and enters into it. The bindu that results from their commingling swells out. Then is produced a special substance called Hārdakalā (heart-ray). That has to be learnt from the lips of a Guru and cannot be written in books" *(Ibid.* ii. 15. *Com).*

Lalitā Sahasranāma bhāṣya quotes from a Śākta work the following elaborate description of the stages of creation. First is (1) the ghanībhūta stage, when karma absorbed in pralaya is not ripe for manifestation and matter is a homogeneous mass. When the ripening is beginning it, is (2) vicikīrṣa. Māyā becomes charged with ripened karma and Brahma becomes endowed with Māyā and is ready to create; this is (3)

Avyakta or Kāraṇa Bindu (the causal seed). From it starts (4) the Kārya Bindu (effected seed), who is Parā Vāk, Cit. Thence issues (5) Nāda, Sūkṣma Vāk, cidacit; thence, Bīja, (gross) seed, sthūla, Acit. Stages 3, 4, 5, 6 form the Avyakta Īśvara, Hiraṇyagarbha and Vaiśvanara of the Vedānta (explained in section 3), as also their Śākta analogues, *vis*, Śāntā, Vāmā, Jyeṣṭhā, and Raudrī, otherwise, Ambikā, Icchā, Jñāna, and Kriyā.

5. VAIṢṆAVA ĀGAMAS

The *Pādma Saṁhitā* describes the cosmic beings and spheres in the following terms "There is the eternal, incomparable, Light, eternally-satisfied, spotless, the all-form, the formless, beyond Tamas, without destruction. On account of (creative activity) comes out from this eternal Being, Vāsudeva, two-handed, single-clothed, like pure crystal, with the sphere of rays, with cakra (discus) and other implements as his marks, with Śrīvatsa (a curl of hair) and Kaustubha (a jewel) on his breast, shining with a garland ornamented with a crown, a necklace, armlets, bangles, etc., wearing a yellow cloth, graceful, the first spotless King. He is known as Vāsudeva; from (His) four-faced Being all created things (came). He is to be meditated on by Yogīs always in the centre of the lotus of the heart. The wise (sūris) see him as the supreme goal of Viṣṇu. From Vāsudeva was born another Vāsudeva, single-faced, four-armed, endowed with the discus and other implements. (He keeps) the discus for the protection (of the world); the all-loving, again, has the lotus for the purpose of creation; the (conch called) pāñcajanya for release (mukti), also the mace for destruction; with the Śrīvatsa and kaustubha on his breast, ornamented with a garland; black like the peacock's neck; with a yellow cloth, born with him. This Lord Vāsudeva is the author of creation, protection, destruction, and release. For some cause or other he divided himself into two; of these one was Vāsudeva, like a pure crystal, the second was Nārāyaṇa, of the colour of a blue cloud. From Vāsudeva (came) Saṁkarṣaṇa, from him (the latter) was born Pradyumna. From Pradyumna (come) Aniruddha. All these are four armed. Vāsudeva is known to have the six guṇas, jñāna and the rest, in equal quantities; the forms (mūrtis) to be serially described, (come) from possessing different quantities of the guṇas. He who has excess of jñāna is named Saṁkarṣaṇa; Pradyumna has an excess of bala; on the excess of Aiśvarya, (comes) Anīruddha; from the four mūrtis are born twenty-four murtis, as many lamps (are lighted) from one lamp" *(Pādma Sam.* ii-7-12).

The functions of these beings are described in the *Lakṣmītantra.* "Aniruddha creates this; Pradyumna maintains what he creates; the Saṁkarṣaṇa eats (destroys) what is thus created and maintained." *(Ibid.* iv. 19.) In variance with this Lakṣmī describes the course of creation in chap v of the same book. "I, desirous of creation, with a small drop (bindu) of mine, start the pure creation, of the full six guṇas. Before my form is altered by the formation of that bindu, I am called Mahālakṣmī, surrounded by the three guṇas. When Rajas becomes predominant, I become the great Parameśvarī. My form filled with Tamas is known as Mahā Māyā; and my form of Sattva is known as Mahā Vidyā. Myself and these two women by meditation created three pairs (of beings), in accordance with our nature. Know that my own mentally-produced beautiful pair, golden wombed, lotus-eyed, beautiful, lotus-seated, is from a part of Pradyumna. (Of this pair), the male is Brahmā (called also) Dhātā, Vidhi, Viriñca; the woman is called Śrī, Padmā, Kamlā, Lakṣmī. From a part of Saṁkarṣaṇa, was mentally produced by Mahāmāyā, a pair, three-eyed, beautiful in all limbs; the male was Rudra, Śaṅkara, Sthāṇu, Kapardī, three-eyed, and (the woman) Trayī, Iśvarā, Bhāṣā, Vidyā, Akṣarā, Kāmadhenu, the (heavenly) Cow, Sarasvatī. From a part of Aniruddha was mentally produced by Mahā-vidyā, a pair; the male there of was Keśava, Viṣṇu, Kṛṣṇa, Hṛṣīkeśa, Vāsudeva, Janārdana, the woman being Maha-gaurī, Satī Candra, Subhagā; by my command Trayī became Brahmā's wife, Gaurī, Rudra's wife, and the (lotus-born) Lakṣmī, of Vāsudeva" *(Ib.* v. 2-23).

Brahmā then created the cosmic egg; it was broken in two by Rudra and Viṣṇu protects all that is within the egg.

The supreme manifests himself in three forms, called Para, Vyūha and Vibhava; of these, the Para (supreme) form is the one described at the beginning of this section. The Vyūha comprises the four forms of Vāsudeva, Saṁkarṣaṇa, Pradyumna and Aniruddha, whose shapes, ornaments etc. are described in detail in chapter ten of this work. They manifest themselves in each of the four states of Jāgrata, Svapna, Suṣuptī and Turīya (waking, dreaming and sleep and trance.)[10]

The vibhava constitutes the various forms in which Viṣṇu manifests himself to man, *e.g.*, Padmnābha, Ananta, Kapila, the horse-faced Hayagrīva, the various avatāras, the tortoise, etc., Dattātreya and so on.[11]

From the complicated pantheon of the Āgamas, the Vedic deities, Indra and Agni, Mitra and Varuṇa, Vāyu and Sūrya and the ancient Dyāvāprithvī, the lovely Uṣas and the intoxicating King Soma have been entirely excluded; yet the modern Hindu devoutly believes his religion to be Vedic and passionately maintains it to be the Sanātana Dharma, the eternal, never-changing religion; because the Vedas are worshipped but not read by him. Whence these Āgama deities arose, when the complicated scheme of Āgama divinities was elaborated, what determined the character of their evolution is wrapped in that scarcely penetrable veil of obscurity which shrouds most Indian History.

References

1. The argument from design.
2. Śaṅkara interprets this Sūtra thus :—'From the perception (of the effect) when (the cause) exists.
3. Brahmā and other Gods are Puruṣas, just like ordinary human beings.
4. Hence the advaita is called the vivartavāda.
5. "Sat denotes the existence of things in the manifold forms of the

external world, the *Daseyn* of Hegel, the *Natura Naturata* of Spinoza and Asat is the opposite of this, or the formless Prakṛti. . . . Sat corresponds in each separate form to the 'being-this' of Hegel . . . By virtue of its predicate of merely being-this, every something is a finite' and therefore it is an *effect,* because otherwise we could only conceive it as absolute being and therefore unlimited . . . Dr. Muir, however, refers to the commentators on the Ṛgveda who explain Asat as moaning 'an undeveloped state', and adds that if we accept this statement there will be no contradiction. Asat does not mean simply an undeveloped state, but the state of pure or formless existence of the primal substance from which all forms have sprung. It is clear, however, that if Asat means an undeveloped state, then Sat must mean, not the essence of anything, but a developed state". Davies. *Hindu Phil,* pp.-136-8. But Davies forgets that sometimes Sat is used for the essence, the noumenal entity as in *Ch. Up*. VI. ii. 1. 2.

6. In some legends Prajāpati came out of the golden egg, *Śat. Brāh.* XI. i. 6. 2.
7. The orthodox explanation of the seven limbs is that they are the Heaven, the sun, wind, Ākāśa, water, earth and fire conceived as vaiśvānara's head, eye, breath, heart, bladder, feet and mouth. The nineteen doors are the ten organs of sense and action, five prāṇas and the four parts of the internal organ manas, buddhi, citta and ahaṁakāram. This can scarcely be the idea of the author of the Upaniṣad, for the division of the internal organ into four parts belongs to the age of Śaṅkara and not earlier, Anquetil's suggestion that they are the five elements, the ten organs, three guṇas and mind is a better guess, but not sufficiently convincing.
8. cf. Pañcīkṛta and apañcīkṛta, aviśeṣa and viśeṣa, of the Sāṅkhya, v. p. 273.
9. Tattva, lit, that-ness has various connotations. Sometimes it means reality, as opposed to phenomenality, a real, ultimate factor of the cosmos. But in the Sāṅkhya and Śaiva Śāstras it more often means a definite stage of evolution, a stage having individual characteristics of its own. The tattva trayam of the Vaiṣṇavas are, again, three real, and ultimate *factors* of the cosmos and not stages of the evolution of *Prakṛti.*
10. The *Māṇḍūkya upaniṣad* with its classification of spheres into four is so thorough goingly advaita in spirit that it presents a

standing difficulty to Viśiṣṭādvaita commentators. Raṅga Rāmānuja identifies Viśva, Taijasa, Īśvara and Ātmā referred to there with the four Vyūhas of the Vaiṣṇava Āgamas, but the representation of these vyūhas as being present in each state of the mind (waking, etc.) in the *Lakṣmītantra,* knocks the bottom out of Raṅga Rāmānuja's argument.

11. Besides Para, Vyūha and Vibhava forms, other Vaiṣṇava works add two other forms, antaryāmi, the all pervasive form (taken from the antaryāmi-brāhmaṇa, *Bṛh. Up.*) and the arca, the forms of temple idols.

GLOSSARY

NOTE This index refers to chap. II and III and deals only with technical terms that have different meanings or refer to things named differently in different schools . The nos. refer to pages.

The following contractions are used in this Index. A. Advaita; V. Viśiṣṭādvaita; D. Dvaita S. Sāṅkhya; Y. Yoga; Va. Vaiśeṣika; N. Nyāya; Ś. Śaiva Siddhānta; Pa. Pāśupata; Pr. Pratyabhijña; Śa. Śākta; Vai. Vaiṣṇava; M. Mīmāṁsā

Acit: unconscious, matter (V.), 98, cor. Mūlaprakṛti(S).

Adṛṣṭśa : unseen : cause cause of actions (Va, N.), 258; karma (Ś.), 296.

Ahaṁkāra: I—maker: the consciousness of Self as opposed to not-self, (S), 269; [treated by ater A. as a sub-division of antaḥkaraṇa, the inner organ; to be distinguished from Ahaṁtā, I-ness, the Śakti of the Āgamas, who is a goddess, the world-mother and not a tattva *merely*].

Aliṅga : without distinguishing marks or which cannot merge into another: primal matter (Y.), 112; cor, Mūlaprakṛti (S).

Anu: tiny, minute: atom, (1) eternal, ultimate sub-division of earth, air, fire and air (Va., N.); Mana also is Aṇu, 203, 204, 208; conception of, 256; (2) Individual self, (Ś.), because he imagines himself to be infinitely small, 156, 294. cor. Jīvātmā (A), cit (V.), etc.

Asat: non-being: proto-matter, root of matter, that state of matter when it cannot be distinguished as matter, a vedic term, 72, 73, 282 n. treated in the upaniṣads sometimes as Parama Brahma, 283; Cor. Mūla-prakṛti (S).

Ātmā: original meaning unknown: (t) name of the substance, Ego, (Va, N.), 00, (2) a class of tattvas (Śa.) 289.

Avidyā: ignorance; (1) ignorance of the non-duality of the Jīvātmā and Paramātmā (A.), 87, 89; (2) consciousness of finiteness (Śa), 156.

Avyakta: indistinguishable, undivided, undiffer-entiated; 78; (I) identical with Avidyā, which in the *manifested* world causes the sense of separation of the individual from the Supreme Self (A.), 89; (2) indistinguishable state of individual selves and matter when there is no *manifestation* (V.) 94.

Bhūta: being; objects (of the world) (Y.) 114; *also,* elements, subtle (Sūkṣma), 271, and gross (Mahā), 273. (S.).

Buddhi: knowledge; (1) the first stage of differentiated consciousness (S.), 267-269. (2) intellection (M.) 223, 236.

Cit: Orig. mean, unknown : conscious, individual self (V.) 93, (Pr.) 172. Cor. Jīvātmā (A.), Puruṣa (S.), etc. The derivative Caitanya (Śa. 152-153, Pr.) 170; another derivative, citi-Śakti, used in Y., 113.

Citta: probably derived from cit, but refers not to the pure consciousness, but (1) to the inner organ (Y.) 111,113-114,115; (2) memory (later A.), *ib;* (3) discriminative procedure of knowledge (P.), 150.

Dharma: What is established: (1) quality (Y.), 114, 276; (2) Vedic ritual (M.), 222.

Draṣṭā: Seer: the 'subject' (Y.), 111; Cor. Paruṣa (S.), cit (V.), Ātmā (Va., N.)

Dṛṣṭi: Sight: cognition (Y.), 111, 112; Cor. Prakāśa, or cit-Śakti (Ś.), jñāna (S.), Caitanyam (Pr.)

Dṛṣṭya: Seen: 'object' (Y.), 111, 112; Cor. prakṛti (S.)

Guṇa: strand: (1) three fundamental properties of the 'object' (S.), 105-107; (2) six special qualities of the Supreme. (Vai.), 181-182; (3) any quality of any object (Va., N.), 196.

Idaṁtā: this-ness: 'object' (Śa.), 141, 143, 144; Cor, Prakṛti (S.), dṛṣya (Y).

Īśvara: ruler: (1) the omniscient being, author of creation, dependent on Avidyā, but different from it(A.), 87—89; (2) an ever-free Puruṣa (Y.), 115; (3) Paramātmā, (Vai, esp. later), 186, 189; (4) Moral Governor of the universe (N.), 208; (5) God, the creator etc, (later N.), 261-262.

Jivātma : self living (in the manifested world) : individual self (A.), 86; frequently contracted into jīva, especially in later A., and D.; Cor. chit (V), aṇu (Ś), paṣu (P., Ś), puruṣa (8.), draṣṭā (Y.), Ātmā (Va. N.)

Kalā: small part: (1) insentient matter (P.) 149-150; (2) that which manifests caitanya partially (Śa), 290.

Kāraṇāvasthā: causal condition: Param-Brahma during pralaya (V.) 94; Cor. Param Ātma (A).

Kāryāvasthā: Effected condition: Param-Brahma during Kalpa (V.), 94; Cor. Iavara (A.).

Kriyā: action, usual sense everywhere: Rajas (Y.), 112.

Kṣetrajña: knower of the field: Individual soul (Vai., Bhag. Gītā), 184; Cor. Jīvātmā (A.), cit (V.), etc.

Māyā : power of causing illusion : (1) a power of Īśvara (A.), 88; same as Avidyā (A.), 89; (2) treated as an entity (later A.), *ib*; (3) the womb of the world (Śa), 158; of two kinds (Śa.) 158—161.

Mūlaprakṛti: root- matter: Nomuenon of material objects (S), 103-5 in some respects like Param Brahma also asat of the Vedānta, ether of science, *ib;* Cor: Aling (Y.), idaṁtā (ŚA), acit (V.), avidyā (A.), avyakta (A.),

Nirviśeṣa Brahma: Brahma free from specific attributes : word used by Rāmānuja, 92, and Śrīkara, 162, in referring to the Param Brahma of A., frequently called especially in later A., Nirguṇa Brahma.

Param Brahma: Supreme Being : used chiefly in Vedānta; in Ṛgveda, 72; in Bhag. Gīta, 72, 244; in Upaniṣads, 74; in Vedānta Sūtras; 77, in (A.), 86; in (V.) 92-94; in (D.), 97-08; Cor. Prakāśa (Śa.), Nārāyaṇa (Vai), Śiva (Ś.)

Pāśa: fetter: (Ś) 155-C, vaguely corresponds to prakṛti.

Paśu: cattle: individual self (P.), 149, (Ś), 154-155; 161-162; Cor., Jīvātmā (A., D), cit (V., Vai.).

Pati: Lord : Supreme Lord (P), 149, (Ś), 153; Cor. Param Brahma (Vedānta), also, Īśvara of various schools.

Prakāśa: light: (1) light of consciousness (S), 291, also generally used; (2) Sattva Guṇa (Y.), 112; (3) the Supreme, (Śa.) 141, 143, 144, Cor. Param Brahma.

Pradhāna: chief: Syn. of Mūlaprakṛti (S.,) q. v.

Prakṛti: [?] how a thing is made : the 'object' (S.), 101; used by most schools also.

Puruṣa : orig. mean, unknown : male : the 'subject' (S.), 101; used by moat schools also.

Sakala : with parts : (I) a class of individual souls (S.), 161;

Śīlā: Syn. of Guṇa(Y.), 112.

Sthiti: rest: (1) name of Tamas (Y.), 112 (2) maintenance of the world (Vai.) 183.

Spanda: Vibration: Name of the Supreme (Pr.), 170 : Cor. Param Brahma, etc.

Vidyā : knowledge : (1) cognition of the identity of the individual and supreme self (A.), 87; (2) method of meditation (upaniṣads), 120; (3) Sentiency (P.), 149; (4) a class of tattvas (Śa.), 292; (5) the 30th tattva (Śa.), 291.

Vikṛti: Alteration : (1) effect (S.), 103; (2) Paramātamā (Vai.), 178.

Viśeṣa difference : (1) species (Va.), 197; (2) elements that produce bodies (S), 273.

INDEX

A

B

L

M

N

★★★